Mechanisms of Aging and Mortality:
The Search for New Paradigms

MONOGRAPHS ON POPULATION AGING

General Editors
Bernard Jeune and James W. Vaupel

Vol. 1
*Development of Oldest-Old Mortality, 1950-1990:
Evidence from 28 Developed Countries*
Väinö Kannisto

Vol. 2
Exceptional Longevity: From Prehistory to the Present
Bernard Jeune and James W. Vaupel (Eds.)

Vol. 3
The Advancing Frontier of Survival: Life Tables for Old Age
Väinö Kannisto

Vol. 4
*Population Data at a Glance:
Shaded Contour Maps of Demographic Surfaces over Age and Time*
James W. Vaupel, Zhenglian Wang, Kirill F. Andreev, and Anatoli I. Yashin

Vol. 5
The Force of Mortality at Ages 80 to 120
A.R. Thatcher, V. Kannnisto, and J.W. Vaupel

Vol. 6
Validation of Exceptional Longevity
Bernard Jeune and James W. Vaupel (Eds.)

Vol. 7
Mechanisms of Aging and Mortality: The Search for New Paradigms
Kenneth G. Manton and Anatoli I. Yashin

Aging Research Center
Odense University

Mechanisms of Aging and Mortality: The Search for New Paradigms

Kenneth G. Manton and Anatoli I. Yashin

Monographs on Population Aging, 7.

Odense University Press

Mechanisms of Aging and Mortality: The Search for New Paradigms
© Kenneth G. Manton, Anatoli I. Yashin,
and Odense University Press, 2000
Printed by Special-Trykkeriet Viborg a-s, Denmark
Cover illustration: My last days are past. Paper-cut by Sonia Brandes
ISBN 87-7838-507-5
ISSN 0909-119X

Odense University Press
Campusvej 55
DK-5230 Odense M
Phone +45 66 15 79 99 - Fax +45 66 15 81 26
E-mail: Press@forlag.sdu.dk
Internet bookstore: www.sdu.dk/press

Table of contents

I. Introduction 13

    1.1. New evidence about aging
    1.2. The need for new models of late-age mortality
    1.3. The monograph

II. Changes in the quality of vital statistical and other data for studying mortality and health at late ages 21

    2.1. Studies assessing the quality of demographic data
    2.2. Changes in the quality of U.S. demographic data: milestones
    2.3. Summary

III. Biological rationales for models of mortality 32

    3.1. The Gompertz Paradigm
    3.2. Stochastic models of mortality and aging
    3.3. Inference about an organism's internal state
    3.4. Evidence for heterogeneity and selection in age trajectories of human mortality
    3.5. Dynamic-state heterogeneity and age changes in chronic disease processes
    3.6. Interventions in chronic disease and mortality processes at late ages
    3.7. Summary

IV. Changing concepts of the biology of late-age morbidity and mortality 46

    4.1. Changes in cause-specific mortality
    4.2. Mechanisms underlying changes in cause-specific mortality
    4.3. The role of pathogens in circulatory disease development
    4.4. The role of pathogens in cancer
    4.5. Cell death and it's contribution to human survival: apoptosis and aging

	4.6.	The effects of micro-nutrients on chronic disease risks and aging
	4.7.	Consumption of animal protein, CVD, and osteo-arthritic changes
	4.8.	Summary

V. Effects of evolution on the age trajectory of human mortality curves 65

	5.1.	Survival and evolution
	5.2.	Evolution and the age dependence of human mortality
	5.3.	Adverse environmental exposures and age changes
	5.4.	The age-related efficacy of immunological surveillance for genetic errors
	5.5.	Atherosclerosis in U.S. African-Americans and whites may represent different pathological processes
	5.6.	Early survival advantages and their effects at late ages
	5.7.	Exogenous modifications of genetic factors and their phenotypic effects
	5.8.	The time scale of evolutionary effects on aging
	5.9.	The loss of the ability to manufacture ascorbic acid
	5.10.	Acquired disease resistance due to ecosystem changes
	5.11.	Changes in the ecosystem and technical disruptions of evolutionary processes
	5.12.	Summary

VI. The role of selection, debilitation, and adaptation in forming age patterns of mortality: a statistical perspective 86

	6.1.	Why does old-age mortality level off?
	6.2.	Fixed frailty in Gompertz-Makeham models
	6.3.	Acquired heterogeneity (debilitation) models
	6.4.	Phase type distribution models
	6.5.	Summary

VII. Analysis of genetic effects on human longevity 96

	7.1.	Longevity as a phenotypic trait

- 7.2. Linkage analysis
- 7.3. Allele sharing analysis
- 7.4. Case control methods
- 7.5. Quantitative trait locus maps
- 7.6. Combining genetic and biostatistical models in analyzing human longevity
  - 7.6.1. Logistic regression models for biologically related individuals
  - 7.6.2. Regression for related individuals
- 7.7. Genetic analysis of duration data
  - 7.7.1. Shared frailty models
  - 7.7.2. Correlated frailty model
  - 7.7.3. Correlated frailty model with covariates
  - 7.7.4. EM-algorithms to estimate parameters of correlated frailty models from twin data
- 7.8. Combining survival and genetic trait analysis in twin data: estimating lower bounds to the limit of human life expectancy from bivariate survival data
- 7.9. Summary

VIII. Human mortality and physiological change at late ages: multivariate dynamic process 109

- 8.1. Mathematical models, biological knowledge, and data
- 8.2. Observational plans determine the predictive power of the MWY model
  - 8.2.1. Analysis of failure-times where age-related mortality is driven by latent processes
  - 8.2.2. Longitudinal data where mortality is driven by observed covariates
  - 8.2.3. Randomly changing hazards and conditional survival functions

8.3. Quadratic hazard models of aging and mortality
8.4. Marginal and conditional hazards

    8.4.1. The hazard as a function of observed and unobserved covariates

8.5. The MWY approach to estimating a quadratic hazard without covariates
8.6. Incompletely observed covariates

    8.6.1 Continuously changing stochastic covariates observed at discrete times

8.7. Generalizations for dependent observed and unobserved processes
8.8. Examples: longitudinal surveys and population studies

    8.8.1. The Framingham heart study
    8.8.2. The national long-term care surveys

8.9. General properties of the age-dependent quadratic hazard
8.10. Summary

IX. Population models of human aging and mortality 135

    9.1. Life table equations
    9.2. Cohort life tables for multidimensional state processes
    9.3. Age trajectories in cohorts; diffusion and mortality selection
    9.4. Summary

X. Discussion 147

    10.1. Aging as a dynamic adaptive process
    10.2. The biology and epidemiology of human aging processes
    10.3. Contribution of genes and environment in the aging process

References 153

List of tables and figures

Tables

2.1. Estimates of sex specific mortality rates at ages 100 and 110 and their mortality percent increase age 100 to 110 30
8.1. Chi-squared values associated with risk factors, $\tilde{x}_t$, and with the senescence process θ for total mortality in Framingham 34 year follow-up 125
8.2. 1982-1984-1989 NLTCS; seven functional scores: total mortality 130
9.1. Life tables and age trajectory of the averages of three disability intensity scores for females in the U.S. NLTCS followed 1982 to 1991 138
9.2. Male and female life tables calculated from the three NLTCS and mortality 1982 to 1991 for high and low education subgroups 140
9.3. A comparison of projections (in millions of persons) based on control of multiple risk factors, a 2% continuing decline in mortality and two Census Bureau variants 145

Figures

2.1. Mortality rates (per 100,000) for white males 26
2.2. Mortality rates (per 100,000) for white females 27
5.1. Three scenarios relating the age distribution of physiological stress to the shape of human mortality rate changes with age 73
7.1. Individual relative risk for Danish female twins, birth cohorts of 1870-1910 107
8.1. Quadratic hazard functions at ages 50 and 95 when covariate information is informative (θ= 8.1% Framingham) and highly informative (θ=4.8% NLTCS) about senescence processes θ. 132
9.1. Trajectories of the population aged 65+ and 85+ for males and females, optimal intervention and highest Census Bureau series 142
9.2. Gender specific ranges of populations in 2010, 2040, 2060, and 2080 assuming a longevity change due to risk factor interventions phased in over 20 to 40 years; median ages and 95% population bounds 143

Authors

Kenneth G. Manton, Ph.D.
    Director
    Center for Demographic Studies
    Duke University
    2117 Campus Drive
    Box 90408
    Durham, North Carolina 27708-0408
    USA
    Phone +1 919-684-6126
    Fax   +1 919-684-3861
    e-mail: kgm@cds.duke.edu

Professor Anatoli I. Yashin, Ph.D., Sc.D.
    Max Planck Institute for Demographic Research (MPIDR)
    Doberaner Strasse 114
    D-18057 Rostock
    Germany
    Phone +49 381-2081-106
    Fax   +49 381-2081-169
    e-mail: yashin@demogr.mpg.de

Acknowledgments

The authors gratefully acknowledge the assistance of Carl Brehmer, Ivan Iachine, Betsy Smith, Cassie Gray, David Gray, and Edward Davison.

Kenneth G. Manton and Anatoli I. Yashin

I. Introduction

1.1. New evidence about aging

The focus of the study of aging depends on the scientific discipline. Demographers studying mortality and survival relate aging to an increase in the risk of death with age (focusing on the relation of age to adult mortality, i.e. deaths occurring after age 30). Demographic models have often ignored the effects of health changes as well as the influence of genetic and environmental factors on mortality. Taking such effects into account may help in the explanation and forecasting of mortality trajectories.

For epidemiologists studying the effects of genetic and other factors on disease, age is a variable associated with the risk of specific chronic conditions which become clinically manifest in mid- or late life. Epidemiologists try to identify the genetic and environmental factors influencing the manifestation of chronic disease over age – as well as the effects of lifestyle or medical interventions that may postpone the age at onset of specific chronic diseases, or slow disease progression and, consequently, delay the age at death.

Geriatricians and other clinicians try to analyze the complex interactions of multiple comorbidities and disabilities in elderly patients and to determine what medical interventions are feasible – and, frequently, which interventions may most improve the quality, as well as the quantity, of life (e.g. optimizing active life expectancy, cf. Manton et al., 1992, Rubenstein and Josephson, 1989).

Biologists and physiologists investigate details of age-related changes in the functioning and interaction of different organs, tissues, and subsystems of the organism – often using data from well-controlled animal experiments. Medvedev (1990) identified over 300 theories and models that attempted to explain age-related changes in subsystems of organisms. Finch (1990) examined the age variation of degenerative biological processes and life span over a wide variety of animal species (Finch and Pike, 1996).

In all these areas significant progress in identifying the basic regularities of the aging process has been achieved. In particular, the population epidemiology of chronic diseases has become better understood. Progress has also been made in identifying the causes of the continuing increase of (historically unprecedented) life expectancy levels of human populations in many developed countries (e.g. U.S.A., Japan, France, cf. Manton and Vaupel, 1995; Vaupel and Jeune, 1996), and in select cultural and religious groups (Seventh-day Adventists, Mormons, cf. Manton et al., 1991). This progress was accompanied by improvements in the quality of vital statistical and other (especially longitudinal survey) data (and data systems) at late ages, combined with rapidly growing scientific insights into the physiology and molecular biology of aging. These changes challenge demographers, biologists, geneticists, and gerontologists to address even more detailed questions about the nature of aging and survival processes. New data and new formulations of the study of aging require a critical review of existing models of disease, functional disability, mortality, and biological senescence in order to generate better and more comprehensive models of aging. New models must not only be substantially more detailed, they also must use new statistical and mathematical principles to exploit and integrate both current and emerging scientific insights and concepts, and the growing availability of improved, and new, types of longitudinal data. These models must link multiple types of longitudinal and cross-sectional data to improve our understanding of complex age-related physiological processes to greater ages than in the past.

With new models and data, past and future changes in human populations can be better analyzed. In particular, the ability to forecast the growth of the elderly and oldest-old population, including groups with currently high health-service needs, can be improved. Furthermore, beyond improving predictions of the size of the elderly population, new models and data can generate better estimates of the age distribution of morbidity and disability in the elderly and oldest-old populations. Such health forecasts will also improve our ability to anticipate future health-service needs and expenditures (Manton et al., 1997). If the structure of the forecasting model is sufficiently parametrically detailed, and biologically realistic, it may help researchers and policy makers to identify and plan more effective strategies for improving the future health of the population and for assessing the cost/efficacy of such interventions (Manton, 1996).

Experiments with aging laboratory organisms as well as models and theories of aging used in different scientific disciplines have produced new data and concepts which allow a more complete, and possibly significantly altered, understanding of the nature of aging and survival to late ages. How can demography, as the scientific discipline most responsible for studying human populations and their dynamics, benefit from new substantive scientific studies and changing biological theories of aging? How can demographic ideas contribute to the development of such theories? Clearly, for demographic analyses to be biologically valid they must be consistent with findings from other scientific disciplines. This requires developing more biologically relevant demographic models of health processes (Manton et al., 1997; Manton and Yashin, 1998). It also raises questions as to what demographic concepts must be changed to meet the consensus of new theoretical and empirical evidence.

The answers to these questions are, in part, dictated by health changes evident in large, free-living national populations. For example, the age range in which specific health events of interest occur is now being rapidly extended in many countries to ages where the current theoretical and empirical demographic knowledge of human aging and mortality processes is still limited – e.g. to ages 85+, or 100+. New, clinically important syndromes are being identified at ever-increasing ages. For example, the deposition of amyloid protein in cardiac muscle, which leads to late-age restrictive cardiomyopathy, has recently been identified, along with possible genetic determinants, and found to have a significant prevalence in populations aged 90 to 99 (Jacobson et al., 1997; Benson, 1997). The immune-function disorder known as "monoclonal gammopathies of unknown significance" has a high prevalence in Caucasians aged 95+ (Radl et al., 1995) and is related to multiple myeloma and other cancer risks (Browner et al., 1993).

1.2. The need for new models of late-age mortality

To illustrate the conceptual and empirical issues involved in the analysis of human aging and survival, we will often use one of the "standard" parametric models of the age dependence of adult human mortality, namely, the Gompertz hazard function. This has been used in many biological (Strehler, 1977; Finch, 1990), demographic (Manton et al., 1986), and actuarial (Spiegelman, 1968) studies. The Gompertz hazard function predicts that human adult mortality rates increase exponentially with age. This model has been accepted by many demographers, biologists, and actuaries as well approximating the empirical distribution of human mortality rates from ages 30 to 85 in many different national, and actuarially select, human populations over a long time (Wetterstrand, 1981). It has also been found to describe the adult mortality of many animal species (Finch and Pike, 1996).

One set of analytic issues arising in using the Gompertz hazard function is whether appropriate principles of statistical inference and formal hypothesis testing are used to evaluate the empirical fit of the Gompertz function – especially at the extreme right tail of the human (and other) survival distributions. Even if appropriate analytic procedures and models are used, study populations and samples have to be designed to yield sufficient data to make statistical tests of differences in the extreme tail of survival distributions with adequate power.

The data available on the biological phenomena that the Gompertz hazard function is used to describe has been rapidly growing and changing in content in the post-WWII period. The age range for which the Gompertz hazard function provides an adequate empirical description of mortality (i.e. ages 30 to 85) encompassed most U.S. deaths in 1960 (the male median age at death was 70.7 years; for females it was 77.8 years; in

1960, 87.4% of U.S. males and 75.0% of females died before age 85). The age range 30 to 85, however, is now a much smaller proportion of U.S. adult deaths. In 1995, the U.S. male median age at death was 75.8 years (an increase of 4.7 years from 1960); for U.S. females the median age at death was estimated to be 82.4 years (an increase of 4.6 years from 1960). The proportion of deaths occurring before age 85 (according to period life table models for 1990) was 78.2% for males (-9.2%); and 58.1% for females (-14.9%; Social Security Administration (SSA), 1992). Thus, fewer deaths now occur in the age range over which the Gompertz hazard function is thought to describe human mortality adequately. As the median age at death in the U.S. population approaches 85 years, the percentage change in deaths from ages below to ages above 85 years accelerates. This is because the "median" represents the dense, "central" portion of the human age at death distribution. The decline in the proportion of deaths occurring before age 85 was larger for females than males from 1960 to 1995. As the U.S. male median age at death approaches 85 years, the proportion of deaths under age 85 for males will decline relatively more rapidly due to the general shape of the human age at death distribution.

The empirical and conceptual limitations of the Gompertz hazard function as a biological model of the force of human mortality increase as the U.S. population of oldest-old persons (those aged 85+) grows – and as survival continues to improve at later ages elsewhere as well (mortality declines have been rapid from ages 80 to 100 in many developed countries; Vaupel and Jeune, 1995). In Japan, female life expectancy at birth in 1993 exceeded 83.3 years; it was 76.5 years for males (WHO, 1994). The U.S. Census Bureau estimated the life expectancy at birth of Asian and Pacific Islanders in 1993 (one of whose major components is persons of Japanese ancestry) to be 86.0 years for females and 80.2 years for males (Day, 1993). Other long-lived population groups (e.g. Seventh-day Adventists, Catholic Nuns, and Mormons, who follow religious tenets restricting exposure to common risk factors such as cigarette smoking and alcohol, and who often practice strict nutritional regimes such as vegetarianism) may have higher life expectancy than even U.S. Asian and Pacific Islanders (e.g. up to 95+ years at birth; Manton et al., 1991).

By 2050, when the largest of the post-WWII baby boom birth cohorts reaches age 85, only 66.9% of males are projected to die (under conservative middle-range SSA projection survival assumptions) before age 85, as compared to less than half (46.8%) of U.S. females (SSA, 1992). The Gompertz hazard function may not be biologically valid as a model of adult mortality when such large proportions of U.S. deaths occur after age 85 (22 to 42% in 1995; 33 to 53% in 2050). This is because the dominant cause-specific mortality processes and the effects of mortality selection on the moments of the population distribution of environmentally and genetically controlled physiological states will change significantly at late ages – and differently for males and females (Manton et al., 1994b; Manton and Stallard, 1996). The proportion of the population that is elderly in many economically developed countries, including the U.S., is rapidly growing (e.g., Japan was projected to have 25% or more of its population aged 65+ in 2025; Nihon University, 1982). This suggests an urgency to develop models that better describe late-age mortality by integrating new scientific knowledge and data on the biology of aging in more rigorous, parametrically detailed mathematical formulations. Population trends with respect to aging are producing effects that are already being integrated into popular cultural norms about aging. A recent U.S. marketing survey found that adults currently aged 50 did not consider a person "elderly" until they were at least 79 years of age. Economic planning for retirement of middle-aged, middle-income persons in good health now often assumes a need to plan for funds to last at least to age 95 for the surviving member of the couple.

An additional problem in creating population models of late-age mortality has been the past reliance on cross-sectional, or period, data in demographic analyses. Cross-sectional data frequently only represent what occurs for individuals under stringent, and often biologically and dynamically unrealistic, assumptions. Yet, cross-sectional data are often used to make inferences about human aging processes and the effects of total and cause-specific mortality on the U.S. population and health-care system (e.g. Olshansky et al., 1991). Cohort data are needed to better model processes at the individual level – especially when mortality selection and health dynamic processes operate over the adult life span (Manton et al., 1997). However, even in cohort analyses the historical basis of health changes up to the time the cohort is assessed may only be partly recognized and described (Manton, 1996; Manton et al., 1997). It will become evident, as we review evidence, that aging processes are undergoing rapid changes because the early health histories of recent elderly cohorts changed significantly in the early and mid- 20th century (Manton, 1996; Manton, 1997; Manton et al., 1997; Fogel, 1994; Lanska and Mi, 1993). This puts a heavier burden on new longitudinal data sources since the multidimensional physiological age and temporal dynamics of multiple cohorts born over a long period of time must be modeled.

1.3. *The monograph*

This monograph is organized into ten chapters. In Chapter II, the trends in the improvement of the quality of population and vital statistics data are discussed. The consequences of improved data quality for analyses of health and mortality changes at age 90+ are examined. In addition, we show that the shape of the empirical mortality curve at older ages observed in developed countries today cannot be explained with traditional demographic concepts and the Gompertz hazard function. The need for a biological rationale in developing models for understanding age changes in survival is emphasized. In Chapter III, the biological foundations of mortality models are discussed. Biological evidence now exists that there are substantial individual differences in susceptibility to diseases and death. This evidence is confirmed by molecular epidemiological studies and by the results of statistical analysis of survival data as well as of data on the age at onset of disease and disability. The modeling of genetic and acquired susceptibility to disease and death thus becomes crucial to understanding their contribution to population aging processes. We examine the special needs of substantive theory describing mortality and health dynamics at extreme ages. This theory must integrate the concepts of human health, disability and frailty into demographic models of mortality events and the risk of death. In Chapter IV new findings about the functioning of physiological mechanisms and their relation to aging and chronic disease processes are examined. Changes in the age patterns of cause-specific mortality are discussed. Possible factors underlying such changes are considered. They include improvements in medical treatment, which contribute to period effects, and the long term effects of improved nutrition, an increased supply of micro nutrients, and advances in hygiene and live stock health protection, which may make a substantial contribution to cohort effects. New results on the role of pathogens in the development of chronic diseases such as atherosclerosis and cancer and the influence of bacterial micro-environments on the aging process are reviewed. The metabolic pathways of consumption of animal protein in the presence of micro nutrients (e.g. vitamins and minerals) and their relation to the etiology of cancer and cardiovascular disease are discussed.

The role of evolution in determining the age dependence of chronic morbidity and related mortality is discussed in chapter V. Traditional evolutionary theories of senescence are reviewed. Their limitations are discussed. Examples of the adverse effects of genetic adaptation of human populations to specific lifestyle and environmental conditions are considered. These include the loss of the ability by humans to manufacture ascorbic acid and the emergence of Lp(a), the development of the MDR1 gene to protect important organs from water-soluble toxins, the genetic development of the P450 superfamily, etc. These examples show how gene-environment interactions may modulate the expression of specific genes at late ages. With Chapters III, IV, and V describing the physiology of human failure mechanisms and their genetic determinants, we have the necessary biological background to review the mathematical models of mortality and aging that have been used to analyze human survival in mid-

and late ages.

These models are discussed in Chapter VI. Several models explaining the deviation at late ages of mortality rates from those predicted by the Gompertz hazard function are evaluated. The role of genetic and acquired heterogeneity as well as individual adaptation is reviewed. Chapter VII examines methodological and data problems in analyzing genetic effects on human disease and mortality. It is shown that survival and longitudinal data on related individuals, together with multivariate survival and health history models, may increase our understanding of aging processes. To make susceptibility (frailty) models identifiable and to better understand the effect of genes on environment and individual susceptibility to disease and death, multivariate models of aging and the survival of biologically related individuals (e.g. twins) are examined. Some models use correlated frailty concepts and proportional hazard functions. An alternate approach is the use of quadratic hazard functions driven by vectors of observed, unobserved, and partly observed dynamic covariates. The importance of stochastically changing individual susceptibilities to disease and mortality, which are unobserved (or sometimes partly observed in longitudinal studies of aging and survival) is emphasized.

In Chapter VIII a multivariate, stochastic process model of human mortality and aging is presented which uses the quadratic dependence of the conditional hazard rate on influential factors. This model can be applied to longitudinal survival data with covariates to directly evaluate the biological mechanisms of human aging and mortality processes. In quadratic hazard models, data on observed time-varying covariates may be used – together with data on genetic markers of disease and longevity. The relationship between individual physiological changes and aggregate population characteristics is considered. Approaches to identifying model parameters using different types of data are discussed. In Chapter IX the use of models with time-varying physiological covariates in forecasting mortality changes in human populations is discussed. In Chapter X we discuss the analytic and conceptual uses to which population health dynamic models can be put.

It is hoped that the material in the monograph will be of use to researchers in many disciplines related to aging. There is a growing need to integrate findings from the biological and basic sciences into demographic and epidemiological models of human population aging and mortality. The material presented offers, for demographers, a review of recent scientific evidence and data on the biology of human disease, disability, and aging processes, i.e. processes that contribute to the observed shape of the age-specific mortality curve. For biologists and epidemiologists the monograph examines methodological approaches for translating research insights developed in the analyses of individual physiological changes during aging to analyses of the age dynamics of human populations. These approaches recognize the limitations of the population data that currently exist for modeling human health and survival processes for individuals. This monograph does not cover comprehensively all ideas, findings and research methods for studying the aging process. The topics discussed reflect the interests and experience of the authors in certain areas of aging studies. The monograph emphasizes the need for demographic research on aging and survival to utilize more completely knowledge and data from relevant scientific disciplines.

II. Changes in the quality of vital statistical and other data for studying mortality and health at late ages

Until recently the quality of mortality statistics at late ages was not well-documented in most countries. The data in official demographic reports often aggregated mortality statistics after age 85. So empirical data about the upper tail of the life-span distribution for humans were often not available. Statistical data on age at death of individuals who died before age 85 often contained errors induced in data collection and registration of death. This inhibited the development of research in aging combining evidence from biological, physiological and demographic studies. To make these studies possible the quality of survival data at late ages had to be improved. Recent demographic studies suggest that significant progress in securing data quality has been achieved during the last few decades. In this chapter we review the quality of demographic data using U.S. sources. Useful information about situations in other countries can be found in the monographs by Kannisto (1994, 1996).

2.1. Studies assessing the quality of demographic data

One difficulty in studying human survival in the U.S. concerns the reliability of age reporting at late ages in both census and death certificate data. In some countries, data quality at late ages is not problematic. Sweden, for example, has had a high-quality population registry, and Britain a good vital statistical system, for a long time (Condran et al., 1991). It appears that age reporting in U.S. vital statistics up to age 100, has improved in quality – especially for U.S. whites (Kestenbaum, 1992). Ironically, if the quality of U.S. data was not good in the past, with age over-reported in death certificate records, recent improvements in data quality should cause estimates of mortality rates to be upwardly biased and the rates of increase of the elderly and oldest-old populations to be downwardly biased.

Evidence of improvements in the quality of age reporting in U.S. data come from a variety of studies. One compares current documents from different sources – such as census records and death certificate data (e.g., for 1960; Hambright, 1969; Kitagawa and Hauser, 1973). A second compares ages reported in earlier census records with ages reported on death certificates for current decedents. Rosenwaike and Logue (1983) compared ages reported for persons found in the 1900 U.S. census to a linked set of death certificates for decedents over age 85 in 1970 in two large eastern states (New Jersey and Pennsylvania). A third study compares ages reported on death certificates to ages reported in Social Security/Medicare files in 1987 in two states (Kestenbaum, 1992). A fourth study compares ages reported on U.S. population census forms with those in special census post-enumeration surveys (e.g., Condran et al., 1991). A fifth examines population changes between U.S. censuses using formal demographic methods and data on mortality and migration.

2.2. Changes in the quality of U.S. demographic data: milestones

A number of conclusions can be reached from the different methods for assessing the quality of age reporting in demographic data. In general, age on U.S. death certificates is believed to be more accurately reported than the age reported in the U.S. decennial census. This is because U.S. census data is collected only every ten years, generally in survey form and possibly from a proxy respondent, without the benefit of ancillary records, and with population coverage (generally undercounts) that is correlated with demographic and socio-economic factors.

In contrast, the death certificate is a medico-legal document. It is filled out by a physician or other legally designated certifier, often with medical and hospital records available (records on health sometimes extending over a number of years) in close temporal proximity to the time of death and with nearly 100% coverage of deaths in the U.S. The U.S. Matched Record Study of 1960 (Kitagawa and Hauser, 1973) showed that the age reported on death certificates tends to be lower than the age reported in U.S. census data when age disagreed between the two types of records. A final conclusion is that ages reported at extreme ages (e.g. 90+) on U.S. death certificates may be higher than the age recorded on U.S. census records in studies matching early censuses (1900) to then current (1970) death certificates.

The use of earlier censuses (e.g. 1880, 1900) in some U.S. studies, while not ideal, was necessitated by a lack of birth certificates for those early dates to compare with the ages reported on death certificates for many elderly persons. The lack of birth certificates for that period was due both to high U.S. in-migration in the early years of the 20th century, and because many state birth registration systems were not complete (i.e. they did not cover 100% of births occurring in the state population) until recently. A concern with record matching studies is that early censuses (e.g. 1880 or 1900) had significant population coverage problems with little ability to directly assess the magnitude or demographic patterns of the under-coverage. For example, the U.S. native white population was estimated to be underenumerated in 1900 by 6.2% – compared to an estimated 11% undercount for U.S. blacks (Coale and Rives, 1973). Coverage problems continue. In the 1990 U.S. census the population aged 85+ was estimated to be undercounted by 2.5% in analyses using post-enumeration surveys and formal demographic models (Day, 1993).

Migrants from foreign countries, or from states other the two studied, precluded making matches for many decedents in the Rosenwaike and Logue (1983) study. This is important in that migrants often reflect a select, mobile population with better than average health characteristics. This has been suggested as one cause of the current advantageous (relative to U.S. whites) mortality rates for U.S. Hispanics (Sorlie et al., 1992). The two states examined in the Rosenwaike and Logue (1983) record linkage study, New Jersey and Pennsylvania, have large metropolitan areas (e.g. Philadelphia, Pittsburgh, Camden, Trenton, Newark). Different racial and socioeconomic groups may have adverse health experiences after moving to these areas.

It was assumed in the Rosenwaike and Logue (1983) study that ages were better reported (they were assumed 100% accurate) on the U.S. census in 1900 than on U.S. death certificates in 1970. But the statistical systems which, in recent years, require consistent age reporting (e.g. qualification for federal programs such as Social Security, Medicare, Medicaid, food stamps, welfare; qualification for private insurance and pension benefits; registration for licensure, certification, and permits, such as for driver's licenses and passports; registration for employment purposes mandated by occupational laws; private cross-linkage and checking of such record systems, such as in commercial credit checks) were not done in 1900. In other words, U.S. census age reports in 1900, which were possibly from a proxy, were not as frequently, routinely, or carefully done by individuals as in recent U.S. censuses and on death certificates. The trend toward computerized cross-system age checking and validation is accelerating in the U.S. as population-based data systems proliferate.

The linkage study (Rosenwaike and Logue, 1983) concluded that, for the U.S. white population aged 85 to 100 in 1970:

> "The figures calculated here imply that if numerators for age-specific death rates for whites were adjusted on the basis of improved age statement on the death certificate, the changes for all five year groups would be small. For only one of the four age groups (90-94 years) would adjustment result in a change in excess of 2%" (p. 582).

Rosenwaike and Logue (1983) also conclude:

> "The findings of the present investigation – at least for the white population – dispute the belief that age reported on death records for persons 85 years and older

are of questionable credibility. On the contrary, it appears that death certificates for those 85 to 99 years in Pennsylvania and New Jersey in 1970 agree remarkably well with an independent check." (p. 584).

Furthermore, empirical results for blacks in 1970 may not be as bad at late ages as one might expect. Among U.S. black decedents aged 85 to 89 (i.e., above the ages when U.S. black/white mortality crossovers are observed; Manton and Stallard, 1997), in contrast to U.S. whites, there was little excess probability of reporting an inflated age on the death certificate. Specifically, 26% of blacks in this age group reported a younger age, and 31% reported an older age. Consequently, the age reporting on U.S. death certificates up to age 90 for U.S. blacks in 1970 should not show a strong bias in age over-reporting. Errors in age reporting for U.S. blacks are more random, and they are likely to be more strongly effected by artifacts of age rounding and heaping (Rosenwaike and Logue, 1983; p. 579).

In Kitagawa and Hauser (1973) corrections for under-coverage in the 1960 U.S. census largely balanced the estimated age reporting errors in 1960 (p. 96). A comparison of Tables 5 and 6 in Rosenwaike and Logue (1983) show a closer correspondence of death-certificate ages reported in 1970 to the 1900 census than to the ages reported in the 1960 census. This suggests improvements in age reporting for U.S. whites aged 85 to 99 and U.S. nonwhites aged 85 to 94 on death certificates filed for decedents in 1960 compared with those filed in 1970. This could in part be due to the start of Medicare and of state and federal Medicaid programs in 1965. It suggests that by 1970, the quality of age reporting by U.S. whites, and possibly U.S. nonwhites, on death certificates up to age 100 is reasonably good.

Kestenbaum's (1992) match of ages reported on U.S. death certificates and Social Security records in two states in 1987 suggests further improvements (after 1970) in age reporting on death certificates – especially for U.S. whites. This suggests that extinct cohort life table methods, which use only death records (and hence are forced, by construction, to have internally consistent morality rate denominators and numerators), may be valuable in assessing mortality at extreme ages (80 to 100+) for recent dates (Manton and Stallard, 1996a; Condran et al., 1991).

Another way to evaluate changes in data quality is to determine if recent U.S. improvements are plausible. Improvements in age reporting on U.S. death certificates may be partly due to the advent of Social Security in 1936-1937 (Bayo and Faber, 1985). The reporting of ages at death for the 1872–1874 U.S. birth cohorts was better than for cohorts born in the 1860s. This was because the 1872–1874 cohorts were the first to qualify for Social Security benefits and thus had to go through a rigorous age determination process – the effects of this age review for persons qualifying for Social

Security benefits were carried forward to later U.S. birth cohorts (Manton and Stallard, 1995b). In addition, the completion of the U.S. vital statistics system with the entry of Texas in 1933, the introduction of Medicaid and Medicare in 1965, and the computerization and cross linkage of all these systems improved age reporting in U.S. data – as will, in all likelihood, increases in the education of the U.S. oldest-old population from 1980 to the year 2015 (Preston, 1992).

Such improvements in U.S. data and data systems may allow us, in the future, to better evaluate claims of persons living to very extreme ages in the U.S. (e.g., an age of 126 years was claimed by a California woman with birth certificate documentation (Kautsky, 1995); and by a man based on Social Security records). For example, the reporting of age at death to Medicare is now done electronically and used to update Medicare payment files. As a consequence, Medicare mortality records may be relatively complete in 2 months – rather than the 6 or more months required in the past (e.g. 1984).

Despite improvements in U.S. data quality and data systems there are intrinsic limitations to the inferences that can be made using cross-sectional death certificate data. This is illustrated in Figures 2.1 and 2.2, where we present the change in U.S. mortality rates (1980 to 1992) for white males and females at ages 75-84 and 85+, respectively.

Figures 2.1 and 2.2 show that, at ages 75 to 84, there was a regular decline in U.S. white male and female mortality rates from 1980 to 1992. 1987 and 1988 are of interest since they are a.) the years for which Kestenbaum (1992) examined U.S. mortality rates, and b.) the last two years of data used to construct SSA life tables for 1990 (SSA, 1992). For ages 85+, mortality rates for 1987 and 1988 are never lower than the average mortality rate for 1980 to 1992. For white males, mortality rates in 1987 and 1988 are higher than in 1982. For females, both 1987 and 1988 have even more extreme mortality rates – with 1988 being higher than any other year in the entire period 1980 to 1992. Thus, efforts to compare period mortality rates for either 1987 or 1988 with long term cohort mortality patterns, or experience averaged over a long period of time (Lew and Garfinkel, 1990), can be misleading.

There are new observational plans whose structure may improve the assessment of both morbidity and health changes to extreme ages. In the 1982, 1984, 1989, and 1994 National Long Term Care Surveys (NLTCS) the age of individuals can be tracked from the age reported in 1982 (based on Medicare-reported dates of birth) to their date of death as recorded in Medicare files (currently up to January, 1996). The NLTCS samples are sufficiently elderly (all sample persons are over 65 years of age; mean age of the four samples is over 80 years), large (about 36,000 persons in the 1982 to 1994 longitudinal file; a total of roughly 18,000 deaths were observed over 16 years, from 1982 to 1997), and followed long enough to allow analyses of survival of multiple birth cohorts to late ages (e.g. ages 115 to 120). For example, if ages up to 95 are reliably reported in

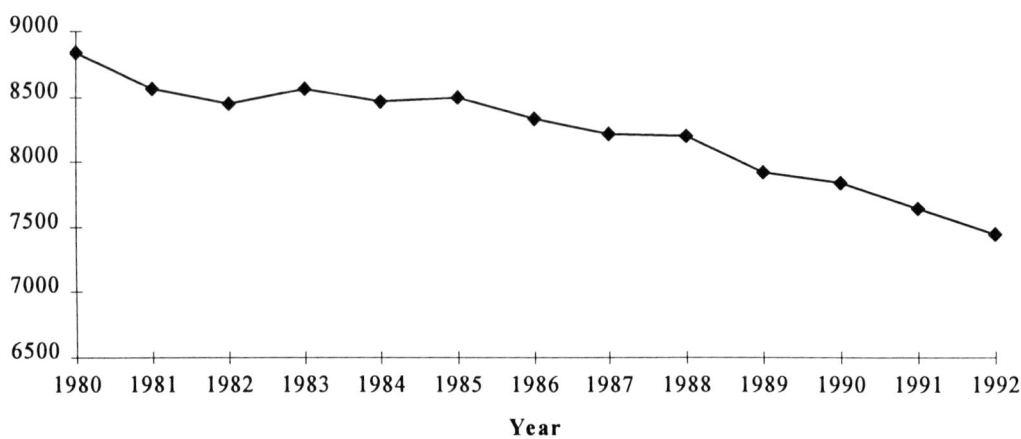

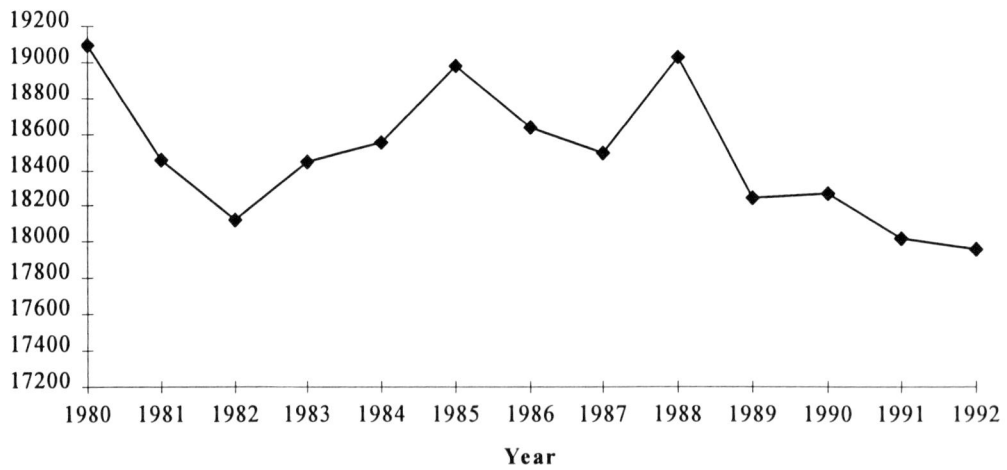

Figure 2.1. Mortality rates (per 100,000) for white males

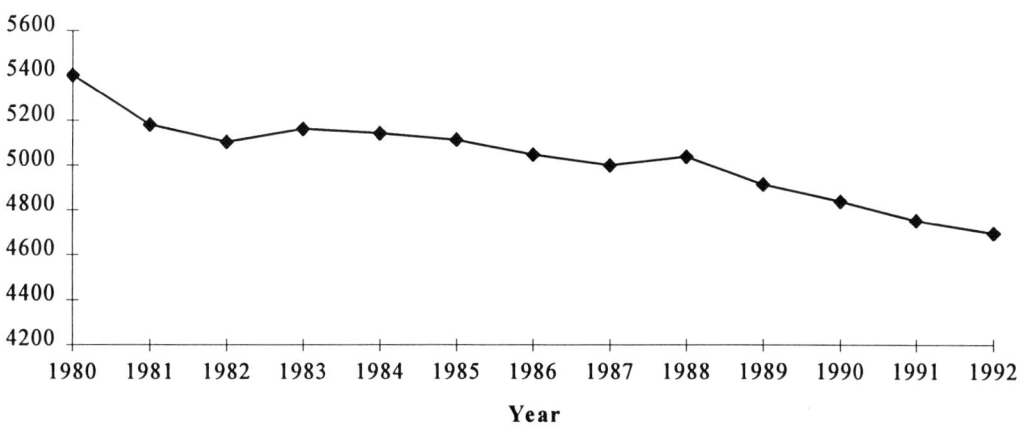

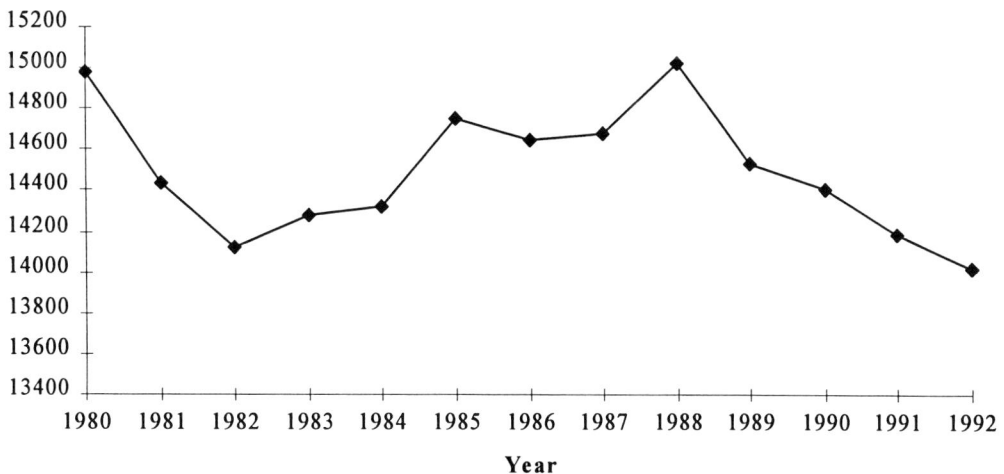

Figure 2.2. Mortality rates (per 100,000) for white females

Medicare data for 1982 (i.e. for persons aged 78 in 1965, when Medicare was started) then ages up to 110 should be reliably reported in the 1996 Medicare files. Extinct cohort analyses using only mortality data from 1960 to 1990 and independent analyses of the 1982, 1984, and 1989 NLTCS data (using only Medicare-recorded deaths, and ages at death, 1982 to 1991) produced similar estimates of life expectancy at ages 65+ and 85+ and of mortality rates to ages 100+ (Manton and Vaupel, 1995; Manton and Stallard, 1996). If ages reported in Medicare data in 1982 were reliable up to age 100 (e.g. Rosenwaike and Logue, 1983) then ages to 115 should be reliably reported by 1996. By the year 2001 it should be possible to track ages to 120.

The NLTCS are longitudinal studies of the U.S. elderly population having the advantages of large sample sizes (about 20,000 persons 65+ in each survey year) and of being nationally representative. There are smaller, more detailed studies of select populations where age is reliably reported – and physiologically more detailed measurements made. One study examined 795 persons aged 90 to 103 (mean age about 93.5 years) who underwent surgery at the Mayo Clinic (Rochester, Minnesota) from 1975 to 1985 (Hosking et al., 1989). Surgery rates for persons aged 90 and over increased fivefold from 1975 to 1985 – while preoperative mortality decreased from 29% in the 1960s to 9% by the late 1970s. Age and other clinical data on the 795 persons were considered highly reliable because the average length of time medical care was provided for each patient at the Mayo Clinic (and, consequently, the length of the continuous medical record history) prior to surgery was 30.6 years.

Mortality within 30 days of surgery was 8.1% for ages 90-94, 9.4% for ages 95-99 and 15.4% for ages 100+. Over 70.5% of patients aged 100+ at the date of surgery survived more than a year. Five-year survival for all patients (i.e. from mean age 93.5 years to roughly 98.5 years) was significantly higher (21%; standard error of estimate 1.4%) than the survival expected from life tables estimated for the general regional population (16%). For those patients with physiological scores assigned by anesthesiologists of 2 (relatively good, but not excellent, surgical candidates), roughly 50% of those aged 90+ survived five or more years past surgery. Thus, this detailed study of medical intervention on an extremely elderly population showed that long-term survival (5 years) was higher than for the same age groups in life tables calculated for the general regional population.

Clinical findings of survival in very elderly populations that is better than in standard demographic data are common. A study of aortic-valve replacement in patients aged 80 years or more (Elayda et al., 1993) found that, for simple aortic-valve replacement, the five-year survival for a group of patients aged 82.6 years on average at the time of surgery and comprised of both genders was 57%. Surgical procedures were done over a 15 year period from 1975 to 1991 (Manton and Stallard, 1996) during which there was improvement in techniques.

A recent study was made of mortality one year after a heart attack for persons aged 75+ in 1984 and 1994. The one-year mortality rate dropped 42% over this time period due to the introduction of reperfusion therapy after 1984 (Gottlieb et al., 1997).

A further confirmation of such clinical observations (i.e. of good outcomes at late ages) is found in multiple estimates of late-age mortality (ages 100+) from different studies, some with high quality data, in Table 2.1.

Mortality rates at ages 100 to 109 and 110+ increased slowly in these data sets. The average increase in mortality past age 100 was 3.1% per year – compared to the 5 to 6% increase per year assumed in SSA life-table estimates after age 100 (SSA, 1992). Age increases in mortality for centenarian males were generally slower than for females. Estimates made from extinct-cohort life tables for three U.S. birth cohorts (born in 1870–74, 1880–84, and 1890–94) calculated from deaths occurring over the 31 years between 1960 and 1990 show age rates of mortality increase that are intermediate to the other data sources, i.e., two sources are lower, and three are higher than the U.S. extinct-cohort estimates for ages 100 to 109 and ages 110+.

The finding of approximately constant mortality rates for U.S. male cohorts at extreme ages is consistent with the finding of constant mortality rates at late ages (relative to the species) in animal and insect experiments (e.g. Carey et al., 1992; Curtsinger et al., 1992). The average annual mortality rate estimate at age 110 (across the human studies) was 45.3% – with no estimate above 50%. A similar finding was made in producing the 1994 Society of Actuaries group annuity life-table estimates. There was no reliable data showing human mortality rates exceeding 50% per year at any age (SOA, 1994). In that study, which used data from 11 large insurance companies, mortality peaked after age 95 at about 25% per year, for both genders – and then fluctuated randomly around the 25% level for later ages. This is consistent with estimates made from U.S. vital statistics data (Manton, 1996) It is also consistent with analyses of the 1982 to 1989 NLTCS, where the mechanism producing the slower increase of mortality rates above age 95 was mortality selection of functionally impaired persons (Manton et al., 1994b).

2.3. Summary

The biological regularities of aging of individual organisms influence their chances of survival. These probabilistic characteristics of the aging process can be estimated from demographic mortality data. The quality of such data become especially important at old ages, where the number of individuals at risk is getting smaller, and where the shape and the trend of the mortality curve are of interest. We reviewed evidence on changes in the

Table 2.1. Estimates of sex specific mortality rates at ages 100 and 110 and their mortality percent increase age 100 to 110

Source of Estimate	Age 100 Rates			Age 110 Rates			% Change in Mortality		
	Male	Female	Total	Male	Female	Total	Male	Female	Total
1. U.S. 1979-81	32,8	29,1	30,1	40,0	37,6	38,2	2,0	2,6	2,4
2. CPS 1960-87	32,0	29,4	30,1	50,3	38,8	40,8	4,6	2,8	3,1
3. Cohort 1890-94	34,3	30,2	31,1	---	---	---	---	---	---
4. Cohort 1880-84	35,6	31,1	32,1	33,5	43,1	41,3	-0,6	3,3	2,6
5. Cohort 1870-74	36,9	33,3	34,2	36,9	43,5	41,8	0,0	2,7	2,0
6. IPSEN 1990-92	43,6	34,6	35,3	---	50,8	48,9	---	3,9	3,3
7. Medicare 1987	36,8	32,0	32,4	---	---	49,4	---	---	4,3
8. Kannisto 1980-90	42,1	36,8	37,8	60,2	48,8	49,4	3,6	2,9	2,7

Average of empirical estimates for age 100 (Sources 2, 3, 4, 5, 6, 7,8) and age 110 (Sources 2,4,5,6,7,8).

Source: Table 2; Manton and Stallard, 1996.

Notes on Data:
1. NCHS (1985) Decennial Life Tables for 1979-81, U.S. White's -- age 100 as reported; age 110 extrapolated from age 109 using NCHS extrapolation formula.
2. Lew and Garfinkel (1990), Cancer Prevention Study 1960-1987 -- age 100 interpolated from 95-99 and 100-104; age 110 extrapolated from 100-104 and 105-109.
3. 1890-1894 Cohort, U.S. whites (*estimates based solely on data from older cohorts).
4. 1880-1884 Cohort, U.S. Whites.
5. 1870-1874 Cohort, U.S. Whites.
6. Vallin (1993), data from IPSEN study 1990-92 -- age 100 as reported; age 110 extrapolated from 100-104 and 105-108.
7. Kestenbaum (1992), Medicare mortality 1987 -- age 100 is average of 99.5 and 100.5; age 110 is estimated from age 107.5-112.5 assuming reported value for 109.5+ is constant above age 109.5 -- figures by sex at age 100 are for U.S. Whites; figures for both sexes at ages 100 and 110 are for total U.S. population.
8. Kannisto (1994), Centenarian life table, 1980-1990, composite of 14 countries' data (Japan plus 13 European countries) -- age 100 as reported; age 110 estimated from 109-111 (males) and 108-112 (females; both sexes).

"---" = Not available.

quality of age reporting on U.S. death certificates and population censuses. U.S. data quality has improved over time. It appears that U.S. data will now support analyses of mortality up to age 100 for white males and females. A fundamental problem in many analyses of human mortality at late ages, however, is that data is often smoothed or aggregated. This may result in a loss of important information and bias the results of analyses of human mortality at late ages.

Several studies have been performed in the U.S. to assess and improve the quality of U.S. mortality and population data before and after age 85. The data verification procedures include the comparison of age reports in death certificate records to age reports from various other sources. New observational plans such as NLTCS improve the assessment procedure for morbidity and mortality characteristics. The results suggests that the U.S. vital statistical data is roughly comparable in quality to European data up to about age 100, and that this data can be used in population studies of aging together with the data from longitudinal studies.

III. Biological rationales for models of mortality

3.1. The Gompertz Paradigm

One of the first models (1825) used to describe the age dependence of adult human mortality, and explicitly relating it to biological principles, was due to the British actuary Benjamin Gompertz. He proposed that age-specific proportional declines in physical vitality caused the adult risk of death to increase exponentially with age, i.e., adult mortality rates increase by a fixed, constant percentage for each year of life. Makeham (1867) added a constant to the Gompertz function to represent exogenous forces of mortality.

The Gompertz function approximates the age dependence of mortality rates between ages 30 and 85 in many human populations (cf. e.g. Wetterstrand, 1981) – as well as the adult mortality of many animal species (Finch, 1990). For this reason many researchers have used and continue to use (e.g. Strehler, 1995; Finch and Pike, 1996) the Gompertz hazard function to model adult mortality.

To further rationalize the Gompertz function, Brody (1924) and Failla (1958) proposed that mortality was inversely related to "vitality" – a hypothetical physiological property of an individual which decreased at a rate proportional to its initial value (Strehler, 1977, p. 113). Simms (1942) and Jones (1956) proposed "autocatalytic" models where age declines in function are proportional to accumulated physiological damage. These models imply that the damage to an organism increases exponentially with age, i.e., more rapidly than has been observed in many longitudinal studies of physiological aging changes (e.g. Shock, 1984). In this chapter we review approaches for combining biological and demographic data to improve our understanding of the regularities of aging. We also examined data on physiological changes in individual organisms at older ages. This information can be used as a background for new approaches to modeling mortality and health – not only for the age ranges usually examined (i.e. 30-85) but also for more extreme age ranges.

Several observations in this chapter are important enough as to justify further study. The first is that models of mortality and aging must have stochasticity represented explicitly: although the age trajectory of the average of many physiological parameters are clear, individual trajectories are influenced by many uncontrolled or weakly controlled external (e.g. weather, social events, environmental pollution, etc.) and internal (e.g. oxidative damage, gene expression) factors. As a consequence they induce significant amounts of both static and dynamic randomness, which influences mortality selection. The presence of such stochasticity is confirmed by experiments with genetically identical laboratory organisms that have different life spans even if external conditions for all individuals were kept the same. Thus, organisms demonstrate both fixed and acquired heterogeneity in susceptibility to disease and death, both types of which have to be taken into account in population studies of aging and survival. The second important observation is that older organisms experience important changes in physiological dynamics: the old and the young organisms of the same individual may have to be considered as different systems. A third observation is that human aging and mortality are quite plastic: external factors can make important contributions to functional improvement and mortality decline. These observations together with new evidence about the shape of population mortality curves at older ages contribute to motivating searches for new paradigms to study human mortality and longevity.

3.2. Stochastic models of mortality and aging

Sacher and Trucco (1962) described age increases in mortality as being due to the accumulation of the physiological effects of stochastic environmental perturbations, or exposures, in an initially homogenous population of individuals. The accumulation of such "damage" causes individuals to randomly deviate further from a homeostatic point in a high-dimensional physiological state space with age until they, by chance, exceed a threshold in that complex state space where endogenous homeostatic mechanisms are no longer sufficient to re-establish physiological equilibrium. At that time (age) the physiological system of the individual, due to the physiological interaction and interdependence of organ systems, begins a catastrophic cascade of events leading to major organ shutdown and system failure, which eventually results in the person's death. This model was based on the assumption that the stochastically perturbed internal states of individuals followed a Gaussian distribution.

Strehler and Mildvan (1960), in contrast, developed a model describing the distribution of accumulated internal effects of random environmental shocks on an initially homogeneous population of individuals as a Maxwell-Boltzman distribution. Both Sacher-Trucco and Strehler-Mildvan recognized that factors such as age-related mortality selection on the distribution of genetic differences in longevity in human populations could cause the age trajectory of human mortality to deviate from a Gompertz function at late age. However, they did not include fixed individual differences in mortality (e.g. genetic determinants of survival) in their model because then mortality would tend to deviate from a Gompertz function at late ages due to the effects of mortality selection on a risk heterogeneous population. They were not convinced (at least not in 1960) of the need to reject the Gompertz hazard function as an empirical description of late-age human mortality. Nonetheless, Strehler-Mildvan (1960) recognized that, at late ages, as the average size of the accumulated effects of stochastic perturbations approximated the insult necessary to cause death, mortality could reach a high constant level;

> "When the vitality has decreased to the point where it is similar to the average energy fluctuation, the rate of mortality should become a constant. Such a course is approached by human mortality figures and is to be predicted on the basis of the integration of the Maxwell-Boltzman equation from large energies to zero" (Strehler, 1960).

It is likely that this "course," which arguably was being approached by human populations in 1960, is now operational in the U.S. population in 1998. Strehler-Mildvan (1960) recognized that models of aging dynamics could not easily

> "be applied to human populations, because variability among individuals and subpopulations, combined with the inherent inaccuracies in the calculated and reported age specific rates at advanced ages will produce unpredictable departures from the ideal. It is hoped that an independent test can be developed on some experimental and more homogenous populations of organisms" (p. 18).

Experimental studies of large populations of *ceratitis capitata*, *Drosophila Melanogaster* and *C. elegans* that approximate the requirements of independent tests all show mortality rates reaching a high constant value at physiologically extreme ages for the respective species. Carey et al. (1992) found that, after 90% of a population of 1.1 million *ceratitis capitata* had died, mortality rates peaked and then declined. Curtsinger et al. (1992), using isogenic groups of *Drosophila Melanogaster*, also found that mortality reached a high constant level. Brooks et al. (1994) found that, in heterogeneous wild populations of *C. elegans*, mortality reached a high constant level (though in isogenic populations no plateau was reached) – second- and third-order polynomial terms (i.e., deviations from a Gompertz hazard function) were, however, significant. These studies used large populations maintained in well controlled conditions, and they followed individuals to ages which were physiologically extreme for the species. Thus data fulfilling Strehler-Mildvan's requirements for experiments on well-characterized animal models confirmed the speculation that mortality would eventually reach a high constant level. This was also supported by simulation studies of expanded theories of the evolution of aging (Mueler and Rose, 1996).

3.3. Inferences about an organism's internal state

Both the Sacher and Trucco (1962) and Strehler and Mildvan (1960) models have been specialized in empirical studies to produce a Gompertz hazard function – a regularity that a model of human mortality and aging dynamics, it was often assumed, must be able to reproduce (Strehler, 1977; Strehler, 1995). The specialization of these more general theoretical models to reproduce a Gompertz hazard function for empirical applications was motivated by various data limitations. Because the many parameters describing an individual's physiological age state, and changes thereof, are difficult to measure over time and are either not available or only incompletely (and infrequently) measured, inference was often inverted with physiological aging rates inferred from the age trajectory of mortality rates.

For example, Simms (1942) experimentally evaluated an autocatalytic model of aging by measuring the insult (e.g. the amount of blood loss) needed to cause death in rats of specific ages. The stress (volume of blood loss) necessary to cause death at a given age was used to measure indirectly the individual organism's vitality i.e., the amount of energy available to maintain homeostasis in the face of the aggregate internal state effects of environmental shocks – and the rate of change in vitality with age. This indirect approach to inferring rates of aging was required by a.) a lack of repeated measurements of physiological changes at late ages and b.) the effort to use a model that was consistent with a Gompertz hazard function – and with the physiological concept of "vitality". However, these models, when estimated solely from mortality data, mathematically confound rates of aging, with age increases in mortality rates. That is, dynamic state model parameters cannot be identified from the age trajectory of mortality (Tolley and Manton, 1991).

Even when frequent longitudinal measurements of physiological function are made, they may not describe changes at physiologically "extreme" ages (age ranges which may not yet have been reached by any individuals in "wild" populations) for a given species. The rate of loss of many physiological functions in early longitudinal studies was roughly linear for the ages examined (e.g. Shock, 1984; Strehler, 1977). The appearance of linear declines in function may have been due to not following physiological changes to sufficiently late ages in humans, or in large enough late-age populations, so as to identify non-linearities in the trajectories at late ages with a sufficient degree of statistical confidence or precision. Studies of populations with significant numbers of very elderly persons (e.g. nonagenarians and centenarians), where direct, detailed, and possibly repeated, physiological measurements are made, are relatively recent. Some examples: the distribution of Apo-E subtypes in 198 Finnish centenarians (Louhija et al., 1994); thyroid auto-antibodies in 34 Italian centenarians aged 100 to 108 (Mariotti et al., 1992); multiple measurements made of 800 French centenarians aged 100 to 115 (Vallin 1993); measures made of fat-free body mass made in healthy centenarians (Paolisso et al., 1993).

The analytic and model construction problems in assessing physiological dynamics in very old organisms are compounded by representing "vitality," or physiological reserve, as unidimensional – and this despite the fact that age changes on multiple dimensions have been observed and measured (Shock, 1984; Strehler, 1977). Rosenberg et al. (1973), for example, used a Weibull (rather than a Gompertz) hazard function to describe adult mortality as being due to the heat-related denaturation of protein. The Weibull function parameter estimates suggested that the activation entropy level (i.e. the mortality threshold) was 190 kcal/mole. Strehler-Mildvan, using a model related to the Gompertz function, estimated a limit of 34 kcal/mole. Thus there is a broad inconsistency in the inferences made from the unidimensional Weibull and Gompertz hazard function about the nature of vitality as inferred from period mortality rates.

Both Rosenberg et al. and Strehler-Mildvan's estimates were based on models of the age trajectory of mortality. Thus, those estimates depend on the parametric structure of the model used to translate multiple functional changes theoretically to a single metric, e.g., measures of the heat energy necessary to maintain physiological homeostasis. The Sacher-Trucco and Strehler-Mildvan models, which describe the internal accumulation with age of the physiological effects (damage or wear) of stochastic environmental influences using thermodynamic equations (or diffusion processes), were more general in form. Thus, the empirical situations which they could describe were much broader than the functions used empirically to reproduce a Gompertz function in cross-sectional (or, less frequently, cohort) human mortality data (e.g. Sacher, 1977).

Energy analogies and metaphors continue to be used extensively in models of human aging and mortality. Recently, aging has been related to the energy-production potential of mitochondria. Mitochondrial DNA is viewed as being vulnerable to the effects of aging because it has fewer repair mechanisms than nuclear DNA. It therefore undergoes mutation more rapidly – possibly up to a thousand times more frequently than DNA in the cell nucleus, where there are more efficient gene repair mechanisms (Cortopassi and Liu, 1995). The mitochondrial DNA mutations tend to accumulate most rapidly in nonmitotic cells (e.g. brain, heart), whose age-dependent loss is often associated with chronic diseases.

One function of the mitochondria is to generate adenosine triphosphate (ATP), a basic chemical in the production of energy for cell function. The generation of ATP is carried out by five enzyme systems, with the adenosine nucleotide translocators localized in the inner membranes of the mitochondria (Wallace, 1992). It is hypothesized that the ability to generate ATP declines with age – possibly due to the accumulation of oxidative damage in mitochondrial DNA, which experiences a rate of oxidative damage 16 times greater than in nuclear DNA. Random mitochondrial DNA mutations often appear to affect the enzyme complex I. The inhibition of this complex induces the formation of mitochondrial superoxide – a potent cell toxin (Cortopassi and Liu, 1995).

The purpose of restricting models of aging processes to one dimension is to simplify them: "Many of these conceptual problems are eliminated if one chooses to focus on longevity as the one scalar, easily measurable parameter that reflects all the above-mentioned aspects of aging." (Schachter et al., 1993). However, many important features of age-related physiological changes may only be explicit when examined over multiple dimensions. Unidimensional mathematical maps of aging processes often cannot adequately describe the multidimensional stochastic dynamics thereof.

3.4. Evidence for heterogeneity and selection in age trajectories of human mortality

The Gompertz hazard function as applied to human population data – and even in some stochastic or diffusion models – assumes that individuals are initially identical. Risk homogeneity may be approximately appropriate for some cases of infant and early adult mortality due to exogenous exposures – such as infectious diseases or accidents. But homogeneity is not an appropriate assumption for chronic diseases dominating mortality at late ages or, for that matter, for early disease with significant genetic determinants (e.g. infectious disease where genetic deficits in immune response or enzymatic function are involved, such as cystic fibrosis or Down's syndrome). Many genetically determined chronic diseases are manifest at relatively early ages (e.g. ages 35 to 60). Marenberg et al. (1994) found the relative risk of CHD mortality in a large number of Swedish monozygotic (MZ) male twins aged 36 to 55 to be 13.4 to 1; for females aged 36 to 65; 14.9 to 1.0. For both genders, mortality selection reduced the relative risk of CHD mortality for MZ twins to 1.0 above age 85.

Elements of the major histocompatability complex (MHC) were found by Kramer et al., (1991) to be subject to mortality selection. The null allele of the B gene in the fourth component of complement (C4B*Q0) was found to negatively affect survival. In persons aged 45 to 60 the prevalence of C4B*Q0 was 16.1%; in persons aged 61 to 90 the prevalence was 5.4%. The differences were due to mortality selection. This selection occurred earlier in life for males than for females. The lack of this allele was associated with increased risk of myocardial infarction – especially in males (Kramer et al., 1994). Similar late-age selection was found for Apo E4 and thyroid auto-antibody prevalence in studies of centenarians (Louhija et al., 1994; Mariotti et al., 1992) as well as for HLA factors determining the risk of auto-immune diseases (Takata et al., 1987) and certain cardiovascular diseases (Thieszen et al., 1990).

Many non-Gompertzian models do not attempt to explain the effects of selection on the age trajectory of mortality. Economos (1982) split adult mortality into a.) initially cumulative mortality which increases exponentially and b.) an exponential decrease in survival (Economos, 1977, 1979a,b). Thus, vitality changes with age were composed of two exponential functions with changes in the age trajectory of mortality caused by the mortality threshold rising above the maximum vitality level (Economos and Miquel, 1979). The rate of functional decline affected the ages over which mortality levels off — eventually reaching a constant. This model also does not explicitly deal with individual heterogeneity or mortality selection. Thus, neither it nor the Gompertz models explain the cross-cohort effects of natural selection on human aging and senescence, or the effects of genetic evolution on the limits of human longevity.

3.5. Dynamic-state heterogeneity and age changes in chronic disease processes

The theoretical models of aging discussed above assumed that late-age mortality could be described as a unidimensional process, e.g. vitality. While some diseases are eliminated from a population early by mortality selection (e.g. certain enzyme deficiency states; type I diabetes mellitus; Hodgkin's disease; hemorrhagic stroke), others emerge to take their place in survivors to later ages (e.g. prostate cancer; multiple myeloma; ischemic stroke; Alzheimer's disease; amyloid-related restrictive cardiomyopathy). As a consequence, human failure processes remain multidimensional over the entire life span – suggesting the existence of multiple, age-dependent equilibrium points in the physiological state space, possibly associated with antagonistic actions between diseases for specific causes of death (Manton and Stallard, 1996).

Even the physiological state manifestation of a chronic disease process may change with age. For example, osteoporosis, a hormonally dependent physiological process affecting bone density underlying much of the risk of hip, spinal, and other fractures at later ages, appears to operate differently in women aged 55 to 75 than in women aged 75 and above. Early-onset osteoporosis (type I) occurs in women with low bone density at menopause, rapid post-menopausal decline in estrogen (due to artificial menopause, for example), or with low production of serum estrone (from body fat) post-menopausally. Late disease (osteoporosis type II) is linked to problems in vitamin D metabolism (in the kidney and liver) and in the intestinal absorption of calcium and vitamin D (Eastell et al., 1991). Even very late stages of manifest disease outcomes may vary considerably over age (and time). Keene (1993) found that, in 1944, the mean age at presentation of hip fracture in Britain was 67 years. The mean age at presentation increased to 79 years by 1990. The 12-year increase in the mean age of hip fracture (roughly a quarter of a year of change in the mean age at occurrence per year of time) caused the dominant type of hip fracture to change from an extracapsular to an intracapsular form. Intracapsular hip fractures are generally more medically complex and expensive to treat, so this change had health-care implications.

The nature of diabetes mellitus also changes over the life span. Diabetes, Type I (often referred to as juvenile-onset or insulin-dependent diabetes) is apparently due to an auto-immune response, possibly triggered by a childhood infection, affecting insulin producing (beta islet) pancreatic cells. Diabetes, Type II, also possibly involving genetic factors (cf. e.g. Takata et al., 1987), is related to insulin resistance in Caucasians at late ages – aggravated by metabolic factors (e.g. obesity; central adiposity) affecting glucose metabolism. In African Americans, however, the nature of the circulatory disease mechanisms involved in diabetes mellitus may be quite different than in whites, possibly relating to an inability to produce sufficient insulin at late ages.

This may cause late-onset diabetes mellitus to relate to circulatory disease changes very differently in African Americans than in U.S. whites (Manton and Stallard, 1996b; McKeigue et al., 1991, 1993). Specifically, in U.S. whites it is believed that insulin resistance and hyperinsulemia occur early in the disease process – which is then followed by progressive impairment of insulin secretion. In African American populations (and other populations of African ancestry), an initial decrease in the mass of beta cells is important in making people susceptible to the insulin resistance produced by obesity, which then leads to further insulin receptor down-regulation and an accelerating decline in beta-cell function – eventually producing profound insulinopenia. This insulinopenia explains why U.S. black diabetics have a lower rate of macro-vascular complications than U.S. white diabetics (Joffe et al., 1992).

The dominant causes of cardiovascular disease (CVD) also tend to change over the life span. Early CVD often involves genetically determined circulatory defects (e.g., cerebral aneurisms or familial hypercholesteremia). In middle age, neuroendocrine factors may interact with atherosclerosis to cause thrombotic events (blood clots; arterial spasms) and catastrophic ischemic failure (i.e. cell death due to impaired circulation) of portions of the myocardium (i.e. heart attacks). At late ages, atherosclerotic changes in circulation, LVH (left ventricular hypertrophy – possibly due to the prolonged effect of hypertension), age-related declines in beta receptor density in the myocardium (Lakatta, 1985), and possibly prior ischemic myocardial damage, produce congestive heart failure (CHF) — a type of heart disease that increased in prevalence until quite recently (Ghali et al., 1990). Recent declines (since 1989) in CHF mortality may be, in part, due to a.) the emergence of more effective drug therapies (e.g. Angiotensin Converting Enzyme (ACE) II Inhibitors) in the last 10 to 12 years (Materson et al., 1994; Paul et al., 1994), b.) more effective exogenous control of cardiac electrical conduction by increasingly sophisticated cardiac pacemakers (Bush and Finucane, 1994), or c.) improvements in surgical and thrombolytic (e.g. streptokinase; t-pa) responses to myocardial infarction in persons aged 80 and over that reduce the loss of myocardium in infarctions (Ko et al., 1992; Gottleib et al., 1997). Anti-thrombolytic therapies are now being evaluated for efficacy in certain types of strokes – when used in the first three hours after the stroke occurrence – and with MRI confirmation of the type of stroke (Fagan et al., 1998).

Recently there has emerged interest in restrictive cardiomyopathies occurring at late ages (e.g. 90 to 99) due to the deposition of amyloid protein in cardiac tissue. This is more prevalent in blacks and was related to transthyretin amyloidosis – especially with a variant sequence in isoleucine 122 (Jacobson et al., 1997). For persons aged 90 to 99, 8.2% of blacks and 2.7% of whites had cardiac amyloidosis at death. It is estimated that isolated ventricular amyloidosis (possibly due to other genetic defects) occurs in up to 25% of persons aged 90+. One-third of patients with CHF, atrial fibrillation, or other conduction disturbances showed no serious pathological evidence of heart disease other than amyloidosis (Jacobson et al., 1997). In the U.S. at least 50 other mutations of transthyretin have been identified, half of which can cause cardiac amyloidosis (Benson, 1997).

Female breast cancer onsetting early in life, often occurring premenopausally, tends to depend on family history, to be histologically aggressive and, consequently (because of a high degree of cellular disorganization), not estrogen-receptor positive. Post-menopausal breast cancer, in contrast, tends to be less dependent on family history, slower developing (an average latency of 14 years for post-menopausal disease vs. 7 years for premenopausal disease), histologically less aggressive, estrogen- and progesterone-receptor positive, and more likely related to long-term changes in reproductive and contraceptive behavior (Manton and Stallard, 1992; Manton and Stallard, 1980).

Hence, for a number of chronic diseases, the adult mortality curve for humans is based on multiple age-related biological mechanisms – many with traits different from failure processes that occur in the same organ systems and dominate mortality at earlier ages.

3.6. Interventions in chronic disease and mortality processes at late ages

The idea that mortality and age-related health conditions can be eliminated or significantly modified at extreme ages (85+) is new (Lakatta, 1985). This concept is receiving increasing empirical support (e.g. Hosking, 1989; Fiatarone et al., 1993, 1994; Ko et al., 1992). For example, a parameter reflecting the loss of a physiological function with age was the age-related decrease in beta receptors in the myocardium, which reduced cardiac responses to stress or physical exertion (Lakatta, 1985). It appears, however, that the new class of inhibitors of angiotensin converting enzyme (ACE II), a hormone responsible for constriction of blood vessels, can significantly increase β-receptor density (Gilbert et al., 1993). Lisinopril, the ACE-II inhibitor used in that study, may reverse age-related declines in cardiac function – and its response to activity-related demand. The use of such ACE-II inhibitors is increasing among the elderly (Psaty et al., 1993).

Body composition, fat distribution, and resting metabolic rate were studied in subjects aged 50 to 100+. After controlling for physical activity and degree of disability, fat-free body mass and metabolic rates were found to be higher in healthy centenarians than in subjects aged 75 to 99. This is supported by several studies showing that physical exercise, and possibly growth hormone replacement, can reverse the loss of fat-free body mass with age (Paolisso et al., 1993).

The notion of the "plasticity of aging" is in distinct contrast to the belief held by many researchers 15 to 20 years ago that U.S. mortality had reached nearly irreducible levels by the late 1950s or early 1960s (NCHS, 1964). The earlier conclusion (of static mortality levels) was reached because male age-standardized mortality rates increased 0.2% per year from 1954 to 1968 (SSA, 1992). Increases were found for 12 of the 15 most frequent causes of death – including chronic diseases like cancer, stroke, and heart disease (Kitagawa and Hauser, 1973). In contrast, U.S. female age-standardized mortality declined 0.8% per year for the 1954 to 1968 period. There was evidence of increases in mortality related to heart disease for males of higher socioeconomic status in the U.S. and Britain in epidemiological studies conducted in the 1930s and 1940s – though such trends began to reverse in the 1960s. Females never manifested a positive association of socioeconomic state and cardiovascular disease risk (Kaplan and Kiel, 1993).

Based on the early epidemiological evidence about cardiovascular disease risks in males and the static national male mortality trends from 1954 to 1968, a variety of authors suggested that U.S. mortality conditions in the 1950s and 1960s reflected increased chronic disease risks produced by the intrinsic nature of industrial societies (Dubos, 1965). Antonovsky (1968) discussed why the mortality risks of cardiovascular diseases might be elevated in such countries. Omran (1971) posited three stages of epidemiological transition. The last characterized economically developed societies as having a high prevalence of chronic degenerative and man-made diseases and a maximum life expectancy at birth of about 70 years.

Many demographers held similar views and generated model life tables to describe mortality in developmentally homogenous sets of countries (i.e., age, gender and cause-specific mortality patterns were assumed invariant once the life expectancy level and stage of economic development of a country was specified) and estimated low absolute upper limits to human life expectancy. Bourgeois-Pichat (1978) projected absolute upper life expectancy limits of 73.8 years for males and 80.3 years for females in 1978 using cause-elimination life tables. A study of the effects of population aging on the Japanese economy (Nihon University, 1982) assumed ultimate life expectancy limits of 79.8 years for males and 80.7 years for females in econometric projections. A mere 11 years later, however, Japanese life expectancy, which was the world's highest in 1993 (76.5 years for males and 83.3 years for females), exceeded the "theoretical" life expectancy limits assumed for females in the 1982 study by 2.7 years (WHO, 1994). Furthermore, the outcomes of the Japanese economic projections (i.e., rates of national economic growth) were quite sensitive to life expectancy assumptions.

These high life expectancies at birth were achieved even though health care for the elderly in Japan is perceived as having serious quality of care problems (Okamato, 1992; Ikegami and Campbell, 1995). In France, life expectancy in 1991 was 73.5 years for males and 82.0 years for females, which exceeded Bourgeois-Pichat's (1978) estimate of the female life expectancy limit by 1.7 years. The quality of care for the elderly in France appears to be quite good relative to that in Japan. Somewhat surprisingly, the U.S. had the best survival from age 80 to 100 among the world's developed countries (Manton and Vaupel, 1995). Clearly, life expectancy limits estimated from recent, total, and cause-specific mortality trends and data alone were inaccurate (Manton et al., 1991). Comparisons with epidemiological and clinical studies are necessary adjuncts to mortality analyses.

Analyses of mortality data show why human life expectancy limits are difficult to estimate (Manton and Stallard, 1996). First, human life expectancy, and life span, are very long relative to most other species – and to the duration of most studies. It will take 130 to 140 years for a recent, large birth cohort to die out completely at current life expectancy levels in the U.S. and Japan. Life endurance (the age to which 1 in 100,000 persons is expected to live) in the U.S. is projected to reach 127 to 129 years by 2050 (SSA, 1992). This will make it difficult to get reliable data on the full mortality experience of a birth cohort (let alone to compare the experience of multiple birth cohorts over a significant period of time) except in a few countries with exceptional registry systems, such as Sweden (Condran et al., 1991). Second, human populations are free-living and cannot ethically be studied in experimentally controlled environments. Hence, the proportion of life expectancy potential realized in any human population is a smaller and less certain proportion of their biological life span potential than can be observed in animal models in controlled, experimental conditions (cf. e.g. Carey et al., 1992; Curtsinger et al., 1992; Johnson et al., 1993).

After U.S. life expectancy at birth had increased significantly from 1900 to 1950 (from 47.3 years in 1900 to 68.2 years in 1950, which was 0.42 more years of life expected at birth per calendar year) the rate of increase slowed for the 20-year period from 1950 to 1970 (from 68.2 to 70.9 years, which was roughly 0.14 years of age increase in life expectancy per calendar year). Increases in U.S. life expectancy at age 65 (from 11.9 years in 1900 to 13.9 years in 1950, or 0.04 years of age increase in life expectancy at age 65 per calendar year) occurred slowly relative to life expectancy changes at birth observed from 1900 to 1950. From 1950 to 1970 the rate of life expectancy gains at age 65 were faster (from 13.9 to 15.2 years, or 0.07 years of age increase per calendar year) but still modest compared to the gains in life expectancy at birth observed up to 1950. U.S. male life expectancy actually declined from 1954 to 1968. From 1970 to 1990, life expectancy gains at age 65 accelerated (from 15.2 years in 1970 to 17.2 years in 1990, or 0.1 years of age per calendar year), representing a larger proportion of the total gain in life expectancy than earlier (total life expectancy gain from birth was 4.5 years; gains above 65 were 2.0 years, or 44.4% of the total).

Some recent gains in life expectancy above age 65 were achieved by reducing chronic disease mortality at extreme ages (85+), i.e. in previously "uncharted" territory. The first reliably documented reports of centenarians date back to about 1800 (Thoms, 1873); the first reliably documented report of a person surviving to 110 was in 1931 (in Britain), with the first documented survivor to age 120 (a French female who eventually survived to be over 122 years of age in August, 1997) recorded in 1995. Recently, a U.S. female died who was documented by the Social Security Administration to be over age 120.

In the last 35 years the centenarian population in the U.S. (Manton and Stallard, 1996) and several other developed countries (Vaupel and Jeune, 1995) has grown 7% or more per year. In the U.S., for example, it grew by 8.5% per annum from 3,000 persons in 1960 to 52,000 persons in 1995 (Manton and Stallard, 1996). As higher proportions of larger, more recent U.S. birth cohorts survive to late ages, reductions in mortality at those ages will contribute proportionately more and more per year of age to overall U.S. life expectancy gains.

Significant – and sometimes conflicting – gender- and cause-specific differences in mortality complicate efforts to predict life expectancy increases. From 1950 to 1970 male life expectancy at age 65 increased 0.3 years (from 12.8 to 13.1 years), with declines from 1954 to 1968. In contrast, female life expectancy increased from 1950 to 1970 from 15.0 to 17.0 years. From 1970 to 1990, life expectancy at age 65 for both U.S. males and females increased 2.0 years – to 15.1 and 19.0 years, respectively.

Yashin and Iachine (1995a,b) recently estimated a lower bound of the biological limits of human life expectancy of 80 years for males and 83 years for females by using bivariate survival data on cohorts of Danish twins born 1870 to 1900. In a later study based on cohort data for Danish twins born 1870 to 1910, these estimates were raised to 83 years for males and 87 years for females. Cohort birth year was used as a covariate in a second analysis (Yashin et al., 1996). An extrapolation of that data suggested that females born in the year 2000 would have a life expectancy of 97 years. Additional increases in estimates of longevity may be generated by using changing (instead of fixed) frailty models for related individuals. The idea of fixed frailty was an important step forward when explaining deviant patterns of human mortality at later ages. However, more sophisticated analyses of mortality and longevity limits will require taking into account acquired, or environmental, components of frailty change with age.

3.7. Summary

When the Gompertz hazard function was formulated in 1825, centenarians were rare biological events. It is difficult to document a person living to age 100 before 1800; or to age 110 before 1931 (Thoms, 1873; Jeune, 1994). While the maximum documented human age attained increased from 100 to 110 years between 1800 and 1931 (a period of 131 years), the first documented case of survival to age 120 was recorded in 1995 (a French female who survived to age 122). The second increase of 10 years in the documented maximum human age required 65 years, which means that the rate of increase of the maximum observed life span from 100 to 110 was more than doubled (Manton and Stallard, 1996). That upper bound increased two years in just two years because the woman in question, who reached age 120 in 1995, eventually lived to August, 1997.

Even higher ages will be observed in the future because the centenarian population in the U.S. and a number of other developed countries has grown 7% or more per year for 30 years (Vaupel and Lundstrom, 1994). The U.S. Census Bureau (middle series; Day, 1993) projects a continuation of the 7.0% annual growth of centenarians observed from 1960 to 1987 (Manton and Stallard, 1995) to 2025: from 52,000 centenarians in 1995 to 392,000 in 2025. If, as the U.S. Society of Actuaries suggests (1994), the maximum credible age-specific mortality rate is 50% – and life tables for recent U.S. cohorts suggest that mortality at late ages (110+) ranges from 30 to 45% (Manton and Stallard, 1995) – then the increase in the maximum observed life span from 120 to 130 may occur in 30 to 35 years, which would mean another doubling of the rate at which the maximum observed life span increased 10 years. Because of the large size of the U.S. elderly population (its mortality rates between ages 80 and 100 are the world's lowest (Manton and Vaupel, 1995)), the rapid growth of the centenarian population, and improvement in data systems, we may be approaching the day when the report of a person surviving to age 130 in the U.S. can be confirmed.

A review of multiple studies of experimental animal populations shows that the Gompertz hazard function overestimated the rate of mortality increase at late ages. Many experimental studies using the Gompertz function either did not statistically test its validity or had design limitations preventing a rigorous statistical test. Perks (1932; see also Beard, 1963) developed logistic models to explain the tendency for human mortality rates to reach an asymptote at late ages. However, statistical tests of the empirical fits of Gompertz and logistic hazard functions are seldom done. Studies using the Gompertz hazard function often do not have populations large enough to allow one to discriminate it from other hazard functions at late ages with sufficient statistical power. Thus, demographic and biological evidence suggests a need for new paradigms for the study of mortality and aging. These paradigms should take into account the following: the presence of deterministic and stochastic components in changes of physiological functioning in the human organism with age, the heterogeneity of the human population in susceptibility to disease and death, the plasticity of human mortality, and its deviance from the Gompertz hazard function at older ages.

IV. Changing concepts in the biology of late-age morbidity and mortality

4.1. Changes in cause-specific mortality

There have been major changes in cause-specific mortality in the U.S. and other developed countries. Cause of death patterns and changes thereof show considerable heterogeneity across countries, which suggests that none of these countries has yet reached its biological limit to life span. For example, U.S. age-standardized heart disease mortality rates declined 52.4% and stroke mortality rates 70.4% from 1950 to 1992 (NCHS, 1995). In Japan, stroke mortality remains much higher than in the U.S. while cardiovascular disease mortality is still lower.

U.S. age-standardized cancer mortality rates increased 6.2% over the same 42-year period. The change in cancer mortality is different for males and females. U.S. male cancer mortality increased from 1950 to 1992 by about 7%, while U.S. female cancer mortality declined 20%. Only recently has the male trend begun to reverse. From 1990 to 1995 total cancer mortality rates declined 3.9%. Actually, if lung cancer mortality due to high levels of smoking in middle-aged white male cohorts is removed from the 1970 to 1990 cancer mortality trends, the mortality rates for all other cancers declined 10% (Cole and Rodu, 1996).

It was difficult until recently to attribute the large declines in U.S. circulatory disease mortality to specific medical interventions in risk factors such as hypertension (Casper et al., 1992; Klag et al., 1989) or elevated serum cholesterol, because many risk factor intervention trials did not show significant reductions in population mortality outcomes until recently – and often not until enough experience from multiple trials had accumulated to conduct meta-analyses. For example, there is consensus that antihypertensive therapy reduces strokes and stroke-related mortality, reduces the risk of CHF (Congestive heart failure), reverses left-ventricular hypertrophy and slows the progression of renal disease. Less conclusive was evidence on reductions in coronary heart disease. Reviews of multiple studies showed that CHD death and myocardial infarction rates were reduced by 14% (assuming a 5mm reduction in diastolic blood pressure) – compared to a 42% reduction in strokes (Moser, 1991).

In studies of cholesterol reduction in 21,515 persons identified from 1975 to 1982 and followed to 1991, ischemic heart disease mortality dropped 24% and all-cause mortality 10% (Law et al., 1994a, b). In 10 cohort studies, a decrease in cholesterol of 10% reduced the incidence of ischemic heart disease by 54% at age 40, 39% at 50, 27%

at 60; 20% at 70, and 19% at 80. Ischemic heart disease reductions in 28 randomized trials (for persons aged 55 to 64) were 7% after two years of follow-up, 22% from 2.1 to five years, and 25% after five years – which is very close to the overall gain (27%) in the 10 cohort studies (Law et al., 1994a,b).

There is evidence that female breast cancer survival has improved. In a study of all breast cancer cases in British Columbia in 1974, 1980, and 1984 it was possible to control for lead-time effects because all women were treated in the same provincial health care system operating under the same treatment guidelines. The treatment regimes may be defined as 1974 (no Adjuvant therapy recommended), 1980 (Adjuvant therapy recommended only for premenopausal disease with positive nodes), and 1984 (Adjuvant therapy recommended for premenopausal node-negative cases and Tamoxifen therapy recommended for women over age 50). Over the seven years of follow-up (to 1991) overall survival increased from 64.8% to 74.6% – a 28% reduction in mortality. In women aged 50 to 89 the overall survival increased from 53.9% in 1980 to 58.3% in 1984 (Olivotto et al., 1994). Significant improvements in survival were also found in long-term prognosis of breast cancer for cases identified from 1955 to 1974 – even though the early treatment of those cancers had not advanced as far as in the Canadian study (Nab et al., 1994).

These results suggest that there were improvements in survival from major causes of death due to advances in medical treatments in the 1970s and 1980s. Progress in the medical management of disease continued, and possibly accelerated, in the 1990s. It is estimated that, if the optimal therapy were delivered to all cases, U.S. female breast cancer mortality could be reduced by a third, from 45,000 to 30,000 deaths per year (Greenspan, 1996). The control of isolated systolic hypertension by medications was demonstrated to decrease the occurrence of strokes in the U.S. among elderly persons (SHEP, 1991). Long-term benefits of thrombolysis for myocardial infarction, a treatment started in 1988, were reported in 1993 (Stevenson et al., 1993). The effect of anti-platelet therapy on death, myocardial infarctions, and stroke was reported in 1994 (Antiplatelet Trialists Collaboration, 1994) based on randomized trials conducted up to 1990.

Period effects might be expected to dominate changes in cause-specific mortality if treatments were the most important factors reducing mortality. In Germany, epidemiological survey data show adverse risk factor trends from 1984 to 1989. The contrast of those trends, with a 19% decline in heart disease mortality over the same period, was interpreted to mean that clinical and treatment innovations were largely responsible for the CVD mortality reductions (Hoffmeister et al., 1994; Brenner, 1993).

The nature of medical conditions also evolved as more persons survived to late ages. For example, up to the 1940 and 1950s most concern was directed to the effects of infectious diseases such as rheumatic fever or syphilis on the heart and to hypertension as a cause of strokes (Kaplan and Keil, 1993). In the 1950s and 1960s, hypertensive heart disease declined while atherosclerotic heart disease increased. The two opposing trends combined to produce a rough net "stagnation" of male mortality trends from 1954 to 1968. Though male heart disease mortality was stagnant overall, on a more detailed level changes in the cause-specific mortality dynamics of different types of heart disease were rapid and significant.

The mean age at which hip fractures occurred in Britain from 1944 to 1990 increased from 67 to 79 years. Concurrently, the nature of hip fractures shifted from intra- to extra-capsular fractures (Keene, 1993). The nature of osteoporosis, the process underlying most U.S. hip fractures, differs from ages 55 to 74, where it depends on post-menopausal changes in estrogen levels, to ages 75+, where it is related to age-dependent defects in the vitamin D endocrine system (Eastell et al., 1991).

4.2. Mechanisms underlying changes in cause-specific mortality

Clearly, more physiological processes are at work, and over longer periods of time, than anticipated by early demographic efforts to estimate life expectancy limits based on total and cause-specific mortality trends, and by efforts to relate mortality changes to significant, but recent, trends in "standard" chronic-disease risk factors (Treasure et al., 1995). Fogel (1994) suggested that U.S. declines in chronic disease prevalence extend back to the mid-19th century. He compared the prevalence of chronic diseases found in physical examinations of Civil War veterans aged 65 to 84 applying for pensions in 1910 (U.S. birth cohorts of 1825 to 1844) with the prevalence of chronic diseases for WWII veterans over age 65, self-reported in the 1985-1988 National Health Interview Surveys (birth cohorts of 1905 to 1923). Fogel found that chronic disease prevalence at ages 65+ declined 6% per decade between 1910 and 1985-1988. The prevalence of medically diagnosed heart disease was 2.9 times higher in Civil War veterans aged 65+ in 1910 than was self-reported heart disease in WWII veterans aged 65+ in 1985-1988. Such declines in chronic disease prevalence may well set the stage for subsequent declines in cause-specific mortality rates up to several decades later.

Many health changes in the population are more strongly related to cohort than period effects, e.g. declines in coronary heart disease mortality in Norway from 1966 to 1986 (Sverre, 1993). Fogel (1994) attributed changes in chronic morbidity to changes in economic and agricultural production factors affecting early and pre-natal nutrition which have also increased the U.S. stature and body mass index (BMI) over time. As a consequence, measures of BMI changes over time were used by Fogel (1994) as population indicators of changes in early and late health characteristics. Many changes between Civil War and WWII veterans predate documented U.S. increases in cholesterol and fat consumption – estimated to have peaked in 1959 (Stern, 1979).

An alternate explanation of long-term effects of nutrition on health may be the impact of maternal protein and caloric deficiencies on fetal development. This was attributed to the effects of maternal nutritional deficiencies (and possibly maternal diabetes) on the development of specific organ systems in the fetus, such that a physiological priority was assumed to exist that dictated which fetal organs received adequate nutrition under conditions of maternal protein and caloric deprivation. If the central nervous system had the highest priority for nutrients, organs like the liver (affecting cholesterol metabolism, and thrombolic factors) and the pancreas (affecting glucose metabolism (Yki-Jarvinen, 1994)) might be susceptible to developmental restrictions that become manifest in chronic disease at later ages.

There is empirical evidence for this in studies relating the ratio of placental to birth weight and of weight at one year of age to chronic disease at later ages (e.g. Barker and Martyn, 1992; Barker et al., 1992; Hales et al., 1991). Barker and Martyn (1992) found higher weight at one year of age to be inversely related to ischemic heart disease, systolic blood pressure, and impaired glucose tolerance in adults, and possibly to fibrinogen levels in men aged 59 to 70. The relation of systolic blood pressure to placental weight for women and men aged 46 to 56 was direct. Other recent studies suggest that the risk of stroke at later ages for a child are due to early maternal nutritional deficiencies affecting the bony pelvis – while deficiencies during pregnancy were associated with heart disease risks (Martyn et al., 1996). Frankel et al. (1996) found a significant relationship between low birth weight and high adult BMI.

Other studies suggest that, in addition to gross nutritional deficiencies (i.e. protein and caloric dietary deficiency), deficiency of micro-nutrients affects the growth and development of specific organs. For example, the effects of folic acid deficiency early in pregnancy (the first trimester) on fetal neurological development have been documented (e.g. increased risk of neurological birth defects like spina bifida and other neural tube defects).

Subtle pathological changes due to smaller levels of micro-nutrient deficiency manifested only at later ages are also possible. For example, a subtle influence of in-utero nutritional factors on a disease manifest at late ages is evident for U.S. prostate cancer. Ross and Henderson (1994) found that African-American females have much higher first-trimester testosterone levels than white females. This may produce high rates of prostate cancer in male offspring by affecting the hypothalamic-pituitary-testicular feedback systems (the "gonadostat"), causing African-American males to have higher circulatory levels of testosterone than white males (Ross and Henderson, 1994; Ross and Bernstein et al., 1992). This in-utero effect may be due to higher fat consumption levels and lower levels of fiber consumption in African-American women than, for example, in Japanese and Chinese women (and men; who have very low prostate cancer risk). There is also evidence that prostate cancer risk may be due to variation in vitamin D nutrition (Corder et al., 1993). There may be many other subtle nutritional deficiencies of micro-nutrients in the early life of older cohorts that produced physiological predispositions toward chronic health problems at late ages. These micro-nutrients may affect chronic disease by mitigating the physiological effects of specific genetic factors or modifying the genetic inducibility of certain proteins by modulating environmental signals.

Others have suggested that nutritional deficiencies affect persons most at the ages when the most rapid physical growth occurs – when protein, caloric and other nutrient needs are highest. This is consistent with Fogel's (1994) use of the Waaler curve to plot temporal changes in BMI and chronic disease risks. It is also consistent with Tango and Kurashina's (1987) findings that Japanese male cohorts born in the 15 years before WWII (i.e. birth cohorts of the early SHOWA period from 1925-1939, aged 5 to 20 during WWII, when there were severe nutritional shortages in Japan) had elevated mortality from diabetes mellitus, ischemic heart disease, peptic ulcer, cirrhosis, and suicide. These results are not consistent, however, with the data on U.S. male cohorts whose peak physical growth was experienced in the 1929-1939 U.S. depression (Manton et al., 1997).

Cohort differences in cause-specific mortality rates are argued to be due to poor nutrition during early, critical stages of adolescent growth spurts – especially for males. The deficiencies probably involve both gross energy (caloric) and protein deprivation as well as deficiencies in micro-nutrients in periods of rapid skeletal growth, when vitamin D serum levels are highest and vitamin C (affecting collagen, and thus cartilage, formation) and B (affecting methionine metabolism and growth hormone release) needs are elevated (McCully, 1983). Recent studies show that high doses of vitamin A in nutritionally deprived children in developing countries can affect infectious disease risks (e.g. of gastro-intestinal disease) by improving immunological status – an effect also found in the elderly. Vitamins A, C, and E improved immune response in the gastro-intestinal mucosa in the very elderly (i.e. centenarians, cf. Beregi et al., 1991). This may have effects, as will be discussed below, because of a.) effects of nutrition on gene expression (e.g. vitamin B_6 modulation of steroid hormonal receptors), and b.) infectious diseases may be important co-factors for many chronic diseases (e.g., atherosclerosis is documented to initiate early in life, cf. PDAY, 1990).

4.3. The role of pathogens in circulatory disease development

Other models suggest that chronic disease and mortality risks in specific birth cohorts may be related to nutritional and hygienic factors operating over extended time periods (Manton et al., 1996; Manton, 1996). One argument is that the effect of viral and bacterial infections on chronic disease changed over time (as well as the natural history of the chronic diseases themselves) due to improvements in food processing and hygiene.

For atherosclerosis there is evidence relating its initiation (that is, the initial injury to arterial endothelium, which starts inflammatory and wound-building activity stimulated by dietary co-factors such as serum cholesterol and aggravating conditions such as hypertension) to viral and bacterial insults (Ross, 1986). This model is supported by evidence that atherosclerotic plaques have a monoclonal origin, which suggests that a somatic mutation is involved in plaque initiation (cf., e.g., Benditt and Benditt, 1973). In addition, infectious agents have been found in plaques by electron microscopy (Grayston, 1993) or in circulating immunological complexes in persons with circulatory disease versus persons without disease. Among the infectious agents implicated are the bacteria Chlamydia Pneumoniae (Linnanmaki et al., 1993), CMV (Mozar et al., 1990; Melnick et al., 1990), and other herpes viruses (Melnick and Schattner, 1992).

A mechanism that could be involved in infectious disease damage to arterial endothelium involves a protein called Platelet Derived Growth Factor (PDGF). Cells in the endothelium produce PDGF. PDGF plays a central role in atherogenesis because it is both a mitogen (i.e., it causes somatic mutations in smooth muscle cells) and chemoattractant (i.e., it attracts macrophages and monocytes to plaques) (Ross, 1986). There is also a strong homology (87%) between the amino acid sequence of PDGF and a protein from an oncogene (v-sis) in the simian sarcoma virus. This homology suggests that PDGF may be important in the proliferation of cells transformed by a virus. Cells transformed by various viruses secrete PDGF. Such virally transformed cells may phenotypically express a previously repressed cellular gene (c-sis) encoding for PDGF (Ross, 1986).

Immune mechanisms may also be involved in malignant hypertension, with data pointing to predisposing genes in the major histocompatability complex, either as secondary to hypertension induced vascular damage (causing a positive feedback loop of plaque growth and hypertension) or as a primary abnormality (Hilme et al., 1993). However involved, reductions in infectious disease exposure might reduce hypertension prevalence (and atherosclerosis) in recent cohorts. Another hypothesis involving immunological factors is that an antiphospholipid antigen, possibly virally induced, increases the risk of stroke and cardiovascular disease (Hughes, 1993).

This data suggests that one might view atherosclerotic circulatory diseases and their catastrophic manifestations as thrombotic, occlusive events leading to ischemia in critical organ systems. This is a multi-staged pathological process during which the initial damage to the arterial intima (possibly a somatic mutation induced by an exogenous pathogen) stimulates inflammatory and immunological responses, where LDL cholesterol becomes oxidized, forming foam cells from monocytes/macrophages that are drawn to the site of the injury and are integrated in the plaque. Also involved in atheroma growth are complex autocrine and paracrine mechanisms of vascular response to injury (Dzau et al., 1993). Other stages of the process involve intracellular absorption of calcium leading to atheroma calcification and inflammatory responses leading to plaque rupture (Buja and Willerson, 1994; Van der Wal et al., 1994). Immunological responses to infectious agents directly stimulating plaque rupture (and thrombotic events) are also suggested by the antiphospholipid syndrome.

Also implicated may be the effects of cholesterol on endothelium-mediated responses in the coronary arteries of patients with atherosclerosis. Thus, part of the effect of cholesterol lowering may be due to cholesterol's effect on vasoconstriction – rather than to structural changes in plaques. Such responses occur more rapidly (within several months) than plaque regression (which requires about five years, cf. Anderson et al., 1995; Treasure et al., 1995; Benzuly et al., 1994). Thus, the effects of elevated cholesterol at late ages may be expressed through impaired vasomotor response. This means that cholesterol lowering may affect a set of intrinsically age-related parameters of physiological change.

To explain how infectious disease involvement with atherosclerosis relates to long-term population health and mortality changes, Mozar et al. (1990) suggested that changes in circulatory disease mortality are traceable to at least 1910. In 1910, 8% of U.S. deaths were due to heart disease. This figure rose to 30% by 1945 and 54% by 1968. A similar trend occurred in the United Kingdom, with diseases of the heart and blood vessels responsible for 11.4% of deaths in 1910 and rising to 36.3% of deaths in 1959. In the U.S. the highest mortality risks for heart disease were reached in 1968. Mozar et al. (1990) suggest that the 1968 peak was due to ingestion of atherogenic viruses during the pre-WWII period. The initial injuries lead to processes with lengthy latency times, as suggested by autopsy studies which have found that fatty streaks and plaques often begin at early ages, as early as age 3 in the aorta (Holman et al., 1958; PDAY, 1990), even in less developed countries, where heart disease risks do not increase late in life. Such infections interacted with increased fat consumption and other risk factors (e.g. increased protein consumption, such as in the methionine-homocysteine model of atherogenesis).

The nutritional (hygienic) factor Mozar et al. (1990) found to be associated with heart disease decline was commercial food processing. Commercial food processing in the U.S. began in the late 19th century. The U.S. Pure Food and Drug Act was passed in 1908. But it wasn't until after WWII that the use of commercial food processing rapidly accelerated, as economic conditions improved, large proportions of the U.S. population moved from rural to urban areas (making food preservation more important), and efforts to control livestock infections such as vesicular xanthema (a viral disease of swine first discovered in 1932) were started, e.g. in California in 1945-1949 – a state showing declines in human circulatory diseases earlier than elsewhere. An outbreak of vesicular xanthema in 1952 mandated the thermal preparation of food fed to swine. A hog cholera eradication program began in 1962. The Swine Health Protection Act was passed in 1980.

The risk of viruses and other infectious agents in chronic circulatory disease is not limited to injuries to the arterial endothelium but may also involve stimulation of auto-immunological factors. An infectious disease important in chronic diseases – which was a major concern in past years – is group A streptococci infections, especially of virulent strains, e.g. M types 3 and 18, which are associated with rheumatic fever, and M1, associated with toxic shock due to production of pyrogenic exotoxin A. Certain streptococcal strains (e.g. M1) disappeared in the U.S. 30 to 40 years ago. They recently reappeared in selected geographic areas in the U.S., which suggests that virulent strains decline and re-emerge cyclically (Kaplan, 1993). This cyclical pattern may be related to the HLA type of individuals. So there have now been studies of how auto-immunological responses relate to rheumatic heart disease (e.g. Carlquist and Anderson, 1993). The disappearance of the most virulent streptococcal strains 30 to 40 years ago is consistent with cardiovascular mortality declines due to atherosclerosis beginning in 1968 – which suggests that viral and bacterial infections are a cofactor of the disease. In addition to food (especially animal protein) as a source for viral and bacterial agents stimulating chronic disease, interactions of nutrition and the behavior of such infectious agents may be important. Nutritional status affects a host's immunological competency – especially at late ages (cf. e.g. Beregi et al., 1991). Poor nutrition, especially in childhood, might cause less effective immunological responses to viral and bacterial challenges at later ages. Second, a physiological response to the acute phase of infection requires considerable energy expenditure. Poor nutrition can reduce the efficacy of the host's response to the disease (e.g. natural killer-cell activity in controlling cancer; Kusaka et al., 1992), allowing it to cause greater physiological damage, thus requiring greater energy expenditures to fight the acute disease and to repair acute physiological damage, which further reduces nutritional resources for normal growth and development (again, possibly setting the stage for future chronic disease).

Hypotheses about the role of infectious agents in chronic diseases are not new: for example, bacterial pathogens were proposed as causes of atherosclerosis in 1911. The reasons they are again receiving attention are 1.) improvements in laboratory techniques and assays (e.g. PCR, electron microscopy) to detect infectious agents in somatic mutations or antigenic responses to specific infectious agents (e.g. B-cell immortal clones due to Epstein-Barr virus; detection of antigens in auto-immunological disease), 2.) the emergence of antibiotic-resistant strains of previously well-controlled agents (e.g. T.B.), and 3.) the emergence, or recent identification, of viral and bacterial agents associated with changes in human ecology (e.g. the spread of lyme disease in the U.S., the identification (1984) of *Helicobacter pylori* in peptic ulcers (Hosking et al., 1992) and in gastric cancers (Forman, 1991), the identification of chlamydia pneumoniae in atherosclerosis (Grayston, 1993)). A positive aspect of these findings is that they suggest that interventions successful against infectious disease may also reduce or even eradicate chronic disease. Thus could be a highly cost-effective approach to population management of chronic diseases (Capron, 1996).

4.4. The role of pathogens in cancer

New genetic and molecular evaluation and assay techniques (e.g. PCR: Polymerase Chain Replication) allow the identification of viruses and other infectious agents causing several types of cancer (Perera, 1996). Epstein-Barr virus is implicated in the etiology of many human lymphoid and epithelial malignancies (Niedobitek and Young, 1994). H. pylori, a causative agent in peptic ulcers (Hosking et al., 1992), is not only associated with gastric cancer, but may be linked to other malignancies (e.g. liver cancer (Nightingale and Gruber, 1994)). Both Rb and P53, growth regulating genes whose normal function is to arrest cell growth when somatic mutations are detected, can be disturbed by viral infections, allowing malignant growth to occur.

The infection rate of *H. pylori* is related to water quality. Long-term improvements in water quality may be responsible for U.S. cohort-specific declines in gastric cancer. Elevation of gastric cancer risks in the upper Midwest may have been due to the use of well water in rural areas (*H. pylori* grows best in still water in wells or cisterns). U.S. gastric cancer mortality rates dropped 85% from 1930 (gastric cancer was the number one cause of U.S. cancer deaths) to 1990 – a decline strongly related to birth cohort. *H. pylori* remains prevalent in developing countries (e.g. in West Africa (Holcombe et al., 1992)) and still has a high seroprevalence (75%) in elderly U.S. cohorts (Safe et al., 1993).

Of interest is how long *H. pylori* infections may have affected man. Is it a "primordial" infection just discovered in 1984 – or have recent ecological changes increased its prevalence? In some areas, access to flowing water may have reduced infection rates. However, in many agricultural areas only standing water was available. *H. pylori* infection may also have been controlled by a biological feedback system in the human gut. *H. pylori* survives gastric acid by neutralizing it with an enzyme, urease, which reduces urea into ammonia (the detection of ammonia on the breath is a diagnostic sign of the infection). If the *H. pylori* colonization of the stomach becomes too great, stomach pH could increase (the stomach becomes less acidic). This not only affects the host's nutritional status (digestion and absorption of nutrients) but also allows *E. coli* bacteria in the intestine to colonize the stomach and compete with *H. pylori*. Once the *H. pylori* colony begins to decrease, the stomach pH declines, reducing the viability of *E. coli* in the stomach. Thus, *E. coli* in the intestine, the control of which requires significant energy expenditures by the host organism, may be in an internal, competitive equilibrium with *H. pylori*.

Recent data suggest that *H. pylori* is linked not only to peptic ulcers and gastric cancer but also to duodenal ulcers and stroke. Effects of *H.* pylori have been evident in human populations for over 200 years (Sonnenberg, 1995). Before the Industrial Revolution *H. pylori* infection may have been widespread but not manifest because of low life expectancy. For cohorts born during the Industrial Revolution, *H. pylori* infection in children would have been nearly universal. At the end of the 19th century increases in life expectancy allowed gastric cancer and gastric ulcer mortality to reach high levels. As hygiene improved, the age at which *H. pylori* was acquired shifted upward, causing gastric cancer mortality to decline (Parsonett et al., 1996). Associated with the rate of *H. pylori* infections was the decline in the use of salt as a preservative starting in the 1930s – when gastric cancer began its decline from being the number one U.S. cancer cause of death. Salt increases the growth rate of *H. pylori* (Joosens et al., 1996). And reductions in salt intake could reduce stroke risk by lowering hypertension. Thus, the interaction of salt intake and *H. pylori* infection could explain correlated declines in stroke (Lanska and Mi, 1993), gastric cancer, hypertension and gastric ulcer mortality beginning in the 1930s.

Important for elderly populations is that NSAIDs, often used to treat joint problems (e.g. osteoarthritis) in the elderly, cause gastric problems. In the elderly those problems are aggravated by *H. pylori* – potentially representing a barrier (if the *H. pylori* infection is untreated) to an effective form of therapy (Safe et al., 1993). The prevalence of *H. pylori* may have been reduced in recent years serendipitously by drugs intended for other purposes. The use of antibiotics for other infections might have cured *H. pylori* infections. Pepto-Bismol, a patent medicine sold to "coat the stomach" and reduce acidity has an antibacterial effect due to its bismuth content – many of the multiple-drug therapies used to treat *H. pylori* contain bismuth compounds (Hosking et al., 1994).

The existence of specific multiply infectious agent-host interactions raises the general issue of how viral and bacterial micro-environments contribute to the aging process in individuals. Aging processes may be related in many ways to yet-to-be-discovered viral and bacterial agents (and to known viral infections, like CMV and Epstein-Barr, that are nearly universally prevalent in humans by adulthood and whose role is incompletely understood). The technology to detect the molecular effects of such chronic infections (Perera, 1996) involve recent technical developments.

Long-term trends in both circulatory and neoplastic disease and mortality may depend on viral and bacterial infections – either as initiating events or as disease co-factors. Reductions in chronic circulatory disease risk factors can only be documented in the U.S. population from the early 1960s (e.g. a decline in smoking, reduction of fat consumption and cholesterol levels, and reductions in hypertension prevalence are documented in the National Health and Nutrition Examination Survey series started in 1960-1962 (NCHS, 1995)). As genetic and molecular biological assays become more sensitive we may find that chronic diseases depend in multiple ways on a variety of infectious agents. Changes in the human environment (e.g. improvement in water quality, which reduces H. pylori infection rates) or in food processing (e.g. elimination of viral infections among livestock, the thermal processing of food) may thus be partly responsible for long-term cohort-related declines in circulatory disease in the U.S (Manton et al., 1997). The high prevalence of certain infectious agents (e.g. CMV) may accelerate dimensions of other age-dependent diseases.

Cancer risks, in contrast to circulatory diseases, may be increasing because a.) different environmental exposures may cause the somatic mutations leading to malignant growth (e.g. smoking or occupational exposures for lung cancer; changing fertility affecting the duration of hormonal exposure of breast tissue for late-onset breast cancer), b.) somatic mutations required for carcinogenesis may be more complex and thus expressed at later ages than circulatory diseases – especially if the risk of early initiating events due to infectious agent exposures were reduced for circulatory diseases, and c.) the co-factors of circulatory diseases may now be better controlled (e.g. LDL cholesterol, hypertension, elevated BMI, folic acid deficency). Infectious disease exposures may represent "missing" risk factors for cohort differences in cancer risk (Davis et al., 1994).

4.5. Cell death and its contribution to human survival: apoptosis and aging

Cutler and Semsei (1989) proposed that there were common physiological processes underlying both cancer and aging. Warner et al. (1995) related those processes to the effects of caloric restriction (CR) on programmed cell death (PCD). Apoptosis (responsible for orderly cell death) is an age-related process of special importance to both chronic disease and aging. It is often not the loss of cells that causes age-related pathology (over currently observed human life spans) but the defective regulation of apoptosis and PCD. Such defects may be involved in the etiology of cancer, auto-immune disease and degenerative diseases of the nervous system.

Specifically, though cell death has been viewed as a chaotic process, it is often controlled by internal cell mechanisms so that a multi-cellular organism can equalize rates of cell generation and death to maintain a stable body size (Carson and Riberio, 1993). Kerr et al. (1972) characterized the morphological changes of dying cells as a.) the nuclei's compaction of chromatin against the nuclear membrane, b.) cell shrinkage with preservation of organelles, c.) detachment from surrounding cells, and d.) nuclear and cytoplasmic budding to form fragments that are rapidly phagocytosed by parenchymal cells or macrophages. This process affects scattered cells in tissue and occurs without releasing proteolytic enzymes or toxic singlet oxygen. There is no leakage of cellular contents into extracellular spaces (a pathological process occurring during ischemic damage during cerebrovascular stroke, i.e. the glutamic "cascade") and, of greater importance, there is no major inflammatory response (or stimulation of local growth factors) triggered. Apoptosis is important in many tissues but especially in the immune system, where it, for example, mediates the deletion of auto-reactive and nonfunctioning lymphocytes.

Apoptosis is clearly differentiated from cell necrosis – the simple destruction of cells. In many cells, calcium activates enzymes contributing to apoptosis. In cancer, when DNA is damaged, various genes (e.g. p53) determine whether apoptosis can prevent malignant cell growth. An important gene determining what happens is the oncogene c-myc, which can trigger apoptosis in certain situations. In contrast, the bcl-2 oncogene is a "cell death suppressor" gene. This gene is found in all haemopoietic and lymphoid cells, many epithelial cells and in neurons. Epstein-Barr virus increases bcl-2 in Burkitt's lymphoma. Cells over-expressing bcl-2 survive longer without growth factor stimulation and better resist ionizing radiation and glucosteroids. And bcl-2 also protects cells from apoptosis induced by the c-myc oncogene.

The p53 gene not only inhibits cell division but it also controls apoptosis. Other factors affect whether apoptosis controls auto-reactive lymphocytes. Apoptosis also occurs in a modified way in neuronal diseases. Thus, apoptosis, or defects associated therewith, play a critical role in a variety of age-related chronic diseases.

Warner et al. (1995) suggest that caloric restriction (CR) up-regulates the expression of anti-oxidant genes and that it also attenuates the formation of reactive oxygen species — and possibly the DNA and mitochondrial damage caused over age. The effects of anti-oxidants on aging and cancer suggests a third model of long-term changes in chronic disease risk and their contribution to late-age health changes.

Another process regulating cell reproduction at a higher level of biological organization is angiogenesis (Folkman, 1995). Angiogenesis, the process by which clusters or colonies of cells are enabled to grow by neovascularization, involves a balance of positive and negative factors. In situ carcinomas may be "dormant" for many years. The production of positive growth factors (e.g. aFGF, bFGF, VEGF and others) is not sufficient to control angiogenesis. A negative regulator of angiogenesis, thrombospondin, is produced by normal cells and is under control of the p53 tumor suppressor gene. A second factor, which is often produced by the primary tumor and which suppresses growth of metastases is angiostatin, a 28 kilodalton protein fragment with 98% homology to an internal fragment of plasminogen. It is a specific inhibitor of endothelial cell proliferation (e.g. endothelial cells in new capilliaries).

Angiogenesis is crucial in other chronic disease processes in both negative and positive ways: a.) in ischemic heart disease it helps develop collateral circulation, whereas b.) in arthritis neovascularization of cartilage is a major factor in joint degradation. Research on the molecular basis of disease is identifying the fundamental physiological processes of chronic disease. For example, P53 gene mutations may affect over half of all cancers, and they may be involved in coronary heart disease. The physiological processes associated with thrombosis may play a significant role both in circulatory disease and in the metastatic progression of tumors. Angiogenesis may be involved in the repair of cardiac ischemic events and in the progression of tumors beyond a dormant phase. Blood lipids may affect the progression of some tumors (e.g. Lp(a)) in breast cancer (Kokoglu et al., 1996) and thrombosis. Specifically, while angiostatin is 98% homologous to a fragment of plasminogen, a thrombolytic enzyme, Lp(a) is able to block the activity of plasminogen and prevent thrombolysis. Thus, Lp(a) can promote both cancer metastases and circulatory disease events. Research into molecular events may eventually lead to the re-organization of chronic disease categories along more basic physiological dimensions – dimensions comprehensively defining the state of an individual's physiology and the dynamics thereof.

4.6. The effects of micro-nutrients on chronic disease risks and aging

As discussed in the prior section, long-term changes in the consumption of micro-nutrients may alter chronic disease risks. Antioxidant vitamins A, C, and E affect cardiovascular disease by lowering the potential for LDL cholesterol to be oxidized, consumed by macrophages, and trapped in atherosclerotic plaques as foam cells or to inhibit vasodilation (Treasure et al., 1995). Vitamins A, D, and E are cellular redifferentiating agents that can repair some genetic damage. Vitamins A, C, D, and E are antioxidants that prevent certain chemical reactions from causing somatic mutations or other cell damage (Prasad and Edwards-Prasad, 1992). They can improve immunological responses at late ages (Beregi et al., 1991).

Vitamin D has a powerful effect on bone metabolism; especially in late-onset (ages 75+) osteoporosis (type II) in females. This may interact with cardiovascular diseases in females by effecting cellular calcium metabolism, parathyroid hormone activity, and hypertension (Browner et al., 1993). It may also interact with iron (Fe) and magnesium (Mg) metabolism (Moon et al., 1992) and is a powerful cellular differentiating agent that may reduce the risk of certain cancers (Lian and Stein, 1993).

The "epidemic" of atherosclerosis and ischemic heart disease in the U.S. can be tracked by the ratio of male to female CHD deaths over time. In the U.S. (also in Canada, England, and Wales) this ratio was near one until the mid-1920s. Then the male predominance in ischemic heart disease increased steadily until 1970. Vitamin D consumption may explain long-term trends in chronic diseases in that milk and other foodstuffs have been supplemented with it since 1924 in the U.S. and Canada.

Moon et al. (1992) point out that the curative effects of cod liver oil on rickets were identified in 1917. By 1923 the U.S. was importing 0.5 million gallons of fish-liver oil annually. By 1930 the figure was 2.8 million gallons. UV-irradiated milk was introduced in the U.S. in 1924. Manufacture of synthetic vitamin D_2 and D_3 increased from 35 lbs. in 1948 to 14,000 lbs. in 1972. By 1970 vitamin D_2 was being added to many foods. There was a concurrent decline of Mg in the U.S. diet due to changes in U.S. agriculture (increased use of nitrogen-based fertilizers). Mg mediates the effects of vitamin D on cellular calcium absorption (Moon et al.,1992). Vitamin D hypervitaminatosis, however, interferes with Mg absorption from food. Thus, over-supplementation of vitamin D may aggravate Mg deficiencies in the U.S. diet and, thereby, enhance the effects of Mg deficiency on acute myocardial infarction.

In the late 1960s, the FDA began to consider limiting vitamin D supplementation. Regulations restricting supplementation were implemented in 1972 – coincident with the beginning of the decline in ischemic heart disease.

The sex ratio of femoral neck fractures can be used to trace the origins of the U.S. osteoporosis epidemic. This ratio suggests (based on data from Rochester, Minnesota) that osteoporosis began it's epidemic upsurge in the late 1920s – about the same time that ischemic heart disease began to increase. Thus, the increase in vitamin D intake from 1920 to 1970 and its subsequent decrease could explain the interaction of atherosclerosis and osteoporosis for females; and their joint trajectories from the 1920s. Specifically, in contrast to the effect of vitamin D on Mg, vitamin D increases Fe absorption. The increased absorption of Fe may lead to increased free-radical generation and oxidation of LDL cholesterol (Sullivan, 1991). This could explain the rapid increase of atherogenesis in post-menopausal females: Fe stores in females increase and with excess vitamin D there is an increased calcification of atherosclerotic plaques.

While the over-supplementation of vitamin D may be associated with increased circulatory disease risks and osteoporosis, it appears that low vitamin D levels are involved in cancer mortality risk. This research began in the 1930s, when Peller (1936) noted that sun exposure tended to decrease cancer risks (Peller and Stephenson, 1937). It was argued that this was due to the activation of 7-dehydrocholesterol in the skin through sunlight. Sunlight activation avoids some of the toxic effects of vitamin D by limiting the production of inactive previtamin D_3-photoisomers (Webb and Hollick, 1988).

The mechanisms by which vitamin D might prevent cancer were examined by Eisman et al. (1979). They found that a human breast cancer cell line had receptor sites for 1,25 dihydro-oxyvitamin D_3(1,25-$(OH)_2$-D_3). Vitamin D also reduces colon cancer risks and, by suppressing the c-myc oncogene, causes leukemia cells to re-differentiate into normal monocytes and macrophages. Low vitamin D levels may also raise the risk of prostate cancer in males – possibly, because of it's similarity to steroid hormones, which means that it can compete for their cell receptor sites (Corder et al., 1993).

While basal and squamous cell cancers are aggravated by sun exposure, melanomas may be suppressed by moderate sun exposure – since melanoma cells also express receptors for 1,25$(OH)_2$-D_3. The administration of vitamin D slowed the doubling time of melanoma cells. Vagero et al. (1986) found melanoma more prevalent in office workers than in persons working outdoors.

Thus, it has been suggested that the rise in cancer mortality (+6.2% from 1950 to 1992) may be due either to a.) a general shift in U.S. occupations from outdoor, daylight activities to indoor, and nighttime activities or b.) recent public health policies to avoid sunlight exposure. There were 600,000 cases of sun-promoted cancers in 1991; those 600,000 cancers, however, only caused 2,000 deaths. On the other hand, there were 413,300 cases of sun-inhibited tumors that caused 137,800 deaths in 1991. Thus, either moderate sun exposure or moderate vitamin D supplementation may reduce the risk of many lethal tumors – with decreased sun exposure possibly explaining trends for certain cancers, e.g. recent increases in the incidence of breast cancer (Ainsleigh, 1993).

Since both high (circulatory) and low (cancer) levels of vitamin D are associated with mortality, it is necessary to keep its consumption in a narrow range. If vitamin D were a drug, it would have a narrow "therapeutic trough." As a hormone, it needs to be kept in strict physiological equilibrium over age. (It is a hormone since it modulates the phenotypical expression of many genes.)

Mg deficiency may have additional effects on circulatory disease because it stimulates renin release by elevating prostaglandin levels; and it suppresses aldosterone production by mobilizing intracellular calcium (Ichihara et al., 1993). This may slow fibrotic changes in the myocardium and in arterial endothelium.

4.7. Consumption of animal protein, CVD, and osteo-arthritic changes

Another explanation of long-term trends in circulatory disease risk is the homocysteine theory of how animal protein stimulates atherosclerosis (McCully, 1983). Ingestion of the sulfur-based amino acid methionine (an essential amino acid for mammalian growth) produces, after demethylation, homocysteine. Elevated levels of homocysteine, due to genetic predisposition or to the dietary deficiency of vitamins B_6 and B_{12}, had toxic effects on arterial endothelium. Endothelial lesions created by elevated homocysteine showed the characteristic fibrous nature of atherosclerotic plaques – but without lipid deposition if cholesterol was not elevated. The theory suggests that fibrous plaques are produced when vitamin B_6 deficiency allows accumulation of homocysteine and a toxic metabolite, homocysteine thiolactone, is produced. The metabolism of homocysteine is moderated by vitamin C. Though ascorbic acid is a potent reducing agent, after oxidative conversion to a free-radical form, semi-dehydroascorbic acid, one of its physiological functions is to oxidize the sulfur atom in homocysteine.

Thus, three stages in a pathway for the utilization of methionine are a.) demethylation and dehydration of methionine to homocysteine thiolactone, b.) oxidation of homocysteine thiolactone to homocysteic acid by semi-dehydroascorbic acid, and c.) reaction of homocysteic acid with ATP to form active coenzymes to synthesize sulfate esters of connective tissue proteoglycans.

Methionine deficiency inhibits growth and wound healing – like scurvy. In scurvy, the lack of dehydroascorbic acid inhibits the formation of sulfated proteoglycans. Increased conversion of methionine to homocysteine thiolactone increases production of sulfated proteoglycans, which apart from involvement in wound healing are deposited in atherosclerotic plaques. Age changes in hepatic homocysteine metabolism may explain why children in rapid growth phases are less susceptible to the atherogenic effects of homocysteine. The stimulation of growth is due to homocysteic acid, which has a similar effect to somatomedin (the serum polypeptide mediating the effect of pituitary growth hormone on cartilage) on sulfate binding in cultured cartilage fragments – suggesting a relationship between homocysteic acid, somatomedin, and growth hormone activity. After normal growth ceases and the epiphyses ossify, the growth stimulation affects the cells of blood vessels (especially smooth muscle cells) rather than the chondrocytes and osteocytes in mature bone.

Thus, the homocysteine model suggests a basis for the age dependence of osteoarthritic diseases and the effects of growth hormone and somatomedin on the aging of connective tissue. Some data suggest that the agent mediating the growth of smooth muscle cells is carried by platelets and released during platelet aggregation and adherence to injured intima. Calcification of fibrous connective tissue is stimulated, as is the disruption of intermolecular cross-linking in newly synthesized collagen fibrils due to the reaction of homocysteine with allysine to form tetrahydrothiazine adducts. This may interfere with intermolecular cross-linking in collagen and elastin.

The relation of this mechanism to increased heart disease in the 20th century may be due to an increased dietary ratio of animal to plant protein (dietary intake of methionine is correlated with cholesterol intake). Increased consumption of animal protein may explain the relation of increasing body size over time (as noted by Fogel, 1994) with atherosclerosis.

Vitamin B_6 levels decrease through life to the eighth decade because serum glutamine oxaloacetic transaminase hepatic activity decreases. When the elderly are treated with pyridoxine (B_6), transaminase levels return to the levels of younger persons (McCully, 1983; von Eckardstein et al., 1994). Also, since pyridoxine is water soluble, pyridoxine availability decreases as the lipid content of the diet increases.

To explain U.S. heart disease trends using the homocysteine model, the quantities of synthetic pyridoxine hydrochloride produced over time were examined (McCully, 1983). U.S. production increased from 1,900 kg. in 1944 to 30,000 kg. in 1963 (the last year for which U.S. production statistics are available). Imports of B_6 increased from 9,100 kg. in 1963 to 22,300 kg. in 1969, to 39,800 kg. in 1972 (a per capita threshold consumption of 0.53 mg/day, which is the minimal dose necessary to control homocysteine levels) and to 275,000 kg. in 1978 (3.42 mg/day). The timing of this increase is consistent with the post-1968 declines in heart disease for males. Since B_6 supplementation will prevent arterial damage but not reverse it, the decline in circulatory disease will increase as more recent birth cohorts who had adequate B_6 dietary supplementation reach older ages.

Though fibrotic changes induced by homocysteine may not be reversible, by attacking co-factors such as LDL cholesterol – or inflammatory and thrombotic responses – atherosclerotic plaques might be reduced in size. Recent data suggests that the effects of LDL cholesterol are under-estimated in prospective studies due to a.) the surrogate dilution effect (total cholesterol is measured, while it is LDL cholesterol that increases risk), and b.) regression dilution bias stemming from the random fluctuation of individual cholesterol measurements over time. These two factors may have led to researchers' underestimating the effect of LDL cholesterol by 35%. This would mean that a 1% reduction in cholesterol lowers ischemic heart disease mortality 3% (Law et al., 1994a) rather than the 2% previously estimated. It has been estimated that most of the effect of LDL cholesterol reduction is manifest after 5 years (Law et al., 1994b). This is consistent with studies which have found that cholesterol lowering begins to improve arterial functioning even before reductions in atheroma size are manifest (Treasure et al., 1995). Furthermore, fibrotic changes due to homocysteine are reversible in that ACE-II inhibitor drugs block aldosterone – the hormone responsible for fibrotic changes in the myocardium (Weber and Brilla, 1991). This involves control of a growth factor's effect on gene action leading to phenotypical changes in smooth muscle cell growth and structure.

Supplementation of B_6 is necessary because thermal food processing (to decrease viral exposures from animal protein consumption) degrades natural pyridoxine. This is controllable by consuming adequate levels of synthetic vitamin B_6 and B_{12} (von Eckardstein et al., 1994; Brattstrom et al., 1990; Dudman et al., 1993). The need for supplementation increases with age due to altered vitamin intake, absorption, and metabolism (Pancharuniti et al., 1994; Selhub et al., 1993).

The effects of B_6 on human physiology may be even more pervasive because B_6 a.) modifies the structure of steroid hormone receptors, and b.) alters the transcriptional capacity of genes (the ability of the hormone to affect or stimulate gene expression). Among the hormones affected by vitamin B_6 are androgens, estrogens, and glucosteroids (Tully et al., 1993). These effects are recognized in FDA regulations calling for the supplementation of food with folates (McCully, 1996). It is estimated that folate supplementation may decrease coronary heart disease mortality by 51,000 deaths per year (Boushey et. al., 1995). That does not include effects on strokes or peripheral vascular disease.

Dietary intake of at least two other trace minerals may affect long-term heart disease and stroke mortality trends by affecting blood pressure. Reduced salt intake leads to lower blood pressure and reduced abnormalities of calcium metabolism, incidence of renal stones, and bone demineralization. Increased salt intake in persons with a genetic predisposition in kidney function towards difficulty in excreting sodium is associated with excretion of calcium, which increases parathyroid hormone, vitamin D and serum osteocalcin. Salt was used in the 1920s and 1930s to preserve foods before refrigeration was available. Thus, reduction of dietary salt could affect not only hypertension but also osteoporosis and other circulatory diseases (MacGregor and Cappuccio, 1993).

A second trace mineral, potassium, found in many fruits and vegetables, decreases blood pressure. Thus, is hypothesized that increases in fruit consumption over time can reduce the incidence of early strokes.

Recently, new classes of organic compounds have been identified with major effects on chronic diseases. These are the bioflavonoids and phytoestrogens (Aldercreutz et al., 1991). One such class of compounds, phenols, may explain low French cardiovascular disease risks despite a level of high fat consumption (Franken et al., 1993). Red wine diluted a 1,000-fold reduced the oxidation products of LDL (hexanal and conjugated dienes) by 86% to 100% – compared to a reduction of such products by alpha tocopheral (vitamin E) of 60%. These phenols and polyphenols inhibit cyclooxygenase and lipoxygenase in platelets and macrophages – further reducing the risk of thrombosis.

Not only are these compounds potent anti-oxidants but phytoestrogens may block hormonal receptors and the expression of oncogenes. This may explain the lower risk of certain cancers in oriental populations, where the intake of such compounds (soy products contain high levels) is higher than in the West (Adlercreutz et al., 1991).

4.8. Summary

The period effects of improvement in survival from major causes of death in the 1970s and 1980s can be related to advances in medical treatment. The long-term effects of improvement in nutrition and in the supply of micro nutrients are major contributors to cohort effects in mortality decline. Historically, nutritional deficiencies leading to chronic diseases were prevalent until the role of specific vitamins and minerals in those diseases were identified and supplemental sources identified. At levels lower than those which cause specific deficiency syndromes (e.g. scurvy, pellagra, osteomalacia, rickets), vitamin deficiencies may contribute to long-term population changes in chronic disease and disability risks. Some actions are basic, involving both the modifications of cell membrane receptors for specific hormones and the transcriptional capacity of genes to produce certain proteins. Thus, these are excellent examples of gene-environment interactions – mechanisms basic enough to affect the expression of genetic factors underlying aspects of cellular senescence (Ramsey et al., 1995). The improvement in food processing and hygiene contributed to the reduction of infectious agents that may be responsible for the development of chronic conditions such as cardiovascular diseases and cancer. The homocysteine model explains how an increased consumption of animal protein and deficiency in micro nutrients may lead to atherosclerosis.

For the ebb and surge of chronic diseases over time to be consistent with the various models, there had to be changes, not only in mortality at late ages but also in the nature of age-related chronic disease processes in the past 150 or more years as nutrition (at both the macro- and micro-nutrient levels), food hygiene (H. Pylori infections, toxins due to food spoilage, e.g. aflatoxin) and viral and bacterial exposures changed. These changes may also affect genetic disease risk by altering gene-environment interactions (Berdanier and Hargrove, 1993). Thus, the average health characteristics of the very elderly population may continue to evolve as new birth cohorts, with different early health experiences, enter the elderly population. In sum, as the profile of chronic diseases affecting elderly populations changes over their life span, there is a potential for further long-term changes in age-related chronic diseases – and in what are currently identified as "natural" aging changes.

V. Effects of evolution on the age trajectory of human mortality curves

5.1. Survival and evolution

Despite numerous experimental and theoretical attempts to understand the forces shaping the age-specific human mortality curve at late ages many problems remain unsolved. Numerous explanations based on the ideas of heterogeneity in mortality, individual adaptation, or on some general properties of complex multistate dynamic systems often contradict each other. Their statistical testing requires additional data from new experiments and observational plans. Several interesting theories about the nature of senescence are suggested in the evolutionary biology literature. These theories, however, do not explain observed age patterns of human morbidity and mortality. In particular, they do not provide a consensus about the causes of the deceleration and leveling off of mortality at late ages. Many other problems associated with aging, chronic diseases and mortality remain unsolved. Why were lethal genetic diseases not eradicated by evolutionary forces? How responsive were genetically modulated physiological homeostatic mechanisms to environmental change during evolution? What is the long-term role of evolution in forging the age pattern of human mortality within, and beyond, the reproductive interval?

In this chapter we discuss several approaches developed in evolutionary theories of biological senescence. We also illustrate the role of evolutionary forces and gene-environment interactions in forming physiological mechanisms controlling human longevity and biological senescence. These mechanisms include changes in glucose metabolism, fat deposition, and insulin production; effects of free radicals; changes in immunological function; changes in cancer risks related to genetic and somatic mutations; effects of hormesis, etc.

5.2. Evolution and the age dependence of human mortality

Many traditional models of human mortality and aging ignore individual differences in the chances of survival. For many demographic applications this is a convenient simplification. The assumption of an initially genetically homogeneous human population is, however, biologically implausible and, furthermore, it precludes study of the effects of evolution on biological senescence and the genetic endowment for longevity. For senescence and late-age mortality to be shaped by evolution, the phenotypic expression of genetic traits must be affected by selection, i.e., the population in a model of the effects of evolution on senescence must be genetically heterogeneous, allowing the age dependence of species-specific mortality and fertility rates to be correlated (Hamilton, 1966).

Senescence and life-span limits are not present in haploid uni-cellular organisms with asexual reproduction. It was necessary for diploid organisms to develop, with sexual reproduction, for aging (senescence) and death to appear in the course of evolution. This is because sexual reproduction confers on diploids the potential to take advantage of increased environmental adaptability resulting from new combinations of genes. This is not possible in haploid cells because, with a single set of chromosomes, a mutation with adverse phenotypic effects causes death. In diploid organisms, because of the redundancy of chromosomes, a recessive mutation may not affect the survival of the organism because of the effects of the dominant gene. Thus, in diploids, different stochastic combinations of mutations can be expressed and acted upon by selection, i.e., "They are mechanisms of recombining accumulated unexpressed genes on a large scale and bringing various combinations of them to expression" (Sonneborn, 1978; p. 366).

Diploids and sexual reproduction (with somatic cells aging and dying while germ cells are "immortal") accelerated evolution. It is estimated that, while it took three billion years to go from the origin of life to unicellular diploid organisms with sexual reproduction, it took only 500 million years for unicellular diploid organisms to progress to the existing plethora of multi-cellular organisms. An unanswered question is how cultural and technological innovations accelerate environmental changes and evolutionary pressures on genetic longevity determinants (e.g. changes in the virulence of microbes due to the pressure of selection of general antibiotic use).

Two evolutionary models of senescence have been proposed. Williams (1957) suggested senescence was due to selection producing genes with different effects on "fitness" or "vitality" changes with age. Williams attempted to explain why senescence, a non-adaptive trait, would be produced by selection. Williams' pleiotropic model differed from Medawar's formulation (1952), where a significant role was envisioned for the accumulation of deleterious mutations in genes to be expressed later in life.

Weismann (1891) argued that a death mechanism evolved to kill off "worn out" organisms from a population to provide better conditions for the rest. Weismann was not specific about the nature of this mechanism but suggested it involved limits to the number of times that somatic cells could divide. Death mechanism theories emerged in the concept of the Hayflick limit and, more recently, by observation of the role of the telomere (and the controlling enzyme, telomerase) in somatic cell division (Kim et al., 1992).

Williams rejected Weismann's formulation because it required natural selection to favor group, rather than individual, survival, i.e., the death of worn-out individuals from a population was argued to increase the average vitality of group survivors. Williams' arguments also implied rejection of the "wear-out" assumption implicit in the Gompertz hazard function. Comfort (1956) rejected Weisman's theory on the basis that senescence was outside the developmental program that concerns natural selection, since no organisms in the wild attain a "senile" state. If no individuals reach a senile state, Comfort argued, senescence could not be regulated by selection. Williams rejected Comfort's argument by differentiating between the processes of senescence (which might initiate early in life) from senile states. Williams suggests that selection could operate on the gradual decrement of vitality in aging organisms during the reproductive life span. This would lead to a stochastic life-span limit (since failure processes would be multi-dimensional and stochastic) which could be modulated by environmental factors.

It has been suggested that aging occurs because selection favored a strategy in which fewer resources are invested in maintaining somatic cells. The "disposable soma" model was proposed to provide evolutionary support for the error theory of aging. The disposable soma theory links genetic selection to individual phenotypic traits by relating survival to reproductive potential. The theory can be represented by modeling the intrinsic rate of population increase, r, as,

$$\int e^{-rx} l(x;s) m(x;s) dx = 1 \tag{5.1}$$

where l, the probability of survival, and m, fecundity, are functions of age (x) and the investment of energy, s, in somatic cell maintenance. The optimum value of s maximizes r, subject to theoretical constraints.

The mortality of adults might be assumed to be described by the Gompertz-Makeham function (Kirkwood, 1990),

$$\mu_x = \mu_0 e^{\beta \cdot x} + \gamma, \tag{5.2}$$

where, μ_0 represents the base level of mortality, γ is a constant representing mortality due to environmental stresses, and β is the rate of aging. When in (5.2) $s = 0.0$ no energy is invested in cell maintenance. When $s = 1.0$ the maximum available energy is invested in cell maintenance (after taking care of other essential functions). These effects can be represented as,

$$\mu = \mu_{0\min}/s, \qquad \text{(a)}$$
$$\beta = \beta_0(s'/s - 1), \quad (s < s'), \quad \text{(b)}, \tag{5.3}$$
$$\gamma = \gamma. \qquad \text{(c)}$$

Fecundity parameters might be related to s by,

$$\alpha = \alpha_0(1-s), \tag{5.4}$$

and

$$f = f_{\max}(1-s).$$

It is assumed that some fraction of juveniles survive to adulthood, with (5.2) describing adult mortality. Reproduction begins at a peak rate f at age a. f declines at the same rate, β, as mortality increases in (5.2). The age-specific relation of survival to s (assuming Gompertz-Makeham mortality dynamics) can then be expressed as

$$l(x;s) = s \, \exp\!\left[-\exp\!\left(e^{\beta x} - e^{\beta a}\right)\mu_0/\beta - \gamma(x-a)\right]. \tag{5.5}$$

For fecundity the relation to age and energy level, s, is

$$m(x;s) = f \, \exp\!\left[-\exp\!\left(e^{\beta x} - e^{\beta a}\right)\mu_0/\beta\right], \quad x > a.. \tag{5.6}$$

The optimum rate of energy investment in cell maintenance, s^*, is different from the s required for $\beta = 0$ (i.e., constant mortality) because a minimum mortality level (γ) is generated by stochastic environmental forces so there is no advantage gained by increasing s to preserve physiological function beyond that level. Thus, instead of investing all of s in somatic cell maintenance it is assumed preferable to invest only sufficient energy for the organism to remain viable through the "normal" life expectation in the "wild" and to use the remaining energy in reproduction.

This model has several limitations. First, though it does not require a Gompertz-Makeham function to be evaluated, some survival function must be selected if the theoretical relations are to be parameterized. The function chosen, in contrast to (5.2), should reflect the interaction of population heterogeneity on longevity with survival if evolutionary processes are modeled. As discussed by Strehler-Mildvan, if there is a constant stochastic rate of environmental insults, mortality can reach a constant level. There is no absolute level of selection against longevity traits in that long-lived persons could survive either by chance, or as environmental stressors were reduced -- and γ is reduced. As recognized by Pearl and Pearl (1934) 65 years ago,

> "The persons of any race or clime who live to age 92 show, as subgroups, extraordinarily little intra-group variability in their average total longevity [CML(92)]. Now it is evident that the immediate reason, things being as they are, why these extremely longevenous subgroups exhibit such small inter-group variation is because age 92 is so near the upper limit of the human life span. In a manner of speaking they have no room in which to vary much. But this is only a statistical aspect of 'things as they are.' Biologically, the upper limit of the human life span is determined only by the inability of human beings, as now bred and

envisioned, to live much more than 95 to 100 years. There is no necessary theoretical or biological reason why some human beings should not have their length of life so distributed that the inter-group variability in respect of CML(92) would be of the same order of magnitude as that in respect of CML(0) now is. There simply are not sufficient numbers of such persons at the present time." (p. 4).

They also argue,
"It is seen that the same identical groups of human beings display an inter-group variability in numbers of survivors to age 92 from roughly 6 to 8 times greater than their inter-group variability in expectation of life at birth. Now a part of this greater variability in numbers of survivors to extreme longevity is doubtless due to the fact that the data are necessarily more meager as the upper limit of the life span is approached, but this can scarcely account for all of the differences. A considerable part of it presumably rests on biological and specifically genetic causes." (p. 5).

Mueller and Rose (1996) show that extensions of evolutionary theories of aging would also lead to a plateau in mortality. Thus, analysis of the disposable soma and other theories of longevity evolution requires a multivariate stochastic state process model with a mortality component to describe genetic selection for specific longevity traits.

Second, the disposable soma theory assumes the existence of a "normal" life expectation in the wild. While possibly valid for animal species, humans exert considerable, and growing, control over their internal and external environment (i.e., γ can be reduced significantly).

The following example illustrates how seasonal variation in mortality can be controlled. In England and Wales there are approximately 20,000 more deaths from ischemic heart disease and stroke in winter than during other times of the year. This effect is pronounced in the elderly, where there is a 30% increase in these causes of death during the winter months. Though seasonal variation in cholesterol is documented, it is unclear how its winter variation might trigger an acute circulatory event. Thus, one might better examine variation in relevant homeostatic subsystems.

A relevant subsystem involves fibrinogen and serum factor VIIc – among others – whose values are elevated in winter. The winter differences observed in these factors could cause 15% (fibrinogen) and 9% (factor VIIc) increases in ischemic heart disease. Fibrinogen was strongly related to neutrophil count, c-reactive protein, and *a1* antichymotrypsin – but not to ambient temperature. Plasma fibrinogen, c-reactive protein, and *a1* antichymotrypsin are all synthesized in the liver during inflammatory processes – mediated by interleukin 6, which is produced by monocytes and macrophages. So it seems that acute respiratory infections which trigger changes in clotting factors by stimulating inflammatory responses are the most likely explanation for the excess mortality risk in winter months – and not temperature per se (Woodhouse et al., 1994). Thus, both immunization against acute respiratory infection (especially in the elderly) and changes in factors affecting the risk of respiratory infections (e.g. drier winter air; cold air inducing bronchial irritation) could affect the seasonal excess mortality risk of important causes of death.

Environmental stress can be modulated and "normal" human life expectancy changed either by reducing exposures through altered behavior, or by altering the environment (e.g. changing water quality; sanitation; internal climate control, migration of retirees to different climates). This alters the amount of energy, s, which should be devoted to somatic cell maintenance because life expectancy potential is increased. It is unclear how the relationship between survival and fecundity is affected by environmental changes that constrain r to values below the threshold maximum (e.g. Calow, 1982).

Third, though the model is verifiable by examining how much energy is devoted to specific maintenance functions (e.g. cell repair in the epidermis after exposure to UV radiation), this does not explain the total energy requirements of the organism. This is especially difficult if there are interactions of organ systems that affect s. For example, the maintenance of circulatory efficiency could reduce the need for energy to maintain kidney function; vitamin C affects the generation of collagen (the only vitamin whose primary effects are inter- rather than intra-cellular). Thus, to represent such effects for humans one must deal with gene-environment interactions, the biochemical interaction of organ and tissue systems on the total energy economy of the organism, and, finally, on longevity.

Schachter et al. (1993) suggest two strategies for identifying genes that influence longevity: "association" or "case-control" studies and "sibling pair" studies. Association studies require selecting an ethnically heterogeneous population and then carefully matching cases and controls. A problem with this design is that the "ideal" controls are already deceased. A suitable control population might be selected from the population aged 25-60 because the probability that such individuals will become centenarians is small. Unfortunately, the probability of a person aged 60 reaching age 100 is changing rapidly in developed countries. The likelihood of a 50-year-old selected in 1996 reaching age 100 may be much higher than expected based on period life tables. The probability cited in 1980 for surviving to age 100 from birth was 2.5% for white females and 0.25%

for white males. Just 15 years later these values increased to 4.75% for females (nearly double) and to 1.26% for males (fivefold) (SSA, 1992). The existence of such changes raises questions about the assumptions used to justify the applicability of such case control methods. The sibling approach has the problem of not specifically describing how genes affect longevity over time.

It is not clear to what extent reproduction stresses male and female organisms differently. If reproduction is low, does that free energy for cell maintenance operate through a non-evolutionary mechanism (behavioral changes affecting the internal environment)? The effects of altered fertility on longevity could operate through complex hormonal systems (e.g. effects of estrogen exposure on breast tissue and on breast cancer incidence rates; effects of histamine release in neoplastic cells) so that a unidimensional "energy" model is insufficient.

A recent study of 19,380 male and 13,667 female British aristocrats born between 740 and 1876 suggests that women with fewer children, and who had children late in life, had greater longevity. This study, one of the few with a long enough time period to reflect genetic differences was interpreted as illustrating the effects of antagonistic plieotropy for females, i.e., that genetic factors favoring early fertility were not advantageous for long life. There are, however, many other environmental factors that could have affected the results (Langreth, 1998).

To evaluate evolutionary models one needs to identify the genes involved, the degree of phenotypic variation in survival due to genetics, and models of environmental inputs. Clearly, a model more complex than (5.2) is required to describe the multidimensionality of the physiological aging and stochastic failure processes. The "inverse genetics" suggested by Schachter et al. (1993) won't accurately reflect such complex dynamics. Nor does this model explain the observed late-age pattern of human mortality. Several recent papers have suggested models of the evolution of age-trajectories of mortality. Charlesworth (1990) developed a quantitative genetic model of senescence. The model predicts that, under mutation accumulation, additive genetic variance for mortality rates increases with age and that mortality rates at older ages should eventually reach 100%. Abrams and Ludwig (1995) extended disposable soma theory and formulated the optimization problem for calculating the age pattern of mortality at later ages. They concluded that a wide variety of mortality curves could be expected if the repair-reproduction trade-off were a major determinant of senescence. Mueler and Rose (1996) presented computer simulations using an evolutionary model of mortality. They concluded that the shape of mortality at late ages (a mortality plateau) can be explained by standard evolutionary theories. Pletcher and Curtsinger (1997) claim that the mutational effects assumed by Mueller and Rose are biologically unrealistic, and that standard theories of the evolution of senescence are insufficient to account for the deceleration and leveling off of mortality at advanced ages.

5.3. Adverse environmental exposures and age changes

The dynamics of phenotypic variation has an analogous expression in demographic studies in the concept of mortality selection operating on the frailty distribution and debilitation causing changes in frailty. Mortality selection suggests that, at late ages, mortality increases slowly because the death of frail persons reduces the average mortality risk for survivors. Debilitation suggests that the average mortality risk in a population is increased by adverse environmental exposures.

There are examples of debilitation in human populations when adverse exposures occurred at young ages. Japanese male cohorts in their teenage years during WWII manifested poor survival in middle age (Nihon University, 1982). This was apparently due to the physiological effects of poor nutrition for males during the period of their most rapid physical growth. However, the later in life that debilitation occurs, the more difficult it is to distinguish it from the accumulation of environmental exposures thought to drive age increases in mortality (cf. e.g. Strehler and Mildvan, 1960; Sacher and Trucco, 1962). This is shown in Figure 5.1.

In Figure 5.1 there are three hazard functions (A, B, C) and three distributions of environmental risks (1, 2, 3). Environmental exposures occurring at the earliest age (1) produce early increases in mortality which, if the environmental exposure ceases (for example, the effects of malnutrition in Japan ended after WWII), will eventually be eliminated from the population by mortality selection. Exposure at later ages (2) causes an increase in mortality risks that, if of the same magnitude as (1) (and assuming that persons at the two ages are of equal susceptibility), will produce a smaller relative mortality increase. Thus, unless the time-frame is narrowed, it becomes more difficult to identify the effect of debilitating events at later ages against "background" environmental exposures driving age increases in mortality. This can be illustrated by differences in the asbestos-induced risks of mesothelioma and lung cancer. Mesothelioma only occurs after asbestos exposure. Thus, its expression at any age can be presumed to be due to asbestos. In contrast, though asbestos raises the risk of lung cancer, there are other lung cancer determinants that can elevate lung cancer risk, such as genetic alterations of the cytochrome P450 enzyme system (Sellers et al., 1990). This makes the estimation of the effect of asbestos exposure on lung cancer difficult.

In the limit such debilitating effects can only be identified when occurring as mortality "shocks" in the population (e.g. the effects of influenza on mortality at late ages). The overall accumulation of environmental damage, on the other hand, becomes large at late ages, so that aging changes become indistinguishable from the slow

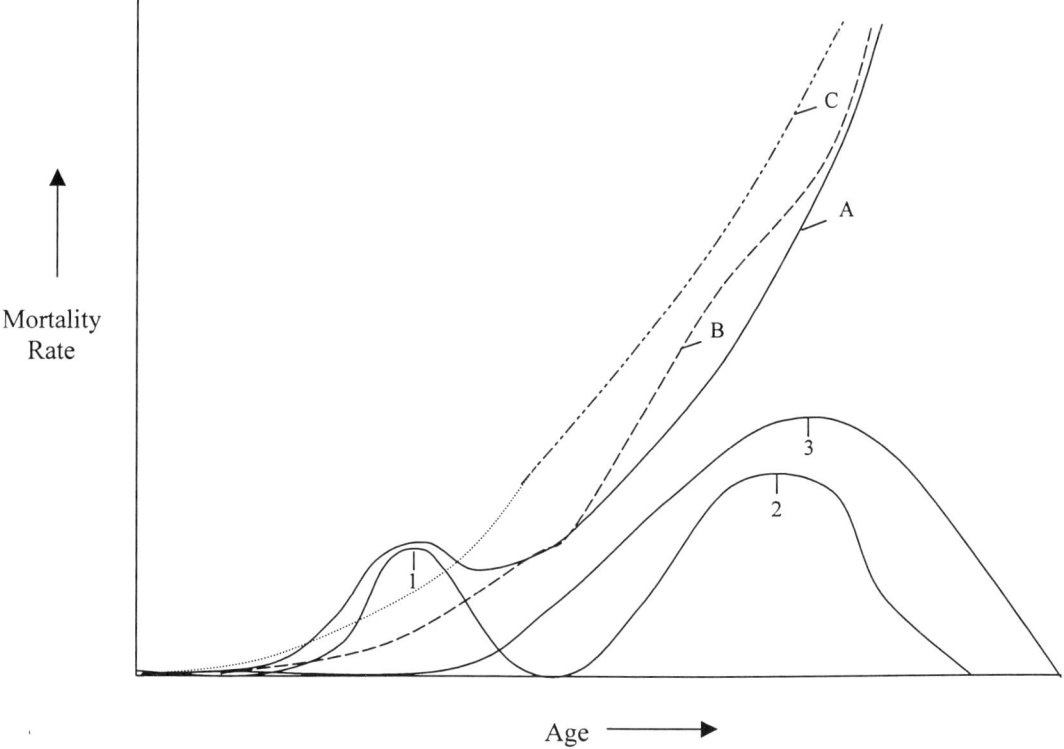

Figure 5.1. Three scenarios relating the age distribution of physiological stress to the shape of human mortality rate changes with age.

accumulation of debilitation due to environmental exposures. There may also be processes of "hormesis" (Stebbing, 1987), by which low-level stress on the organism increases its "vitality" or "fitness". Stress can produce debilitation if it is above an energy response threshold, and hormesis (and increased longevity) if it is below the threshold. An example of a physiological system where "hormesis" is likely is the B-cell production of antibodies in the human immune system due to challenges from exogenous factors.

5.4. The age-related efficacy of immunological surveillance for genetic errors

A similar problem emerges in analyzing the cellular mechanisms of chronic diseases. One model suggests that cancers are caused by m genetic errors in a cell allowing growth control to be lost (Armitage and Doll, 1961). Some genetic errors may be inherited. Knudson et al. (1971) found familial retinoblastoma to increase linearly with age ($m = 1$) while non-familial disease increased quadratically ($m = 2$) (Knudson, 1996). It was hypothesized that this was due to one of the genetic errors being inherited in familial cases. However, some of the same genetic errors that are inherited (e.g. mutations of the p53 growth regulatory gene in the Li and Fraumeni syndrome; Vile, 1993) can be induced during an individual's lifetime by environmental exposures (e.g. to DNA tumor viruses).

If the emergence of such errors is viewed as a stochastic process occurring in genetic material that is biochemically unchanging with age, then such events may occur throughout life with the initiation of a cancer due to a.) the age accumulation of mutational events, and b.) age-related degeneration of immunological surveillance processes. That is, the risk of a tumor is the product of the age-variable equilibrium of multiple processes. The immune system's decline could, in part, be the result of evolutionary pressures where, as the number of dysfunctional cells with some complement of genetic errors increases with age, the immune system has to decrease the intensity of response to prevent the emergence of lethal auto-immunological diseases. For example, systematic lupus erythematous had very high early mortality rates until treated with cortico-steroids (Fries, 1989). Auto-immunological responses are contributing factors in many other diseases – for example, as mechanisms in diabetes mellitus types I and II.

Both induced and inherited genetic errors play a role in atherosclerosis. Atheromas may develop initially as natural repair responses to arterial damage, but they go out of control as excess oxidized LDL cholesterol in macrophages is trapped as foam cells in the atheroma and inflammatory responses stimulate the production of growth factors increasing arterial wall thickness (Buja and Willerson, 1994). Of interest in the inflammatory process is whether macrophage activation leads to the release of hydrolytic enzymes (collagenases, elastases, cathepsins) that degrade the surface connective tissue of the plaque. Evidence was found for this by Henney et al. (1991). He demonstrated the presence of a gene for stromelysin in atheromas. Stromelysins are extracellular matrix metalloproteinases that break down the plaque capsule. Metalloproteinases (and their inhibitors TIMP) are involved in the ability of cancer cells to migrate through artery walls to establish metastatic sites (Gralnick, 1992). This suggests that a repair response mechanism out of control, and costing more energy, can increase the risk of death from multiple disease mechanisms. This also suggests that virally induced somatic mutations in connection with declines in immunological surveillance are two mechanisms underlying many aging changes.

5.5. *Atherosclerosis in U.S. African-Americans and whites may represent different pathological processes*

The rate at which atherogenesis progresses is influenced by many factors such as inherited tendencies to hypercholesteremia (Thieszen et al., 1990). Differences in glucose metabolism may lead to differential expressions of atherosclerosis in response to blood lipids. In blacks this may lead to insulinopenia, which reduces the rate at which smooth muscle cells proliferate in atheromas – thereby reducing the rate of atherogenesis in blacks. Blacks may also have a higher level of renin-induced hypertension and of Lp(a) (a lipoprotein affecting the ability to dissolve clots). Thus, while hypertension increases the risk of arterial damage, blacks may be more likely to experience a thrombosis once an atheroma is formed. Immunological responses are also involved in that macrophages stimulate inflammatory responses leading to the production of growth factors causing arterial smooth muscle to grow – further accelerating atherogenesis. Such growth of arterial intima may be viewed as a neoplastic process (Benditt and Benditt, 1973) – as may other cellular proliferative states that are out of normal physiological control. It is other factors that accelerate atheroma development in whites. These involve lower levels of HDL cholesterol in white males, higher level of body iron stores in whites in general (McCord, 1991), and a different physiological response to glucose intolerance in white diabetics.

The evidence suggests that glucose metabolism (and the glycosylation of protein – one model of aging changes; Cerami, 1985; Mooradian and Wong, 1991a,b) and factors affecting wound response (Lp(a)) may have evolved differently in blacks and whites (Manton and Stallard, 1996). This is also suggested by Lp(a) differences that are under genetic control: the distribution of Lp(a) is different in black and white populations (Marcovina et al., 1993).

5.6. Early survival advantages and their effects at late ages

Given the identification of genetic differences in disease risk between population groups and ways of representing those effects in a multivariate stochastic process model, are there plausible evolutionary mechanisms that determine the development of genetic differences? For example, immunological responses may start at early ages as adaptive reactions to high levels of exposure to infectious agents (e.g. poor water and food quality, poor sanitary conditions). However, as anti-microbial therapy developed along with immunological therapy against childhood infectious diseases, the contact rate with many pathogens may have decreased, so that persons with the most reactive immune system no longer have early survival advantages. Specific disease mechanisms where this occurs are sickle cell trait (for malaria) and cystic fibrosis (where the gene may have produced defenses against cholera). In both cases, the presence of a recessive trait may have once improved survival chances against an infectious agent. Those responses may now form either the primary (e.g. rheumatoid arthritis) or secondary (inflammatory responses to tissue damage) stimulus to genetic diseases.

Plasma-cell disorders known as monoclonal gammopathies of unknown significance (MGUS) are an example of a process linked directly to age-related immunological dysfunctions. These are highly prevalent at advanced ages in Caucasians (about 19% past age 95; Radl et al., 1975; Bowden et al., 1993). In about a third of cases they lead to multiple myeloma – a malignant myeloproliferative disorder whose prevalence increases with age. A comparison of this disorder across racial groups suggests that it is genetically linked – being highly prevalent in oldest-old Caucasian populations but having a low prevalence in Japanese populations. Normal immunoglobulin inflammatory responses are more often observed in Japanese people than in whites, which suggests that it is not less exposure to immunologically stimulating events that causes gammopathies in whites but poorer control of the production of immunoglobulins in plasma cells. Blacks have higher rates of MGUS than whites, suggesting they have both greater environmental exposure and poorer regulation of B-cell function (Browner et al., 1993). This suggests that genetic differences in plasma-cell function arose because of evolutionary differences between the population groups.

Another example of such a mechanism is found in restrictive cardio-myopathy occurring at late ages (90 to 99 years) due to amyloid deposition. A number of genetic errors related to deposition have been identified (Benson, 1997; Jacobson et al., 1997). Amyloidosis at early ages has been linked to genetic errors causing plasma-cell dysfunction in producing such protein. Treatments using cytotoxic therapy – including bone marrow (or umbilical cord blood cell) transplants – may lead to effective therapies by "re-initializing" the immune system, i.e., re-establishing it without the genetically defective stem cells.

5.7. Exogenous modification of genetic factors and their phenotypic effects

The processes described above seem consistent with William's pleiotropic model of senescence: inflammatory and immunological processes enhancing survival at early ages become maladaptive and are then expressed in chronic auto-immunological diseases at late ages. These auto-immunological processes are selected out by mortality at extreme ages (e.g., thyroid auto-antibodies by age 87; Mariotti et al., 1992; HLA types associated with diabetes, Takata et al., 1987; if immunological responses are involved in atherogenesis, mortality selection for this trait largely occurs by age 85, Marenburg et al., 1994; null alleles for MHC complement, Kramer et al., 1991, 1994). Only MGUS continues to progress to extreme ages (e.g., 95+) – though in the longitudinal data examined, selection forces tend to peak at about age 95. Immunological dysfunctions may be enhanced by free radical damage. Anti-oxidants seem to improve the function of certain cell types at late ages (cf. e.g., Beregi et al., 1991). Common anti-inflammatory drugs (e.g. aspirin) may reduce the risk of myocardial infarction (by reducing clotting factors), colon, esophageal, and possibly other cancers (by decreasing the ability for tumors to become vascularized or to metastasize) and possibly Alzheimer's disease (again, due to anti-inflammatory effects (McGeer et al., 1996)). Thus, there are multiple exogenous factors that modify the age-specific manifestation of genetically regulated disease processes.

If such mechanisms are involved in longevity and its evolution, how do we describe the interactions of so many processes, with some of them uncontrolled or only partly controlled? Three factors are required. The first is to realize that within an organism there are multiple stochastic processes that must remain in equilibrium (e.g., bone marrow generation of lymphocytes (Freedman, 1996); hematopoiesis (Abkowitz et al., 1996)). Thus, the hazard component of a state-space model must be multidimensional – and have multiple homeostatic points in the state space. Second, it is important that, when modeling the trajectory of multiple state variables by dynamic equations, the trajectories represent the temporally dynamic phenotypic expression of genetically controlled physiological processes.

Cholesterol levels may reflect the operation of several integrated metabolic subsystems affecting the trajectories of multiple-state variables (e.g. the effects of the liver on metabolizing fats; the production of lipases to mobilize energy from adipose tissues (McKeigue et al., 1991, 1993)), with the trajectory of physiological measures reflecting, in part, the genetic determination of the age dependence of physiological changes and, in part, the stochastic influence on those processes of environmental factors. Kidney function and its loss with age may be determined by levels of dietary protein. Fat consumption (amount and type) may affect the production of bile salts – which can raise the risk of certain cancers – as well as hormonal levels. Phytoestrogens and bioflavonoids (Adlercreutz et al., 1991) may affect cancer risks by blocking cell receptor sites. Vitamins A and E are cellular redifferentiating agents that can reverse genetic errors (Prasad and Edwards-Prasad, 1992).

Finally, the effects of evolution in human populations, at least in recent times, differ from models of "natural" selection. The ecological range of humans as a species is far broader than for any other animal. This is because humans as a species culturally accumulate endogenous and exogenous resources. The accumulation of selective advantages in other animal species is temporally limited, e.g. the accumulation of energy in fat or in other increased physiological reserves (lean muscle mass; increased organ weight).

Beginning with post-hunter-gatherer agrarian society, accumulation of survival advantages in humans could be extended beyond the soma of particular organisms, e.g., initially to food storage in abundant years or to the storage of plant-energy equivalents in livestock. (Since farm animals are self-maintaining organisms, this was a way of storing the energy in grain and other plant foodstuffs in a biological mechanism that avoided waste due to spoilage by utilizing the protective immunological systems of these organisms.)

As cultures become more complex this storage of prior environmental "advantages" becomes more efficient and complex. This makes possible the technological transfer and preservation of survival advantages at early ages to later ages. Thus, the calculus of natural selection is affected by cultural, exogenous factors that have to be related in a model. A third difference is the self-image of functional changes with age, which generates the motivation to adapt behavior to change survival at late ages.

5.8. *The time scale of evolutionary effects on aging*

A crucial factor in developing a multidimensional-state stochastic process model of human aging representing genetic effects is the ability to describe the time scales of the effects of evolutionary processes on aging and survival. Typically, evolutionary time is thought of as being long relative to available human data. A trait conferring a 2% survival advantage between generations will become dominant in 30 generations – or 700 to 800 years. However, there are important aspects of the internal environment that may dominate physiology and emerge in less time. Likewise, there are "imprints" of evolutionary events on current genetic material that go back millions of years. Thus, the study of evolutionary pressures on the life spans of specific species requires us to consider time scales of very different magnitudes.

Perhaps the most fundamental dimension of evolution is an organism's response to nutrients in the environment. In micro-organisms, sugar, amino acids and inorganic compounds (e.g., phosphate ion) start or stop transcription from specific genes by affecting DNA-binding proteins (Berdanier and Hargrove, 1993). The notion that a DNA-regulating segment can control genetic responses to nutrition by affecting the rate at which gene products are synthesized comes from studies of microbial metabolism. In the space that separates the bacteria cell wall from the plasma membrane there are two dozen proteins binding to sugar isomers, amino acids, etc.

Yeasts are eukaryotic organisms, so many of their structural and metabolic features are similar to those of mammalian cells. Yeast DNA has histones and other proteins typical of chromatin, separated from the cytoplasm by a nuclear envelope. Yeast cells contain mitochondria and endoplasmic reticulum. They differ from mammals in being able to grow in anaerobic conditions, having a cell wall, and in their ability to synthesize complex organic cofactors and amino acids from simple precursors. They are like bacteria in that environmentally prevalent nutrients, or their metabolites, directly activate or inactivate genes so that hormonal coordination of tissue function (large collections of cells with similar structure) is less important.

In multi-cellular organisms, functionally distinct groups of cells are found, including some specializing in storing or mobilizing nutrient reserves. Specialization requires a means for intra-cellular communication. Though secretion of metabolites and other small molecules may play a role, the fine control of metabolism requires paracrine and endocrine control of intra-cellular mechanisms. It is in the feedback of these finely controlled, biochemical communication mechanisms that we may find selective advantages favoring the development of longevity traits not directly related to reproductive age (e.g. hormesis).

For example, another time scale extending back 300 million or more years involves genes with multiply-coded sequences that are resistant to mutation. Some of these are involved in neoplastic processes. Cancer cells, as they are freed from growth control, revert to a more primitive functional state, becoming less dependent on inter-cellular regulation – as occurred in the free living conditions of cells 300 million years ago.

One such oncogene (c-myc) expresses multiply-repeated sequences to protect against mutation. C-myc may also be involved in aging. In contrast, two genes, p53 and Rb, control the growth of cells in the G_2 growth phase so that if they are intact, adverse genetic mutations cannot be expressed. Thus, there is at least one level of error control redundancy in the cellular regulation of somatic mutation.

Consequently, an important mechanism in the evolution of the biological control of life span is the rate at which environmental factors are imprinted onto the genetic machinery of cells. It has been hypothesized that endogenous retro-viruses found in the DNA of all humans (about 0.5 to 1% of the entire human genome; more than the sequences for retro-viruses) may both promote cancers and protect the cell from expression of exogenous retro-viruses.

5.9. The loss of the ability to manufacture ascorbic acid

Genetic factors can be species-specific. These may have evolved over millions of years as multi-cellular organisms differentiated. For these genes to remain in place they must perform specific functions. Three examples of such functions are Lp(a), the MDR1 gene, and changes in the cytochrome p450 enzyme system.

Lp(a) is a lipoprotein that accelerates wound healing and cellular repair mechanisms and prevents lipid oxidation. It blocks the activity of plasminogen, the effect of which is to stabilize blood clotting at wound sites. Lp(a) is found in humans, other primates, and guinea pigs which lost the ability to manufacture ascorbic acid (vitamin C) because of a mutation in a required enzyme (L-gulonolactone oxidase). It is hypothesized that Lp(a) was an evolutionary adaptation to the loss of the ability to generate ascorbic acid endogenously. It is, however, associated with heart disease risks, probably because it stabilizes clots formed in the circulation due to the damage caused to circulating blood cells by atheromas. Thus, this is an example of a pleiotropic mechanism with adverse consequences for adaptation when Lp(a) is elevated in older organisms with more extensive atherosclerosis (Rath and Pauling, 1990). The production of Lp(a) differs over racial groups. It is higher in African-American and other black populations Elevated Lp(a) is found in female breast cancer and may explain elevated early breast-cancer risk in black females (Kokoglu et al., 1996). Its elevation in blacks is of interest in that it may be affected by hepatocyte production of G6PD – an enzyme that helps control oxidative stress, whose expression is controlled by insulin, and which is adaptively deficient in humans exposed to malarial risk.

MDR1 is a gene that codes for glycoproteins that pump water-soluble toxins from cells. It evolved to protect such organs as the kidney, liver, and stomach from water-soluble toxins in vegetables and fruits. This gene is one reason why kidney and liver tumors are difficult to treat: the molecules of many effective chemotherapeutic agents (e.g., adriamycin) are water-soluble and are thus removed from cells with a high level of MDR1. This is why lipid-soluble metabolic chemotherapy agents have more effect on drug-resistant tumors (e.g., in "stealth" liposomal delivery of Adriamycin; Stewart, 1997). Clonal selection by the pressure of chemotherapy will also lead to a selective advantage for tumor cells manifesting this trait, so that MDR1 can cause drug resistance to evolve (by gene amplification) in other tumor types. This may be dealt with by blocking the action of the gene (e.g., using calcium channel blockers; Gottesman, 1994).

The P450 gene superfamily generates the largest number of enzymes for drug and exogenous chemical metabolism. Many chemicals are non-polar and soluble in lipids. P450 enzymes convert those chemicals into water-soluble products so that they can be excreted. This biochemical reaction occurs in two phases. Phase I (functionalization) involves attaching a functional group (such as OH) onto the molecule by a P450 enzyme. In Phase II the functional group is used to conjugate with, e.g., glucuronic acid, sulfate, glutathione, glucose and cysteine to form a water-soluble product. The P450 superfamily contains 20 families, 10 of which are present in all mammals. The operation of P450 enzymes is often due to induction by the chemicals to be metabolized. The action of P450 genes is influenced by pituitary and sex hormones.

One question about the P450 superfamily is its genetic development. Three major mechanisms affected its evolution: genetic drift (diffusion of mutations), natural selection, and molecular drive. The first two are based on population dynamics. The third involves the internal dynamics of irregular DNA behavior. Molecular drive is thought to be a major basis for the evolution of the P450 gene family. It is thought that P450 enzymes may have evolved with time in animal-plant "warfare," co-evolving parts representing members of different species. Such molecular drive allows animal species to exploit new plant species (Gonzalez and Nebert, 1990). A consequence of P450 evolution is polymorphisms in drug and other chemical metabolism. The study of such factors is referred to as pharmacogenetics. Such changes may explain many carcinogenic phenomena. The expression of the P450 system varies by age, gender, and racial group. Thus, there is tremendous variability in the genetic determinants of P450 behavior across human populations. Such variation may be related to the age rate of progression of select pathological processes. Unique to this gene family are the effects of dietary selective pressures.

5.10. Acquired disease resistance due to ecosystem changes

A third time scale involves changes arising from the transition from hunter-gatherer to agrarian society. This shift means forests were cut down to clear land. Cleared land provides a better environment for some disease vectors. Examples are malaria, asthma and diabetes mellitus.

For malaria the clearing of land provided sun-exposed pools of water that created a favorable climate for the anopheles mosquito. This seems to have been first manifest in the Yam Culture peoples inhabiting South Central Nigeria 12,000 to 16,000 years ago. The Kwa-speaking peoples were hardest hit by malaria and it is likely that they developed the sickle-cell hemoglobin trait as an evolutionary response to the disease. While conferring malarial resistance, this trait also affected the oxygen-carrying capacity of blood.

Another adaptation is the modification of a red blood cell enzyme, glucose-6-phosphate dehydrogenase (G6PD). Persons with deficient G6PD have less glutathione in their red blood cells, which is necessary for the metabolism of the malaria parasite. However, glutathione is an enzyme that reduces oxidation – oxidative processes are a major factor in various models of longevity. Declines in glutathione levels are found in healthy aging adults (Lang et al., 1992). Glutathione levels are about twice as high at ages 60 to 79 years as from age 80 to 99. In addition, there is a survival level of 400 μ g/10^{10} erthrocyte, which all subjects greater than age 80 exceeded. Low blood glutathione has been associated with diabetes, renal function, cancer, and cataracts. Thus, to gain malarial resistance, a longevity-enhancing trait may have been compromised.

A third disease mechanism possibly produced by evolutionary processes is asthma – and other allergic responses. These may have emerged to protect the body from ingesting environmental toxins. The agent causing the greatest release of histamine in asthma sufferers was not standard household dust mites but an evolutionary cousin, *dermatophaigoides farinae*, the grain mite (Mercer and Van Nieker, 1991). Reactions were found to other mites involved with grain storage and to the effects of molds growing in moist grain (e.g. soybeans). Of particular relevance in allergic responses are molds known as Aspergillus. Asthma and other allergic reactions may be evolutionary adaptations to the domestication of grain about 14,000 years ago. What began as a gatekeeper, defense reaction, however, becomes maladaptive when the toxins invading the organism cause the primitive defense system to over-react producing an overly potent allergic response and auto-immune diseases.

Of more recent vintage is genetic susceptibility to diabetes. In Paleolithic times (30,000 years ago) the ability to metabolize sugars readily and to store fat in periods of excess food availability was an adaptive trait. As food production became better organized genes predisposing to diabetes may have been subjected to less selective pressure so that it remained highly prevalent in some populations. An example of such a gene is the HLA DR4 gene in Japanese diabetics (which has little effect in other groups, such as the Swiss).

A prime example of this are the Pima Indians, who settled near the Gila River about 2,000 years ago. This was a desert area with a subsistence economy of hunting and some farming. An adaptation of insulin production allowed them to tolerate high levels of insulin with little glucose-lowering effects. High insulin production creates a number of adverse, nonadaptive physiological conditions that lead to heart and other diseases. The Pima Indians' insulin resistance requires other physiological triggers to become operational (possibly during pregnancy).

A related but more recent genetic adaptation is lactase deficiency, i.e. the lack of the enzyme to metabolize lactose, the primary carbohydrate in milk. Lactose is a disaccharide unique to milk. This deficiency is prevalent in most areas of the world except Northern Europe and North America. It emerged as an adaptation to the emergence of a dairy culture about 8 to 10,000 years ago. In most human populations, phenotypes with low lactase are most prevalent (e.g. 100% in Vietnamese; 95% in American Indians; 65% in Blacks, 22% in U.S. whites).

Lactase production may be higher in Northern European populations because of the reduced sunshine, which decreases vitamin D levels and lowers calcium absorption. In human groups that express an age-related decline in lactase, the decline occurs at about ages 5 to 7 years. In select geographic areas, groups maintain lactase production. This is due to an autosomal dominant trait (Sahi and Launiala, 1977) that persists into adulthood. In these populations, lactase-specific activity rises late in gestation and remains at that level throughout adult life. A juvenile trait with possible longevity-enhancing characteristics is maintained in northern climates (Flatz, 1987).

5.11. Changes in the ecosystem and technical disruptions of evolutionary processes

More recent are ecosystem disturbances that spread major epidemics by changing the relation of human host to disease vectors. The plague of 1347 is thought to have been brought about by the deforestation of large areas of Europe, which brought plague-carrying woodland rats into contact with unsanitary conditions in new urban centers. Similar factors set the stage for the Great London Plague of 1665 and, more recently, for diseases arising from the deforestation of Vietnam from 1965 to 1970. Recent examples of new diseases emerging due to ecosystem disruption are Lyme disease in the U.S. (where many suburban communities are built in wooded areas) and Dengue fever in Latin America.

One factor not fully recognized in analyses of the effects of evolution on senescence is the acceleration of the rate of evolution in the 20th century. The pace of evolutionary change has been disturbed by several factors. First, the density-dependence of pathogens, which causes them to be self-limiting, is mitigated by the speed of modern transportation. The Ebola epidemic in Africa was effectively halted only by the imposition of tribal procedures that enforced quarantine. Second, the use of antibiotics on a mass basis and from multiple classes of agents accelerated the emergence of antibiotic-resistant strains of bacteria (e.g., T.B., staphlococcous). Likewise, chemotherapy affects the rate of selection of cell strains with a survival advantage. In this context, it is important to understand processes favoring new diseases emerging from tropical rain forests (such as AIDS) or the mutation of viral strains in livestock (e.g., swine flu viral mutations).

New immunological therapies (e.g., vaccines) may prove to be protective against emerging diseases, as well as the use of multiple agents to protect against resistant mutations of diseases, or the use of agents like retinoids as redifferentiating agents in cancer.

Summary

Two concepts have dominated evolutionary thinking about senescence during the last several decades: antagonistic pleiotropy and mutation accumulation. Both propose that natural selection declines at older ages. Williams' idea of antagonistic pleiotropy suggests there will be an age-related mortality increase during the reproductive ages. It does not, however, explain the shape of the human mortality curve observed at late ages. The pattern of mortality at late ages was not discussed in the context of mutation accumulation theory. The evidence of teleomere shortening during cell division can be used to explain the Hayflick limit which, in a certain sense, supports Weismann's hypothesis on "programmed" life span. These facts, however, do not clarify the reasons why the age pattern of mortality at late ages tends to level off. The shape of the curve, especially after the reproductive period, remains incompletely explained by evolutionary theories. Wear-out hypotheses used in reliability theory can mathematically describe the deviation of the mortality curve from the Gompertz function at later ages. This description is too mechanistic, however, since it ignores the role of evolutionary forces and does not explain the biological regularities of the aging process. The disposable soma theory combines natural selection with the wear-out hypothesis. This theory is methodologically close to Dawkins' (1995) idea of "selfish genes." It requires further understanding of energy metabolism in the organism, and, in its current form, cannot explain the observed mortality pattern.

The role of evolution in shaping the human mortality curve might be better understood if the interaction of environmental forces with physiological homeostatic processes were explicitly described. To gain pathogen resistance in the organism during evolution, longevity-enhancing traits were often compromised. For example, the presence of the sickle-cell hemoglobin trait in human populations is an evolutionary response to malaria. The deficiency in the G6PD enzyme also plays a protective role against malaria, but it increases oxidative processes in organisms. The decline of the immune system with age may be an evolutionary response to the stochastic increase in the number of genetically defective cells at advanced ages. The presence of some recessive genes in the human genome may be explained by their protective role against infectious agents. There is an evidence of the "imprint" of evolutionary events on current genetic material. The rate of such imprinting is an important subject of evolutionary studies. Three major mechanisms of this genetic evolution are genetic drift, natural selection, and molecular drive. To study these mechanisms, a multidimensional stochastic process model of mortality and survival is necessary.

VI. The role of selection, debilitation, and adaptation in forming age patterns of mortality: a statistical perspective

6.1. Why does old age mortality level off?

To explain the deceleration and leveling off of mortality rates at late ages, new demographic mortality models have been developed and applied to data. These models exploit the ideas of selection and debilitation in heterogeneous populations, as well as that of adaptation of individual organisms to environmental and internal changes. One model exploits the concept of fixed frailty. Another deals with randomly increasing frailty (i.e. acquired heterogeneity). The third model includes the ability of individuals to adapt. Below we examine the formal basis of the explanations of mortality offered by the different models.

6.2. Fixed frailty in Gompertz-Makeham models

Strehler and Mildvan (1960) noted that the heterogeneity of individuals produces a trajectory of the average population mortality rate that deviates from the age trajectory of the mortality risk for an individual. One way to represent population risk heterogeneity is to assume individuals have different chances of survival to specific ages because of fixed, innate differences in "frailty." Beard (1950) and Vaupel et al. (1979) describe mortality for individuals of frailty Z at age x by:

$$\mu(x, Z) = Zae^{bx} + c, \qquad (6.1)$$

where a, b, and c are parameters to be estimated. If Z is assumed to be a gamma-distributed, random variable with mean 1 and variance σ^2, the average frailty ($\bar{Z}(x)$) among survivors to age x is:

$$\bar{Z}(x) = \frac{1}{1 + \sigma^2 \frac{a}{b}(e^{bx} - 1)} \qquad (6.2)$$

and population mortality (i.e. the average risk of death for individuals age x) $\bar{\mu}(x)$ is

$$\bar{\mu}(x) = \frac{ae^{bx}}{1 + \sigma^2 \frac{a}{b}(e^{bx} - 1)} + c \ . \tag{6.3}$$

Equations (6.1) and (6.3) assume frailty is fixed, unidimensional, and continuously distributed. The gamma-mixed Gompertz in (6.3) produces $\bar{\mu}(x)$, which increases as a logistic function of age.

A more general mixing distribution (Dubey, 1967) can be used where a parameter n is set to determine the distribution of frailty (Manton et al., 1995c). For $n = 1.0$, the mixing distribution is a gamma which produces a constant coefficient of variation for Z (i.e. both the mean, $\bar{Z}$, and the variation of Z decrease with age). When $n > 1.0$ the coefficient of variation decreases, e.g., $n = 2$ produces an inverse Gaston distribution of frailty, where the variation of Z declines faster than $\bar{Z}$. When $n < 1.0$ the coefficient of variation increases (i.e., $\bar{Z}$ decreases faster than the variation of Z, so relative heterogeneity increases with age). In all cases, mortality selection can cause $\bar{\mu}(x)$ to reach a constant value at late ages (e.g. $x > 95$). Manton et al. (1982, 1986) showed (6.3) fits U.S. and Swedish cohort mortality better than a Gompertz-Makeham model without heterogeneity. Yashin et al. (1994) confirmed these results, fitting the gamma-Makeham to recent Swedish mortality data.

6.3. Acquired heterogeneity (debilitation) models

Another approach to modeling mortality deceleration at old ages assumes that mortality risks increase stochastically with age. Assume an individual age x can be in state 0,...,n, corresponding to n+1 levels of frailty. In state $i<n$ a person faces both the risk of death and of moving to state $i+1$, where the death rate is higher. Survival parameters can be calculated for special cases of this model (Le Bras, 1976; Gavrilov and Gavrilov, 1991).

Specifically, assume newborns in a cohort start from state 0, i.e., everyone has the same chance of survival at birth. This is similar to the assumption of "initial" homogeneity made by Sacher-Trucco and Strehler-Mildvan. Let λ_0 be the transition rate from state 0 to state 1; and μ_0 the transition to the death state. For the ith state let the transition rates be $\lambda_0 + i\lambda$ and $\mu_0 + i\mu$. Transitions through states could be explained by the accumulation of frailty, as in the Sacher and Trucco and Strehler-Mildvan models – except that they described accumulated damage as changes in a continuous-state variable controlling survival rather than as the accumulation of discrete traits. The discrete state transitions do not depend on age but increase monotonically across n. If $P_i(x)$ is the probability that individual age x is in the ith state, Le Bras (1976) shows

$$P_0(x) = P_0(0)e^{(-\lambda_0+\mu_0)x}, \qquad (6.4)$$

and

$$P_i(x) = \frac{P_0(x)}{i!}\left\{\frac{\lambda - \lambda e^{-(\lambda+\mu)x}}{\lambda+\mu}\right\}^i \prod_{k=1}^{i}\left(\frac{\lambda_0}{\lambda}+(k-1)\right), \qquad i > 0. \qquad (6.5)$$

Survival to age x is

$$S_n(x) = \sum_{i=0}^{n} P_i(x). \qquad (6.6)$$

As $n \to \infty$, $S_n(x)$ tends to

$$S(x) = e^{-(\lambda_0+\mu_0)x}\left(\frac{\lambda+\mu}{\mu+\lambda e^{-(\lambda+\mu)x}}\right)^{\frac{\lambda_0}{\lambda}}. \qquad (6.7)$$

Taking the logarithmic derivative of (6.7) the population mortality rate is

$$\bar{\mu}(x) = \mu_0 + \frac{\mu\lambda_0\left[1 - e^{-(\lambda+\mu)x}\right]}{\mu + \lambda e^{-(\lambda+\mu)x}} \qquad (6.8)$$

When $\mu < \lambda$, (6.8) is approximated by

$$\bar{\mu}(x) = \left(\mu_0 - \frac{\mu\lambda_0}{\lambda}\right) + \frac{\mu\lambda_0}{\lambda}e^{(\lambda+\mu)x}, \qquad (6.9)$$

which is equivalent to (1), where $\left(\mu_0 - \frac{\mu\lambda_0}{\lambda}\right)$ corresponds to the constant (e.g., γ),

$\frac{\mu\lambda_0}{\lambda}$ to the scale parameter (μ_0), and $(1+\mu)$ to the shape parameter (β). This model can represent many types of mortality age trajectories, including those where mortality levels off at late ages. Unless the data deviates from a Gompertz-Makeham curve, however, four parameters cannot be estimated (as for the gamma-mixed Gompertz). Even if not directly estimable, the more detailed parametric structure may be a better description of health change and mortality mechanisms. It may, for example, better explain health changes in epidemiological studies.

Fixed frailty models (like the gamma-Makeham model) can describe genetic effects on mortality and longevity. The influence of environmental factors and a randomly developing health deterioration process can be represented using the Le Bras or Strehler-Mildvan models. However, mortality data alone cannot identify which effect is more important (Yashin et al., 1994). For example, (6.8) can be written

$$\bar{\mu}(x) = \lambda_0 + \mu_0 - \frac{\lambda_0(\lambda+\mu)}{\lambda + \mu e^{(\lambda+\mu)x}}. \tag{6.10}$$

Equation (6.8) is equivalent to (6.10) when

$$\mu_0 = a + c,$$

$$\lambda_0 = \frac{b}{\sigma^2} - a, \tag{6.11}$$

$$\lambda = b - \sigma^2 a,$$

$$\mu = \sigma^2 a.$$

Solving these equations for a, b, c, and σ^2 produces,

$$a = \frac{\lambda_0}{\lambda}\mu,$$

$$b = \lambda + \mu,$$

$$c = \mu_0 - \frac{\lambda_0}{\lambda}\mu, \tag{6.12}$$

$$\sigma^2 = \frac{\lambda}{\lambda_0}.$$

Equations (6.11) and (6.12) establish a one-to-one correspondence between the Le Bras and gamma-Makeham parameters. Both fit the data equally well. So how can statistical results be interpreted? Yashin et al. (1994) show both genetic (fixed frailty) and health deterioration (acquired frailty or debilitation) models can describe mortality, if $\bar{\mu}(x)$ reaches an asymptote at late ages.

These two concepts may be distinguished by experiments in which "stress" is applied to laboratory animals (e.g., insects) to see how aging and mortality processes react. To use such data, models of mortality representing the mechanisms of how stress influences survival are needed. One problem is that some effects, such as "hormesis", are associated neither with selection nor debilitation. The concept of hormesis (see p. 110) suggests that, when subjected to low levels of stress, organisms may manifest either greater population growth or greater fitness and longevity.

Specifically, if the homeostatic (or, more precisely, when the equilibrium point is age-varying, homeorhetic) mechanisms of an organism respond to a stress of low intensity with a fixed level of energy the organism may have greater "fitness" if energy is put into maintenance rather than reproductive functions. Stebbing (1987) suggests,

"Following perturbation, it has been shown that (population) growth rates may sometimes exceed the equilibrium growth rates of unperturbed organisms or cultures, resulting in hormesis at certain concentrations. It might be assumed that organisms growing at a submaximal rate would be selected against, in favor of those growing faster. However, it is becoming clearer that the capacity of the control mechanism to counteract the perturbing effect of environmental variables is a function of the residual margin between actual and possible growth rates; and that homeorhetic or homeostatic capacity (or "fitness" in Calow, 1982) has greater survival value than the ability to merely maintain a higher growth rate" (pp. 546-547).

Thus, in contrast to the disposable soma model, there may be a survival advantage in increasing the longevity of adult organisms by utilizing the energy generated in responding to low-level stress (i.e., s^* in the disposable soma model discussed in Chapter V is increased) than by always investing that energy in an increase in r (see (5.1)).

Calow (1982) elaborates this "adaptationist" approach and suggests that maximum feeding, growth, and reproduction rates are unlikely outcomes of natural selection. He presents four arguments for models of hormesis.

1.) Organisms can accelerate growth after illness or starvation – if increased feeding can compensate for deferred growth then metabolism must be elevated above normal levels, and hence, initially had to be operating at "submaximal" levels.
2.) Endocrine systems can regulate growth. Growth could not be regulated if feeding and growth rates were at maximal levels.
3.) Feeding processes adjust to the quality of nutrition intake through neuroendocrine regulation. More primitive regulatory mechanisms involve direct interactions of genetic expression and the nutritional environment
4.) Catabolic processes can be controlled.

The issue then becomes: what traits are likely to promote a positive relation of homeostasis/homeorhesis and fitness? There are six possibilities.

1.) Maximal growth rates of offspring can put parents at risk (by metabolic exhaustion or susceptibility to predators).
2.) Predator-prey models suggest that larger animals should be selected as food – making submaximal growth rates optimal.

3.) Variation in food supply (e.g. seasonal availability) would select for a submaximal growth rate.
4.) Susceptibility to physical and climatological stresses varies with size.
5.) Trade-offs between the rate and efficiency of metabolism.
6.) The possibility of group selection.

Calow (1982) concludes "the possibility of selection for active regulation according to homeostatic principles also remains a plausible outcome of neo-Darwinian selection" (p. 418).

Thus, the concept of hormesis also implies that the relation of s^* and r (see equations 5.1-5.6 in Chapter V) is more variable than in the disposable soma theory (where increases in s above a threshold are channeled into reproductive capacity) because physiological responses to low-intensity environmental stress may confer more survival advantages than by increasing r, since life expectancy in the "natural" state is altered when that state is changed. An increase in r, if the organism uses all of the energy made available by the response to an environmental stress, would reduce the survival of the stressed organism and perhaps block future increases in r. Specifically, if all excess energy is consumed by raising r to the maximum level, then the mortality rate of the organism is increased because the adaptability to environmental stress is lost.

The tendency for stress to increase the fitness of the organism is due to the feedback structure, and time lag of responses in the organism's homeorhetic mechanisms. A closed-loop feedback system tends to increase fitness because the energy necessary to survive variable degrees of stress will be produced in fixed quanta, not as an absolutely continuous response, since information on environmental stress is subject to time delays as it is processed through the system. For example, if the stressor increases the production of heat-shock protein in the cell as the biochemical response to stress, there is time involved, both in the production of the heat-shock protein and in producing the adaptive response. This can be illustrated in *Drosophila*, where older organisms produce more heat-shock proteins in response to heat stress than younger organisms because older organisms have more protein susceptible to heat shock. A similar response is induced in young flies by experimentally altering their proteins before applying heat stress. Maintenance functions may be improved with age by low intensity environmental stress (Fleming et al., 1988).

Thus, hormesis may be a mechanism that increases longevity due to evolutionary factors. The more variable the environment, the greater the chance an organism will receive a stressful shock before reproduction and offspring-rearing functions are fulfilled. Examples of environmental stresses of human populations cover a wide range of time frames; from the stress of long-term climatological changes (e.g., the Ice Age) to shorter-term climate changes (e.g., a 10 to 11 year cycle in El Niño in the Americas); and from viral and bacterial pathogens, which undergo selection as their exposure raises the immunological responses of survivors to particular microbial changes (e.g., influenza cycles; possible cycles in streptococcal infections).

Such phenomena can be frequently observed in humans. Influenza epidemics used to kill many people. Those in robust health survived and developed B-cell antigens against the virus. They subsequently have better immunological responses to similar viruses. Thus, the initial stress of infection modified the immune system so that the organism was protected against similar future infections. We now make use of this mechanism by injecting altered viruses (to reduce the intensity of stress) to induce B-cell antigenic responses. A lower expenditure of energy in response to stress provides a greater difference between the energy allocated to respond to stress and the efficacy of future responses. Influenza shots are recommended for persons who are young, elderly, pregnant, or have a chronic illness: We thus use the mechanisms of hormesis and increase its efficiency for vulnerable subgroups. This affects both the rate and nature of evolutionary selection for longevity by environmentally modifying physiological mechanisms.

There are mechanisms in humans analogous to the heat-shock protein response in *Drosophila*. When homeorhetic systems do not produce hormesis, they "over-react" to the stress and produce a pathological state. In a number of human auto-immunological diseases a prior inflammatory response (due to infection or injury) may produce heat-shock proteins. This may lead to a chronic auto-immune response which may be expressed in arthritis due to Lyme disease, and possibly in other more general auto-immune diseases (e.g., systemic lupus erythematous; SLE). Auto-immune diseases are expressed because the immunological stimulus may be similar to proteins occurring naturally in the organism (Friedman et al., 1990).

In this context, the adaptive properties of apoptosis and programmed cell death become apparent. That is, apoptosis controls the amount of internalized damage due to environmental stress by removing cells not capable of being repaired without a major inflammatory response. However, apoptosis is an active process requiring energy – as is the genetic regulation of the apoptosis mechanisms controlling the disassembly of the constituents of affected cells.

The mechanisms described above suggest that a mixed model with a Dubey-type distribution (Dubey, 1967) with $n < 1.0$ (an increasing coefficient of variation) may fit data in organisms with such responses whereas a debilitation model, in which states must be ordered in terms of decreasing vitality, would not. They also suggests that more general models that describe state feedback and use a quadratic hazard function to describe mortality are needed (i.e., mortality is lowest when there is stress of low rather than zero intensity, to which a response maximally deviates from the energy expenditure for fixed r). Thus, a satisfactory model must allow for function to improve – as well as decline – with age in response to external stress.

A quadratic hazard function may be required to model mortality in most species because

> "hormesis can be caused by virtually any kind of toxic agent, and second, that there is apparently no taxonomic limitation to the organisms that exhibit it, as examples are known from every major taxon of plants and animals. Any control mechanism whose behavior might account for hormesis therefore must operate at the lowest level of organization and be common to all forms of life. Biochemical control mechanisms abound which could account for such observed behavior" (Stebbing, 1987; p. 547).

Thus, a quadratic (or convex) hazard function is needed to develop a theoretically satisfactory model of human mortality because almost any risk factor can cause a mortality reduction between zero and a low-level exposure.

6.4. *Phase-type distribution models*

To use of a quadratic hazard one requires measurements of the state of the organism. However, we may wish to use demographic models using only mortality data which are flexible enough to represent the mortality age patterns induced by hormesis. The LeBras model cannot describe mortality if hormesis exists since transitions in that model represent monotonically deteriorating health. More general models must include the possibility of health improving: health-transition functions that are non-monotonic functions of age must be represented. Such non-monotonic health transitions can be described by "phase-type" distribution models.

A phase-type distribution describes the timing of events for a finite-state, time-homogenous Markov chain (Neuts, 1975). Let Y_t be a time-homogenous Markov chain with state space $\{1,2,...n+1\}$. States $\{1,2,...n\}$ are transient; $n+1$ is absorbing, A is a matrix of transition intensities of order n; $p = (p_1, p_2, ... p_n)$ is the distribution of Y_0. T is the time at which Y is absorbed in $n+1$. T is said to have a phase-type distribution with representation (p,A) where n is its order. Phase-type distributions can approximate many failure distributions (Aalen, 1995).

Markov chain theory allows the survival function of a phase type distribution to be represented by

$$S(x) = \sum_{k=0}^{n} \sum_{r=0}^{m_k-1} c_{kr} \frac{x^r}{r!} e^{\rho_k^x}, \qquad (6.13)$$

where $\rho_1, \rho_2, ..., \rho_N$ are eigenvalues of A with multiplicities $m_1, m_2, ..., m_n$ and the c_{kr} are constants (Aalen, 1995). Since all eigenvalues have negative real parts, and the dominant eigenvalue is unique and real, the hazard for large x approaches a constant minus the dominant eigenvalue. This model may approximate mortality patterns associated with hormesis.

One can see from the three mortality models that the nature of mortality and aging cannot be fully understood by analyzing mortality data alone. Additional information is needed to make assumptions about the nature of aging processes testable prior to catastrophic failure. Such information is collected in longitudinal studies. It includes data about regularities of physiological and biological processes in individual organisms during the aging process as well as genetic data.

6.5. Summary

The leveling off of mortality at late ages observed in humans and other species may be the result of mortality selection operating on heterogeneous cohorts. Fixed-frailty models can describe this effect. These models, however, often cannot be used to rationalize the shape of the underlying hazard function or of the form of a frailty distribution. Multistate models of changing frailty can produce exactly the same age patterns of marginal hazards as in fixed frailty models without introducing age-dependence in the conditional transition rates. Such models can be used to describe the influence of both genetic factors and wear-out processes on longevity by combining fixed and acquired heterogeneity in one model. The use of such radically different models to describe the same biological processes illustrates the fundamental nonidentifiability problems with such models: One cannot decide whether fixed or changing frailty models give better descriptions of age-specific mortality using only data on the times to death. The explanation can also involve adaptation effects. To determine the roles of each of these mechanisms in aging, mortality and longevity, additional data on state changes prior to death are needed. For example, in addition to death time data, longitudinal or follow-up studies provide more information about changes in susceptibility to death with age. Such data, however, are based on observational plans that differ from those used to collect traditional demographic data. They also require more detailed mortality models and more sophisticated statistical methods. An increasing amount of data about the nature and regularities of aging as well as the development of chronic diseases and longevity is available from genetic epidemiological studies.

VII. Analysis of genetic effects on human longevity

7.1. Longevity as a phenotypic trait

In genetic epidemiology the characteristics of chronic diseases that manifest themselves at late ages are referred to as "complex phenotypic traits". This term refers to a phenotype that does not exhibit classic Mendelian recessive or dominant inheritance attributable to a single gene locus. Clearly, a characteristic of human physiology as general as longevity is a complex trait.

There are at least four standard, semi-parametric approaches (i.e., approaches where time- or age-dependent disease process parameters are not directly estimated) that are currently used to analyze complex traits in genetic epidemiology. They include linkage analysis, the allele-sharing method, association studies, and cross studies in model organisms. We review these approaches before examining methods to examine the effects of genetic factors on state "duration" measures.

7.2. Linkage analysis

Linkage analysis identifies the location of a gene causing traits observed in a specific pedigree based on models explaining the inheritance of genotypes. It compares a model based on a "no-linkage" assumption forming the null hypothesis, H_0, with a model which assumes a location for a trait-causing gene (by assumption; or the alternate hypothesis, H_A). The evidence for H_A against H_0 is measured by the likelihood ratio statistic $L = \frac{P(Data \mid H_A)}{P(Data \mid H_0)}$ or, equivalently, by the LOD score, $\log_{10}(L)$.

Sometimes parameters estimated from prior studies are employed to improve estimates by conditioning on ancillary data. Penetrance functions may be estimated from segregation analysis of marker allele frequencies in a prior study. Remaining unknown parameters can be directly estimated by maximum likelihood. Hypothesis H_A is accepted when the LOD score is "large" (exceeding 3.0 in most practical applications). Using this strategy, one gene identified as being related to early-onset breast cancer (BRCA1) was linked to chromosome 17q. This approach is crucial in human genetic mapping. However, applying it to complex polygenic traits that affect dynamic characteristics (e.g., aging or longevity) is difficult since models describing inheritance patterns become complex.

7.3. Allele-sharing analysis

Allele-sharing methods evaluate whether affected relatives inherit a chromosomal region identical-by-descent more often than expected under a null hypotheses of random Mendelian segregation. The methods are based on the calculation of the identical-by-descent affected-pedigree-member statistic, 0, where $X_{ij}(s)$ is the number of copies of a chromosomal region at position s inherited by relatives from a common ancestor within the family pedigree. The sum is taken over all distinct pairs of affected relatives. Assuming random segregation (H_0), $T(s)$ tends to be normally distributed with a mean and variance calculated from the kinship of affected relatives. A deviation from random segregation is indicated when the normalized T-statistics exceed a given threshold. The affected sib-pair analysis is a simple variant of this method. It was used to confirm the role of an HLA region in the development of type I diabetes mellitus. Excess allele sharing for this trait has been found at a locus on chromosome 11q as well (Lander and Schork, 1994).

7.4. Case-control methods

Association studies are similar to epidemiological case-control studies. They do not directly use data on familial relations. They compare affected (case) and unaffected (control) individuals in the population. An allele A in a given locus is assumed to be associated with a trait if it occurs significantly more often among affected than control individuals. The statistical analysis uses variants of 2x2 contingency table methods.

Such methods were used to implicate an HLA segment in the etiology of autoimmune diseases, apolipoprotein E4 in Alzheimer's disease, and the angiotensin-converting enzyme gene in heart disease. A positive association between an allele and a phenotypic trait may not mean the allele causes the disease. The allele can, for example, be in linkage disequilibrium with the actual cause. Population admixtures can also cause errors when making inferences about the relation of events to genetic factors.

7.5. Quantitative trait locus maps

Experimental crosses in animal and insect studies can be used to dissect quantitative traits into discrete genetic factors. Dense genetic linkage maps can be used to construct quantitative trait locus (QTL) maps. An important application of QTL mapping is the identification of modifier genes affecting single-gene traits. The approach may improve understanding of the genetic basis for variation in such traits as cancer susceptibility, drug sensitivity, resistance to infection, etc. (Lander and Schork, 1994).

7.6. Combining genetic and biostatistical methods in analyzing human longevity

Genetic epidemiologists deal with a complicated statistical problem using data that are often incomplete. In addition, the data contain observed covariates and may be influenced by unobserved randomly acting influential factors which, themselves, may have genetic and environmental origins. The methods described above do not capture this complexity – especially when gene-environment interactions vary over age as a.) the relative accumulative effect of environmental influences increases over genetic effects as exposure accumulates, and b.) as mortality selection removes individuals whose genetic risks are magnified by increased environmental exposure more rapidly.

To study the genetic and environmental nature of the human life span, for example, a model of unobserved susceptibility to disease and death and its association with observed covariates is often necessary to explain mortality in populations at late ages, where a significant degree of attrition has occurred. Such models require some parametric specification of the disease process operating in a population to identify the effect of unobserved susceptibility (Tolley and Manton, 1991). To model the effects of unobserved variables the concept of "liability" has been used in quantitative genetics (Falconer, 1992). A similar concept is used in the demographic (Vaupel et al., 1979) and biostatistical (Oakes, 1989) literature and is called "frailty". We will examine the parametric specifications used to implement both types of concepts – and then discuss differences.

In analyzing survival data for twins, it is necessary to estimate the correlation of phenotypic traits. One way to do this is to infer a genetic effect in twin studies by comparing concordance rates (McGue, 1992). Concordance is defined to exist if both members of a twin pair are affected. Discordance exists if only one member of a twin pair is affected. If environmental influences shared by members of monozygotic (MZ) twin pairs are similar to those shared by dyzygotic (DZ) twins then a higher concordance rate for MZ than DZ pairs provides evidence of a genetic influence. However, when a genetic trait is unobserved, estimating the phenotypic effect of the trait requires us to use mathematical assumptions to parameterize an estimable model.

For example, the "liability" model has been used to analyze dichotomous traits in twins. If liability is assumed to be the result of large numbers of small genetic and environmental influences, the overall effect (liability) is asymptotically normally distributed because of the law of large numbers. For computational convenience (and to improve the identifiability of parameters) the liability variable can be assumed to have zero mean and unit variance. For twins, liability is assumed to have a bivariate normal distribution with an unknown correlation. The expected proportion of concordant positive twin pairs is found by integrating the bivariate normal distribution over the portion of the density function above the threshold on both axes (Kendall and Stuart, 1969). This produces a tetrachoric correlation for liability variables which is estimated from the proportions of concordant and discordant MZ and DZ twin pairs.

The model can be extended for multivariate analyses by using a canonical correlation model where each root of a hermite tsbeyscheff polynomial generated in the canonical solution refers to a bivariate normal distribution with the set of bivariate normal correlations describing the relation between discrete variables with more than two levels of response.

7.6.1. Logistic regression models for biologically related individuals

Liability threshold models can be made compatible with continuous trait models. If the risk of a disease, given liability values Z, is described by the conditional probability $P(Y=1|Z)=F(Z-T)$, where $F(\cdot)$ is a cumulative distribution function, then the model is equivalent to a threshold model with liability $Z_0 = Z + Z_1$ and threshold T, where random variable Z_1 has distribution F. For Z_0 to be normally distributed F must be normally distributed. This is equivalent to decision threshold models used in econometric studies. In those models often the threshold variable is assumed to be logistically rather than normally distributed.

Thus, to analyze phenotypic traits, a logistic regression model of liability with covariates can be used. The conditional probability of being affected by a trait is,

$$P(Y=1|Z) = \frac{e^z}{1+e^z}, \tag{7.1}$$

with

$$Z = a + b_G + B_G U, \tag{7.2}$$

where b_G and B_G are functions of the unmeasured genotype G. U represents (an) observed covariate(s). A likelihood can be produced by averaging the product over all combinations of unobserved genotypes for pairs of biologically related individuals (e.g., twins; sibs). N is the number of pairs of related individuals.

This type of logistic regression model can be generalized by adding variables for unmeasured, residual (non-Mendelian) genotypes, G_1, and unmeasured residual environmental effects, E_1. Using this generalization, Martin et al. (1987) represented liability as

$$Z = a + B_1 G + B_2 E + B_3 GE + B_4 G_1 + B_5 E_1 + B_6 GG_1$$
$$+ B_7 EE_1 + B_8 GE_1 + B_9 EG_1 + B_{10} E_1 G_1. \quad (7.3)$$

To estimate (7.3) constraints are needed. G_1 can be assumed to be bivariate normally distributed with a correlation of 1.0 for MZ and 0.5 for DZ twins. E_1 is assumed bivariate normally distributed with zero correlation for both MZ and DZ twins. This model was used to analyze breast cancer in female twins (Martin et al., 1987).

7.6.2. Regression for related individuals

Discrete variables in concordance studies are often derived from continuously measured phenotypic traits. Changing a continuous variable into a categorical variable may lose information on individual differences and create heteroschedastic error variances (persons near the threshold have a larger likelihood of an erroneous classification than people far from the threshold). Thus, for continuously measured traits, regression is often preferable (LaBuda et al., 1986). Regression provides a statistical test of genetic etiology which is often more flexible and powerful than concordance analysis. The contribution of heritable factors to observed differences in values of phenotypic traits can also be estimated.

The use of regression in twin studies depends on the statistical properties of the correlation (or covariances) of normally distributed variables (cf. e.g., Anderson, 1958). For example, let Z_1 and Z_2 be normally distributed random variables with a common mean m and variance σ^2. If Z_2 is observed, the conditional mean of the unobserved variable $\hat{Z}_1 = E(Z_1 | Z_2)$ is,

$$\hat{Z}_1 = m + \frac{Cov(Z_1 | Z_2)}{\sigma^2}(Z_2 - m), \quad (7.4)$$

Assuming Z_i, $i = 1,2$ can be decomposed into additive genetic, A, common environmental, C, and unique environmental, E, components, then a^2, c^2, and e^2 are proportions of the total variance σ^2. For MZ twins, $CORR_{MZ}(Z_i, Z_2) = a^2 + c^2$. For DZ twins $CORR_{DZ}(Z_i, Z_2) = .5a^2 + c^2$. If $Z_2 = P$ (proband) and $Z_i = C$ (cotwin) one can use these results to predict the co-twin's covariate value. Let R be the coefficient of familial relation – which is R =1 for MZ twins and R = .5 for DZ twins. C can be written

$$C = m + (a^2 R + c^2)(P - m), \quad (7.5)$$

or

$$C = \alpha_0 + \alpha_1 P + \alpha_2 R + \alpha_3 PR. \quad (7.6)$$

where $\alpha_0 = m - mc_2$; $\alpha_1 = c^2$; $\alpha_2 = -ma^2$; and $\alpha_3 = a^2$. Assuming an additive model describes the genetic effects, and assuming equal shared environmental influences on MZ and DZ twin pairs, α_3 is a direct estimate of population "narrow sense" heritability, a^2. Coefficient α_1 is an estimate of c^2 (LaBuda et al., 1986; DeFries and Fulker, 1988).

7.7. Genetic analysis of duration data

Regression is a convenient tool for many analyses when data are complete. Unfortunately, survival data (i.e., times to system failure or death) are often systematically censored. To deal with censored data, specialized survival models are preferable to traditional regression models. Survival models should also be adjusted for unobserved heterogeneity produced by genetic and environmental factors. To study genetic effects the survival models should also be able to analyze duration data from related individuals (e.g., twins or other relatives where the times to specific events are correlated). These features can be realized in multivariate survival models with random effects, i.e., in multivariate frailty models. We examine several survival models below.

7.7.1. Shared-frailty models

Models have been proposed to analyze data where the time to events may be dependent, shared relative risk, or shared frailty (Clayton, 1978; Clayton and Cuzick, 1985; Oakes, 1986; Self and Prentice, 1986). If U_i, $i = 1, 2$ are observed covariate values for twins, and Z the latent frailty variable which is shared, then conditional on Z and U_i, the risk of an event at age x is,

$$\mu(x, Z, U_i) = Z \lambda_0(x) e^{\beta U_i}. \tag{7.7}$$

If frailty Z is assumed to be gamma-distributed with, for convenience, mean 1 and variance σ^2, then the bivariate survival function, conditioned on U_i, is,

$$S(x_1, x_2 | U_1, U_2) = (S(x_1 | U_1)^{-\sigma^2} + S(x_2 | U_2)^{-\sigma^2} - 1)^{-\frac{1}{\sigma^2}}, \tag{7.8}$$

with $S(x | U_i) = (1 + \sigma^2 e^{bU_i} H(x))^{-\frac{1}{\sigma^2}}$. The univariate form of the shared-frailty model described by (7.7), with a finite mean for the frailty distribution, is identifiable (Elbers and Ridder, 1982). If frailty is gamma-distributed the parameters σ^2, β, and the hazard $\lambda_0(x)$ can be found from the univariate survival distribution.

This property poses a conceptual problem associated with the application of shared-frailty models to bivariate duration data: When the univariate model is "true", the bivariate shared-frailty model cannot be "true" for related individuals who share less than 100% of the relative risk. The shared-frailty model cannot be correct even for hypothetical survival data on individuals with different familial relations (e.g., MZ and DZ twins). This means that large sample estimates of the coefficients of covariate functions, β, calculated from a.) univariate subsets of bivariate data; b.) bivariate data on MZ twins; and c.) bivariate data on DZ twins will be different. This complicates evaluating the effects of covariates on survival in biologically related persons. In genetic epidemiological studies, differences in σ^2 calculated, say, for MZ and DZ twins can reflect differences in the amount of genetic material shared between individuals in a pair. However, the interpretation of these values in genetic analyses of dependent survival durations is unclear. Similar problems in the genetic interpretation of association parameters arise for the positive-stable-frailty distribution (Hougaard, 1986, 1987). The association parameter estimates calculated in these models cannot be used to determine, say, heritability estimates. For this purpose, estimates of the correlations of phenotypic traits are used.

7.7.2. Correlated-frailty models

A multivariate survival model should link biostatistical and quantitative genetic methods and be flexible enough to describe the joint distribution of durations for individuals with different biological relations. The shared-frailty model has conceptual limitations. A more easily interpreted model is based on correlated frailties (Yashin et al., 1995; Yashin and Iachine, 1994). In these models, the correlation of the frailties of biologically related individuals are parameters of the model.

Correlated-frailty models use the same concept of frailty as in the univariate case. Let T_i and Z_i be the life-span and heterogeneity variables for two related individuals ($i = 1, 2$) with dependent individual hazards $\mu(Z_i, x)$. Assume that, conditional on Z_1, Z_2, life-spans T_1, T_2 are independent and the force of mortality for each related individual corresponds to the proportional hazards model $\mu(Z_i, x) = Z_i \mu_0(x)$. Assume Z_i are both gamma-distributed, $\Gamma(k_1 + k_2, \lambda)$, with variances σ_1^2 and σ_2^2 and correlation ρ_z. The marginal survival function of the bivariate gamma distribution of frailty (Yashin and Iachine, 1994) is,

$$S(x_1, x_2) = S_1(x_1)^{1 - \frac{\sigma_2}{\sigma_1}\rho_z} \tag{7.9}$$

$$(S_1(x_1)^{-\sigma_1^2} + S_2(x_2)^{-\sigma_2^2} - 1)^{-\frac{\rho_z}{\sigma_1 \sigma_2}},$$

where $S_i(x_i)$ are univariate survival functions, and

$$\rho_z \in \left[0, \min\left(\frac{\sigma_1}{\sigma_2}, \frac{\sigma_2}{\sigma_1}\right)\right]. \tag{7.10}$$

For same-sex MZ and DZ twin survival data one assumes $\sigma_1^2 = \sigma_2^2 = s^2$ and $S_1(x) = S_2(x)$ (Yashin et al., 1995). The shared-frailty model is thus a special, and restricted, case ($\rho_z = 1.0$) of the correlated-frailty model.

Including correlations as parameters in the model allows questions about genetic and environmental effects on individual frailty to be evaluated. To do this a genetic decomposition of frailty is incorporated in the correlated-frailty model. In six different correlated-frailty models the estimated proportions of the variance of the frailty distribution associated with genetic and environmental components (Yashin and Iachine, 1995a,b) showed that the environment determined 50% of the variability in individual frailty associated with the life spans of Danish male and female twins born from 1870 to 1900.

7.7.3. A correlated-frailty model with covariates

With data on covariates, the parameters of a bivariate frailty distribution and the effects of covariates on survival can be estimated simultaneously. The presence of covariates changes properties of both shared- and correlated-frailty models – though the advantages of the correlated-frailty models remain. If the individual hazard is described by (7.7) then the bivariate survival function $S(x_1, x_2 | U_1, U_2)$ is

$$S(x_1, x_2 | U_1, U_2) = S_1(x_1 | U_1)^{1-\frac{\sigma_2}{\sigma_1}\rho_z} S_2(x_2 | U_2)^{1-\frac{\sigma_2}{\sigma_1}\rho_z}$$
$$(S_1(x_1 | U_1)^{-\sigma_1^2} + S_2(x_2 | U_2)^{-\sigma_2^2} - 1)^{-\frac{\rho_z}{\sigma_1 \sigma_2}} \tag{7.11}$$

Here $S_i(x | U_i) = (1 + \sigma_i^2 e^{\beta U_i} \tilde{H}(x))^{-\frac{1}{2\sigma_i^2}}$ and $\tilde{H}(x) = \int_0^x \mu_0(u) du$. To estimate the parameters of this correlated-frailty model different computational strategies may be used. One is to modify the EM algorithm for the correlated-frailty model (Iachine, 1995).

7.7.4. EM-algorithms to estimate parameters of correlated-frailty models from twin data

To estimate parameters in the shared-frailty model, Clayton and Cuzick (1985) suggested modifying the EM-algorithm by transforming observations into expected order statistics computed for a generalized rank vector using a parametric model. Gill's (1985) version of the EM-algorithm extended Cox's (1972) partial likelihood techniques to hazards with random effects. Klein (1992) considered how this technique could be applied to data from the Framingham Heart Study.

To evaluate covariate effects in the shared-frailty case, the M-step is similar to Cox's estimation scheme. In the E-step, conditional expectations of the frailty variable Z and its logarithm (log Z) given the data are calculated. A property of the gamma distribution can be exploited in the algorithm, i.e., frailty among survivors is also gamma-distributed. Thus, the function maximized in the M-step depends on two sets of parameters. One is the conditional distribution of frailty among survivors. The second is the log likelihood function of the complete data (constructed as if frailty were observed). The values of these parameters are chosen at the M-step, i.e., when maximizing the conditional log likelihood of the complete data. These values are used as new parameter estimates.

The procedure for the shared-frailty model cannot be applied to the correlated-frailty model because the conditional distribution may have different properties. For example, gamma-frailty distributions are not gamma-distributed after conditioning on covariates. However, a modified EM-algorithm can be used for the correlated-frailty model (Iachine, 1995). Performing the E-step when $0<\rho_z<1.0$ is complicated since the frailties Z_1, Z_2 of related individuals who survived to ages x_1, x_2, respectively, are not gamma-distributed. At each iteration, however, the frailty distribution can be represented as a mixture of gamma-distributions for the additive frailty components Y_0, Y_1, Y_2. The number of terms in the mixture depends on censoring information for two related individuals (Iachine, 1995). The procedure has the advantage that estimation of the covariate function coefficients and the underlying hazard performed in the M-step can be separated from the estimation of parameters of the frailty distribution.

7.8. Combining survival and genetic-trait analysis in twin data: estimating lower bounds to the limit of human life expectancy from bivariate survival data

Many attempts have been made to estimate the biological limits to life expectancy in human populations (Manton et al., 1991; Manton and Stallard, 1996a). Siegel (1980) constructed synthetic mortality patterns from the lowest age and cause-specific mortality rates observed in developed countries. The limits to life expectancy at birth calculated by that method were 79.4 years for females and 73.8 years for males. Bourgeois-Pichat (1978) partitioned underlying causes of death into endogenous and exogenous categories. Then exogenous causes of mortality were eliminated to estimate lower limits of age-specific mortality. The life expectancy calculated with this procedure was 80.3 years for females; 73.8 years for males. Other approaches are discussed by Myers and Manton (1984a,b), Gavrilov and Gavrilov (1991), and Olshansky et al. (1990). Olshansky et al. (1990) suggested the upper limit to human life expectancy was 85 years. This was estimated using cause-elimination life tables (Chiang, 1968). It was also suggested that, to reach a life expectancy of 85 to 90 years, 70% of the force of mortality had to be eliminated at all ages – equivalent to eliminating all cancer and circulatory disease deaths. These estimates required the assumption that hazards were proportional – an assumption unlikely to hold at late ages if mortality is genetically determined.

A difficulty with many analyses of life expectancy for human populations is that they use period, not cohort, data. In addition, independence of exogenous and endogenous causes of death is often assumed and models often do not a.) reflect the effects of known risk factors or b.) provide estimates for genetically determined mortality components. To estimate realistic life expectancy limits a more fully parameterized model is needed which describes each cause of death as being due to an underlying process whose parameters could be modified to change the age distribution of morbid events underlying mortality. For example, a life expectancy of 90 years can be reached by eliminating a quadratically decreasing proportion of the force of mortality after age 72 (Manton and Stallard, 1996a). This nonproportional reduction of mortality over age (the proportion of the force of mortality eliminated drops from 70% at age 72 to 35% at late ages) produces results closer to the age pattern of mortality decline observed in human populations than do proportional-hazard models.

A model must also be consistent with a wide range of data. The longest lived person now documented survived to age 122.4 (a French female), which is thus the empirical lower bound to the human life span. The highest life expectancy for a large, heterogeneous national population is in Japan, where life expectancy observed at birth is 83.3 years for females and 76.5 years for males (WHO, 1994). The life expectancies of national subpopulations can be significantly higher. U.S. Asian and Pacific Islanders, for example, have a life expectancy estimated to be 86.0 years for females and 80.3 years for males (Day, 1993). Subpopulations defined by religious or other variables (e.g., occupation; S.E.S.) affecting health habits and nutrition may have even higher life expectancies (e.g., over 90 years; Manton et al., 1991).

Many analytic complexities of such highly parameterized models are avoided if longitudinal data with multiple observed covariates are available because such data contain considerably more information from which to estimate parameters. Manton et al. (1994b) estimated a two-component multivariate stochastic process with a non-Gaston diffusion component from data from the 1982, 1984, and 1989 National Long

Term Care Surveys and using the 34-year follow-up of the Framingham Heart study. The lower limit to mortality in that study was estimated, after generating maximum likelihood estimates of the parameters of the component processes, by fixing the vector of observed covariates at an analytically determined physiological "optimal" point in the space of observed risk factors. The life expectancy corresponding to the hypothetical age-specific mortality rates at that point in the risk-factor space was estimated to be 99.2 years (Manton et al., 1994b).

An advantage of using cohort data on the 10 risk factors that were measured biennially over 34 years in the Framingham Heart study to estimate the parameters of a multidimensional stochastic process model with randomly changing covariates is that longevity predictions can be made by fixing risk-factor profiles at specific levels, e.g. as derived from the National Health and Nutrition Examination Surveys (done four times between 1960 and 1994). In that analysis genetic effects were not analyzed because only survival and risk-factor data was available from the Framingham Heart Study.

To model the effects of genetics interacting with the stochastic accumulation of environmental exposures over age, data on related individuals needs to be combined with multivariate stochastic process models of survival with temporally evolving covariates. For example, in a bivariate survival model, genetically determined frailty estimates of lower limits of mortality (or upper limits of human longevity) can be obtained using estimates of the heritability of individual frailty (Yashin and Iachine, 1995a,b). When covariate changes are measured, one can evaluate the potential for mortality reduction in greater detail. With such data, the lower life expectancy limit can be estimated not only by hypothetically eliminating the environmental component of frailty but also by fixing observed covariates at an "optimal" point in a multidimensional physiological-state space.

This strategy was used to analyze survival data for Danish twins born from 1870 to 1910. A correlated frailty model with observed covariates was used to estimate parameters. Birth year of the cohort was used as a covariate. This was combined with a genetic model of frailty. In the case of a model $Z=A+E$, where A is an additive genetic and E is the independent environmental component of Z, heritability of longevity was estimated to be 50%. (This model provided the best fit to bivariate data on Danish MZ and DZ twins (Yashin and Iachine, 1995a,b).) Relative risk estimates for specific female cohorts are shown in Figure 7.1 together with the fitted exponential functions.

In Figure 7.1 the optimal point in the covariate space corresponds to the last cohort. Estimates of life expectancy limits at this point (i.e., for the cohort of Danish twins born in 1910) are 80 years for males and 87 years for females. If the temporal trends in Danish female mortality rates are assumed to continue, one can make estimates

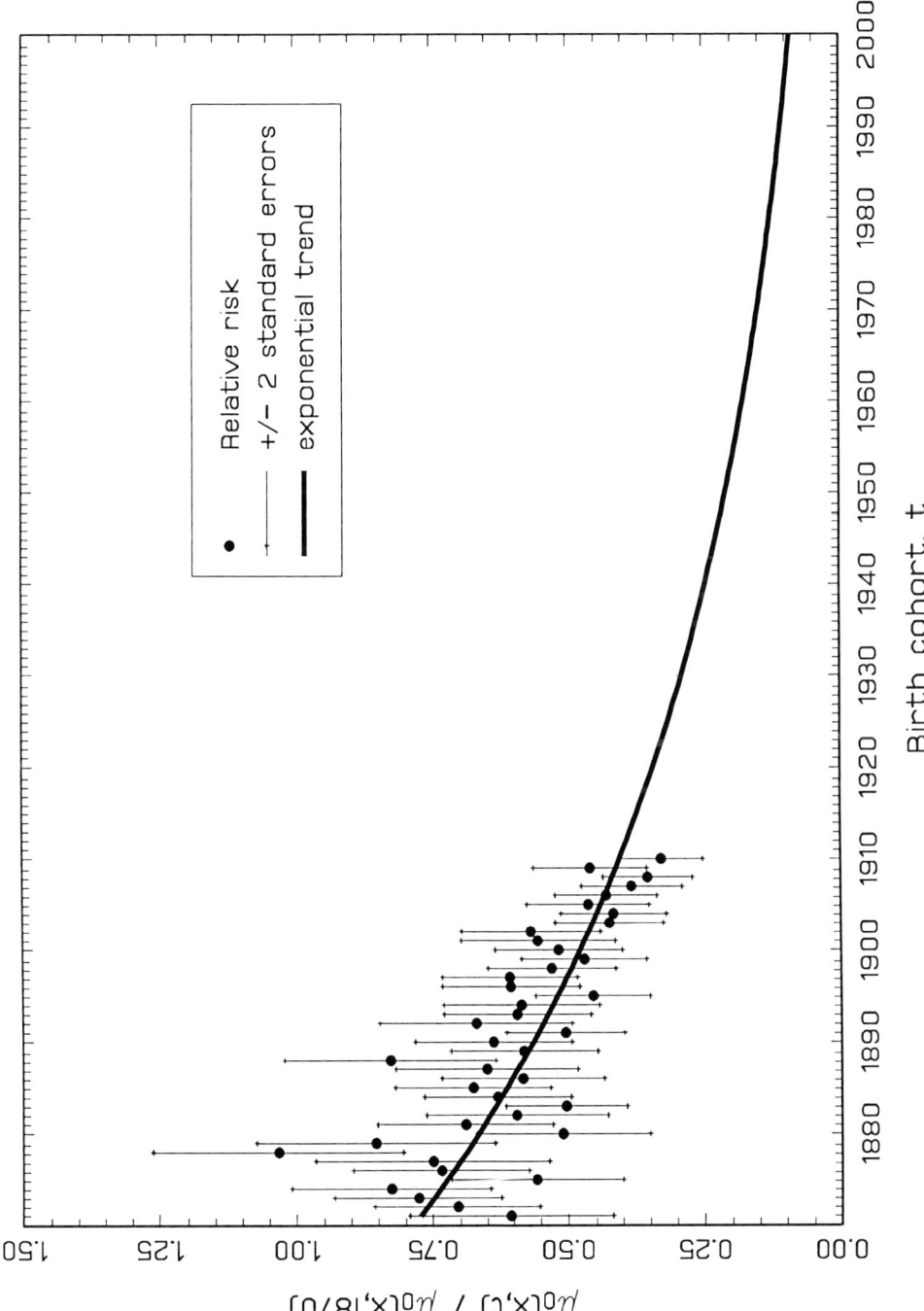

Figure 7.1. Individual relative risk for Danish female twins, birth cohorts of 1870-1910.

for later dates. For females born in 1940, 1970, and 2000 lower bounds to life expectancy limits were projected to be 90, 94, and 97 years, respectively.

Trends in relative risks for males were not determined as precisely as for females. Maximum likelihood estimates of the exponential coefficients are .017 (females) and .0027 (males), with standard errors of .002 ($t = 8.5$) and .023 ($t = 0.12$). Because of the statistical uncertainty of the male parameter, we did not predict future longevity for males.

Additional opportunities to study mechanisms of aging and mortality open up when a multivariate stochastic process model of mortality and aging is used in the analysis of longitudinal data on aging.

7.9. Summary

Attempts to understand the effects of genes and the environment on life span, age at onset of disease, disability, or other durations associated with individual life and health histories require new concepts, data, analytic and statistical methods. The fact that many chronic diseases are concentrated in families indicates the presence of either genetic or common environmental influences on disease etiology. To understand these relations, the regularities of gene transmission in families should be taken into account. Data on genetic markers and environmental covariates have to be used to model dependent failure time data. The use of this data requires multidisciplinary approaches: Genetic-epidemiological concepts and methods have to be merged with the ideas and approaches exploited in demography and biostatistics. New insights and ideas concerning the origin of chronic diseases and their relation to fundamental physiological processes related to age require new efforts in the modeling and statistical analysis of data on biologically related individuals.

Thus, the standard statistical paradigm assuming the independence of individuals in a population has to be shifted towards modeling dependence among individuals in aging studies. This new paradigm opens up new opportunities for studying the role of genes and the environment in aging.

VIII. Human mortality and physiological change at late ages: a multivariate dynamic process

8.1.   Mathematical models, biological knowledge, and data

Using only survival data restricts analyses to simple mortality models. More data are needed to estimate theoretically satisfactory models of human aging and mortality. New longitudinal epidemiological studies and national longitudinal surveys contain information necessary for a better understanding of the regularities of mortality dynamics. Some requirements regarding such information have been discussed by Strehler and Mildvan (1960). By measuring age-related changes in health and physiological covariates together with life span these studies open up new opportunities for analyzing the dynamics of aging processes and mortality.

Unfortunately, most survival analyses still ignore the dynamics of unobserved, or partly observed, stochastic covariates – and the data available on them from empirical studies or theory. Below we review the statistical and mathematical principles necessary to develop a multidimensional stochastic process model for analyzing human mortality and aging. This model can be estimated from longitudinal population studies and survey data by using ancillary theoretical and substantive information about the structure of those processes. We present the likelihood for – and illustrate – a multivariate stochastic process model referred to as the MWY approach (Woodbury and Manton, 1977; Yashin, 1980, 1985). This model has properties necessary for estimating the risk of "health" failures (i.e., death or the emergence of disease or disability) conditional on the past trajectory of the system's state from longitudinal data – possibly augmented with ancillary information (e.g., estimates of system parameters) from prior studies of a system's structure (cf. e.g., Singpurwalla, 1995). We show that this model can be used to extract information on the age rate of changes in physiological-state parameters and that it can be constructed to isolate the effects on aging and mortality of genetic factors and gene-environment interactions.

When trajectories are unobserved, or incompletely observed, the conditional risk of failure must be "averaged" (or, equivalently, mathematically integrated) over influential, unobserved variables in this model. The difficulty and burden of computation in generating averages for these latent variables depends on whether the averaging (the numerical evaluation of specific integral forms) can be expressed in closed analytic form. Several methods that produce closed analytic averaging solutions, such as the Cameron-Martin (1944) method and its generalizations (e.g., Myers, 1981), can be used to evaluate marginal survival distributions. The general conditional hazard model in MWY and models for more complicated observational plans may require sophisticated mathematical methods and theory (e.g., martingale techniques; cf. Lipster and Shiryayev, 1977). Thus, the MWY model significantly extends the survival analyses most often done in demography, epidemiology, and biostatistics at present, which assume that unobserved heterogeneity is fixed (the concept of frailty) to approximate the influence of latent multidimensional stochastic processes (cf. e.g., Vaupel et al., 1979). In MWY, influential, incompletely or fully observed state variable process components may also be used – making the approach useful for analyzing longitudinal studies of covariate changes and mortality and for describing age-related changes in state variables prior to death.

Below we examine the properties of likelihood functions which use ancillary information on the conditional (random) hazard and on the probabilistic properties of unobserved or partly observed covariates. The techniques that generalize Kalman filters to deal with failure processes are reviewed. These lead to the formulation of the MWY model appropriate for analyzing longitudinal data (Woodbury and Manton, 1977; Woodbury et al., 1983; Yashin, 1980, 1985).

8.2. Observational plans determine the predictive power of the MWY model

Two observational plans illustrate most methodological issues: a.) analyses of the age dependence of the times to death (or age-related changes in major health traits; or in the level of functioning) with only ancillary, or indirect, information on latent, influential covariate processes and b.) longitudinal studies of aging and mortality where covariates are observed and measured at multiple fixed times and mortality is tracked continuously. In both cases one can use the same stochastic process model of human mortality and aging. The marginal hazards used in the likelihood functions of the MWY model for statistical estimation of parameters are, however, different for the observational plans. This is because the averaging procedures used to derive the marginal hazards are determined by the information generated by each observational plan.

8.2.1. Analysis of failure-times where age-related mortality is driven by latent processes

Let T be a failure time (e.g. time to death, disease onset, or disability) and $Y=(Y_t)_{t \geq 0}$ an unobserved covariate process defining the randomly changing physiological state of a complex biological organism. Define the survival function, conditional on the unobserved state process $Y_0^t = \{Y_u, 0 \le u \le t\}$, as,

$$P(T > t | Y_0^t) = e^{-\int_0^t \mu(Y_u, u) du}, \qquad (8.1)$$

where $\mu(Y_u, u)$ is a non-negative hazard function – and where $E\mu(Y_u, u) < \infty$ for any $u > 0$. The probability distribution of the physiological state of individuals over time, Y_t, and the structure of the hazard function $\mu(Y_u, u)$ are assumed to be known – but not the numerical values of the two function's parameters. While trajectories of Y_t are unobserved, T is measured for each organism. The problem is to estimate the parameters of the distribution of Y_t and of the conditional hazard function $\mu(Y_u, u)$ when only failure times (e.g. age at death) for N organisms are observed. The marginal survival function averaged over Y_t is,

$$P(T > t) = e^{-\int_0^t \bar{\mu}(u) du}. \qquad (8.2)$$

The marginal hazard function $\bar{\mu}(u)$ (in a form consistent with the distribution of Y_t and the structure of $\mu(Y_u, u)$) is needed to form an estimable likelihood. Either Cameron-Martin (1944) or a martingale version of MWY can be used to define $\bar{\mu}(u)$ and to estimate parameters of $\mu(Y_u, u)$ and of Y_t's distribution from failure times. In other words, trajectories of Y_t need not be observed.

In longitudinal data where covariates are observed, the Cameron-Martin approach is complicated by boundary conditions on the differential equations describing state changes. In the martingale version of MWY, the Kalman filter (Lipster and Shiryayev, 1977) is generalized by adding terms reflecting systematic attrition. This transforms the problem of finding a form for $\bar{\mu}(u)$ to one of solving ordinary differential equations from initial state conditions.

8.2.2. *Longitudinal data where mortality is driven by observed covariates*

Let X_{tj}, $j>0$ describe observations of the state of the system at $t_1, t_2, \ldots$, which are related to an unobserved process Y_t by

$$X_{t_j} = A(t_j) + A_1(t_j) Y_{t_j} + B(t_j) \varepsilon_j \qquad (8.3)$$

where coefficients A, A_1, B are fixed functions of time and $\{\varepsilon_j\}_{j \ge 0}$ are J independent normally distributed random variables. The survival function conditional on state changes observed over time, $X_0^t = \{X_{t_j}, 0 \le t_j \le t\}$ is

$$P(T > t \mid X_0^t) = e^{-\int_0^t \bar{\mu}(X_0^u, u) du} \tag{8.4}$$

The marginal hazard $\bar{\mu}(X_0^u, u)$ (in a form consistent with the distribution of Y_u given X_0^u and the structure of $\mu(Y_u, u)$) is needed to estimate the likelihood. We show how the MWY model is used to estimate $\bar{\mu}(X_0^u, u)$, the parameters of the conditional hazard $\mu(Y_u, u)$, and the probability distribution of Y from data on X_{t_j} and T for N systems.

The unobserved process Y_t may describe either stochastic age-trajectories of external environmental factors or endogenous physiological state measures. Some components of the covariate process may be fixed for the life of the individual (e.g., genotype). Not all expressions of genotype are fixed. For example, the expression of some genes may emerge over age or may require an environmental stimulus before they are expressed (e.g., certain genes determining expression of Cytochrome p450 enzymes are activated by developmentally related or gender-related hormones; Gonzalez and Nebert, 1990). Before examining the relation of $\bar{\mu}(u)$ and $\mu(Y_u, u)$ or of $\bar{\mu}(X_0^u, u)$ and $\mu(Y_u, u)$, we briefly review properties of conditional survival functions.

8.2.3. Randomly changing hazards and conditional survival functions

For T, if $P(T>t)$ is absolutely continuous, the survival function has the form,

$$P(T > t) = \exp\left(-\int_0^t \mu(u) du\right) \tag{8.5}$$

where $\mu(u)$, $u \geq 0$ is the hazard – which is related to (8.5) by

$$\mu(t) = -P(T > t)^{-2} \frac{dP(T > t)}{dt}. \tag{8.6}$$

Different forms of (8.6) may be used in martingale representations of processes (cf. e.g., Andersen et al., 1993; Arjas, 1989). If Y is a latent random variable (i.e., not a process), the conditional survival function is,

$$S(t \mid Y) = P(T > t \mid Y) = \exp(-\int_0^t \mu(Y, u) du) \tag{8.7}$$

where $\mu(Y, u)$ is a *random hazard*. In proportional hazard, frailty models (e.g., Manton et al., 1986) $\mu(Y, u)$ is a linear function of Y; e.g., $\mu(Y, u) = \mu_0(u) Y$. When Y is a stochastic process, as in the MWY model, and $\mu(Y, u) = \mu(Y_u, u)$, one can use the conditional survival function $S(t \mid Y_0^t) = P(T>t|Y_u, 0 \leq u \leq t)$, i.e., the probability of living to t when Y_u is observed from 0 to t. This survival function is,

$$S(t \mid Y_0^t) = P(T > t \mid Y_u, 0 \leq u \leq t) = \exp(-\int_0^t \mu(Y_u, u) du). \tag{8.8}$$

Sufficient conditions for (8.8) to be exponential are discussed by Yashin and Arjas (1988). One such condition is that $S(t \mid Y_0^t)$ is almost surely absolutely continuous over time. Since Y_0^t is unobserved, ancillary information is required to average $S(t \mid Y_0^t)$ over Y_0^t to define a marginal survival distribution and then a marginal probability density function to construct an estimable likelihood function.

8.3. Quadratic hazard models of aging and mortality

With these concepts and definitions we can now formulate models of human aging and mortality that can be estimated from longitudinal data. In some studies covariates are measured from the start. Covariates may also be observed at multiple fixed times during the study. The National Long Term Care Surveys (NLTCS) involved examining a large national sample of persons aged 65+ up to four times (in 1982, 1984, 1989, and 1994) over 12 years. New study subjects who enter the sample by passing age 65 between surveys, say, between 1989 and 1994, are either reassessed in 1994, drop out of the study before 1994, or die before 1994. All three situations occur in the NLTCS. When covariates are not measured during a study (e.g., between 1989 and 1994 in the NLTCS), one may assess the properties of unobserved state variables, Y_t, and evaluate the observed population mortality rates, $\bar{\mu}(u)$, using, under certain assumptions, the Cameron-Martin (1944) approach. Other longitudinal observational plans (e.g. where measurements are made, at fixed times, of multiple stochastic covariates) require the MWY approach.

Woodbury and Manton (1977) suggest modeling the temporal evolution of covariates and changes in their distribution function due to state-dependent mortality by two linked stochastic processes. The evolution of physiological-state variables are described by a k-dimensional diffusion process $Y = (Y_t)_{t \geq 0}$ that satisfies a stochastic Ito differential equation

$$dY_t = a(t)Y_t dt + b(t) dW_t, \tag{8.9}$$

with initial conditions Y_0, Wiener process $W = (W_t)_{t \geq 0}$, and matrices $a(t)$ and $b(t)$ (describing deterministic and stochastic influences over time) with elements that are continuous functions of time. If $a(t) \equiv b(t) \equiv 0$, (8.9) reduces to the special case of a random variable Y_0. More generally, the state-dependent mortality process is assumed to be described by a time-dependent, quadratic function (Woodbury and Manton, 1977)

$$\mu(Y_u, u) = \mu_0(u) + Y_u^* Q(u) Y_u \qquad (8.10)$$

with conditional survival function, where $Q(u)$ is a positive definite matrix of hazard coefficients

$$P(T > t \mid Y_0^t) = \exp(-\int_0^t \mu_0(u)du - \int_0^t Y_u^* Q(u) Y_u du). \qquad (8.11)$$

In (8.11) there is a state variable position, $Y_u \equiv 0$, which is associated with the lowest mortality rate. The point in the state space at time (t) with the lowest mortality rate may not (is likely not to) be equal to a numerical value of zero for any observed covariate. The difference between the "optimal" value and the origin of the state-variable space can be adjusted for in the hazard by adding "location" parameters to Q_t. The location parameters may also vary as a function of genotype. To deal with the problem of estimating location parameters for Y_u one would, in empirical analyses, add linear terms to Q, i.e., use an expanded matrix Q^* of hazard coefficients.

We show below how (8.11) can be applied to a mortality analysis when measured covariates X_t are generated by an unobserved process Y_t. The use of a hazard like (8.11) (augmented with location parameters) can be justified in several ways. Empirically, the relation of risk to risk factors (or their transforms) is often J- or U-shaped – especially in elderly populations (cf. e.g., Witteman et al., 1994). These observations are consistent with theoretical arguments that a complex system such as a human organism has homeostatic mechanisms keeping it from straying to either extreme positive or negative state-variable values. Fundamentally, since any physiological process under homeostatic control operates within (in a topological sense) "interior" state-space regions, U-shaped hazard functions will describe the age/time evolution of populations of complex systems with well developed state-variable feedback control mechanisms. This also implies that an optimal point exists which minimizes risk in the interior of the state space – a point identified by the location parameters in Q^* (Woodbury et al., 1983).

A second argument, based on the behavior of state-variable dynamics for a U- (or J-shaped) hazard with a minimum point in the interior of the state space, is the biological principle of hormesis (Stebbing, 1987) referred to in earlier chapters. Hormesis suggests that low levels of exposure to environmental stresses stimulate the organism and increase its "fitness", i.e., the physiological ability to survive environmental shocks or stresses. Hormesis emerged as organisms evolved and increased in structural complexity.

As biological complexity increased, specific collections of cells (organs) developed specialized functions, with that specialization increasing the efficiency of individual organs in performing their function. As the functional specialization of an organ increases, however, each organ (except for select specialized organs such as those involving sensory function) tends to be further removed from contact with the environment – requiring complex hormonal control systems to coordinate organ functioning in changing environmental conditions. The greater functional separation of organs from the environment and the resulting increasing complexity of hormonal control implied lag times in responding to environmental stress, and it required that the energy marshalled to adjust to these stresses be produced in discrete quanta – not as a continuously varying response.

Stress may imprint the organism with response "templates" to reduce the temporal lag in responding to a future recurrence of the stressor. For example, the response to viral infections in childhood may produce a *B*-cell mediated antibody response from the immune system that may be lifelong – if the organism survives the initial stress. We now consciously take advantage of this mechanism by using the minimal stress necessary to produce the maximal antibody response in vaccination programs. Certain genetically controlled enzymes in the cytochrome p450 system may not be expressed (i.e., the gene is quiescent) until the chemical it metabolizes is encountered. Only then may the "latent" genotype be phenotypically expressed.

An interesting aspect of this phenomena is its stochastic nature: exposure to a virus may induce an antibody which, because of a near structural similarity to the viral protein, may attack natural endogenous proteins (as occurs, for example, in rheumatoid arthritis or in SLE). In this case the energy expenditure may have negative survival implications. At any level of stress there is stochasticity in the hazard induced due to stochasticity (uncertainty) in the response at the molecular level. This suggests that the lowest levels of risk for a biological system, on average, do not occur at zero exposure, even for noxious stimuli, but at a positive, *low* level of exposure.

In cases where this model is biologically valid the quadratic hazard represents the effects of covariate interactions on risk – conditional on location parameters. In contrast, including quadratic and higher-order interactions in a Cox model, with its exponential relation of covariates to the hazard function, produces location-dependent quadratic coefficients. That is, location parameters interact with quadratic (nonlinear) terms (Pekkanen et al., 1992). Because of their location independence, the numerical values of the coefficients in (8.10) can be compared across study populations. This is not true in the Cox model.

In addition, the quadratic function has the property of additivity. Specifically, if health failure is multidimensional, then different hazard coefficients may relate, say, cancer and heart-disease risks to serum cholesterol. In a Cox model, because of its exponential form, one cannot estimate a cancer and a heart-disease hazard and add them together because the combined hazard has a different form (sums of exponentials). The quadratic hazard in 8.10 has additivity properties similar to χ^2 variables, so that two quadratic functions can be added together to produce a combined function that is also quadratic.

8.4. Marginal and conditional hazards

These definitions are sufficient to construct a state-dynamic model of human mortality and aging that can be estimated from longitudinal studies. We start with an expression for marginal survival functions (Yashin, 1985). If $Y = (Y_u)$, $u \geq 0$ is a random process and $\mu(Y,u)$ a non-negative functional satisfying measurability conditions then, for $t \geq 0$,

$$E \int_0^t \mu(Y,u) du < \infty . \tag{8.12}$$

This property allows us to write the equality,

$$E[e^{-\int_0^t \mu(Y,u) du}] = e^{-\int_0^t E[\mu(Y,u)|T>u] du} , \tag{8.13}$$

where T is related to Y_u, by,

$$P(T > t \mid Y_s, s \leq t) = e^{-\int_0^t \mu(Y,u) du} . \tag{8.14}$$

The relation of observed and conditional hazard functions is

$$\bar{\mu}(t) = E(\mu(Y,t) \mid T > t) . \tag{8.15}$$

The random hazard $\mu(Y,t)$ could depend on either current values of Y (e.g., $\mu(Y_t, t)$) or the trajectory of Y up to t (e.g., $\mu(Y_0^t, t)$, where $Y_0^t = \{Y_s, 0 \leq s \leq t\}$). Equation (8.15) shows that to calculate the value of the marginal hazard at age t one needs to integrate over unobserved genetic, physiological and environmental factors described by Y_t for individuals surviving to t.

Equations similar to (8.13) and (8.15) are used by demographers to analyze mortality in human populations where risk heterogeneity is assumed "fixed" (e.g., Vaupel and Yashin, 1985). The relation of observed and conditional hazard functions, however, holds for both fixed and stochastically changing "frailty" distributions.

Formulas (8.14) and (8.15) are the "natural" parameterizations of a marginal failure distribution when the probabilistic properties of Y are known.

8.4.1. The hazard as a function of observed and unobserved covariates

When some covariates are observed (X_t) and others are not (Y_t) a likelihood can be constructed if the form of the survival function (averaged over Y_t), conditioned on X_t, is known. Data can be analyzed if X_t and Y_t are components of a stochastic process influencing a hazard $\mu(X, Y, t)$ that satisfies the measurability condition in (8.12) and

$$E \int_0^t \mu(X,Y,u) du < \infty ,$$

where T is associated with X_u and Y_u by

$$P(T > t \mid X_s, Y_s, s \leq t) = e^{-\int_0^t \mu(X,Y,u) du} .$$

If trajectories of X are observed to t, then

$$P(T > t \mid X_0^t) = e^{-\int_0^t \bar{\mu}(X_0^u, u) du}, \qquad (8.16)$$

where

$$\bar{\mu}(X_0^t, t) = E(\mu(X,Y,t) \mid X_0^t, T > t). \qquad (8.17)$$

The proof of (8.16) and (8.17) is in Yashin and Manton (1997). Equation (8.13) is a special case of (8.16) when there are no X_t, i.e., when population mortality age trajectories are known.

Equation (8.17) shows that, for specific observational plans, the risk of death is dependent on covariates. To obtain the marginal hazard function for the likelihood, the conditional hazard is averaged with respect to unobserved genetic, environmental or physiological factors for survivors to age t.

8.5. The MWY approach to estimating a quadratic hazard without covariates

Yashin (1985) proved that, in the MWY model, $P(Y \leq y \mid T > t)$ has Gaston properties. To calculate a marginal survival function for a stochastic process model subject to a quadratic hazard, assume that the k-dimensional process Y_t satisfies

$$dY_t = [a_0(t) + a_1(t) Y_t] dt + b(t) dW_t , \qquad (8.18)$$

where Y_0 is a k-element vector of unobserved Gaston random variables, with a k-element vector of means m_0, and a $k \times k$ variance-covariance matrix γ_0. $Q(t)$ is a symmetric $k \times$

k non-negative definite matrix whose elements satisfy the condition in (8.12). Then, the "filter" equations, adjusted for mortality, are

$$E[\exp\{-\int_0^t (Y_u^* Q(u) Y_u) du\}] = \exp\{-\int_0^t (m_u^* Q(u) m_u + tr(Q(u)\gamma_u)) du\}, \quad (8.19)$$

where m_u and γ_0 are solutions of k ordinary nonlinear differential equations:

$$\frac{dm_t}{dt} = a_0(t) + a_1(t) m_t - 2\gamma_t Q(t) m_t, \quad (8.20)$$

and $k \times k$ equations,

$$\frac{d\gamma_t}{dt} = a_1(t)\gamma_t + \gamma_t a_1^*(t) + b(t) b^*(t) - 2\gamma_t Q(t) \gamma_t, \quad (8.21)$$

with initial conditions m_0 and γ_0.

Equation (8.18) covers random, deterministically changing, and fixed covariates as special cases. Equations (8.20) and (8.21) can be solved (i.e., trajectories m_t and γ_t estimated) by numerical methods for ordinary differential equations if $a_0(t)$, $a_1(t)$, $b(t)$, and $Q(t)$ are known from ancillary data or theory. These resemble Kalman-filter extrapolation equations (Liptser and Shiryayev, 1977) except for those terms containing $Q(t)$ which represents the probability of loss from the population as a function of state-variable values (Yashin, 1985). Eqns. (8.19) - (8.21) can be used to calculate the marginal survival function if T (ages at which health fails) and Y_0 (the initial state) are known.

8.6. Incompletely observed covariates

Processes are often incompletely observed in a longitudinal study. Measurements may be right-censored by loss to follow-up, end of study, or mortality. In left-censoring differences between censored and uncensored cases are not described by covariates measured at study inception (i.e., data on initial conditions are incomplete). To adjust for incomplete information, an ancillary model relating the probability of the event of censoring to the observed data is needed. Wu and Carroll (1987) modeled right-censoring as a function of the initial value and slope of a latent variable in a linear, random effects model. For longitudinal data, Diggle and Kenward (1994) combined a multivariate linear model of observed covariate changes with a logistic regression describing the dependence of censoring on Y_t. The quadratic hazard can be used not only to deal with left- and right-censoring but also with incomplete information on covariate changes between times of measurement.

8.6.1. Continuously changing stochastic covariates observed at discrete times

To represent covariates whose changes are incompletely observed over time, define $Z(t)$, an n-dimensional process measured k times. Assume mortality is a quadratic function of $Z(t)$,

$$\mu(Z(t),t) = \mu_0(t) + Z^*(t)Q(t)Z(t), \tag{8.22}$$

where $Q(t)$ satisfies (8.12) and $Z(t)$ satisfies

$$dZ(t) = (a_0(t) + a_1(t)Z(t))dt + b(t)dW_t, \tag{8.23}$$

where $a_0(t)$ is a n-dimensional vector function of time (t) with bounded elements for any $t \geq 0$, $b(t)$ is a bounded nxr matrix, and W_t is an r-dimensional Wiener process independent of $Z(0)$. For $Z(t)$ measured at $t_1, t_2,..., t_k$, Yashin et al. (1986a,b) examined the conditional survival function

$$S(t \mid \hat{z}(t)) = P(T > t \mid \hat{z}(t)), \tag{8.24}$$

where

$$\hat{z}(t) = (z(t_1), z(t_2),..., z(t_p(t))); t_p(t) = \sup\{t_j : t_j < t\}, \tag{8.25}$$

with $z(t_i)$, the value of $Z(t)$ observed at time t_i. Between covariate observations, mortality is

$$\hat{\mu}(\hat{z}(t),t) = -\frac{\partial}{\partial t}\ln S(t \mid \hat{z}(t)), \tag{8.26}$$

where $\hat{\mu}(z(t_i),t)$ is the right-continuous mortality rate for $S(t \mid \hat{z}(t))$. Yashin et al. (1986a,b) showed that the relation of $\hat{\mu}(\hat{z}(t),t)$ to $\hat{z}(t)$ is

$$\hat{\mu}(\hat{z}(t)t) = m^*(t)Q(t)m(t) + tr(Q(t)\gamma(t)) + \mu_0(t), \tag{8.27}$$

where for intervals $t_j \leq t < t_{j+1}$ the relation for the K conditional means, $m(t)$, is

$$\frac{dm(t)}{dt} = a_0(t) + a_1(t)m(t) - 2\gamma(t)Q(t)m(t),, \tag{8.28}$$

and the relation of the $K \times K$ covariance elements, $\gamma(t)$, is,

$$\frac{d\gamma(t)}{dt} = a_1(t)\gamma(t) + \gamma(t)a_1^*(t) + b(t)b^*(t) - 2\gamma(t)Q(t)\gamma(t), \tag{8.29}$$

with initial conditions, $m(t_j) = z(t_j), \gamma(t_j) = 0$. Both (8.28) and (8.29) involve dynamic and mortality terms. Equation (8.27) is a special case of (8.17) where $X_0^t = \hat{z}(t)$, i.e., the information in the observed trajectory is the value of z measured at t_i.

An important feature of (8.27), (8.28), and (8.29) is that they specify the dependence of the hazard function on the available (but incomplete) covariate information. This is not represented in the Cox regression model often used in epidemiological, biostatistical and demographic studies of aging. Since the dynamics of observed and unobserved influential processes are represented the predictive power of the quadratic hazard in the general MWY model is greater than for a Cox-regression function.

The hazard $\hat{\mu}(\hat{z}(t),t)$ is used in the likelihood

$$L = \prod_{i=1}^{N} \hat{\mu}(\tau_i,\hat{z}_i(\tau_i))^{\delta_i} \exp(-\int_0^{\tau_i} \hat{\mu}(u,\hat{z}_i(u))du) \prod_{j=1}^{k_i} f(z_i(t_j)|\hat{z}_i(t_{j-1})), \quad (8.30)$$

where $f(z_i(t_j)|\hat{z}_i(t_{j-1}))$ is the Gaston density of $z_i(t_j)$ conditional on prior observations, and τ_i, $i = 1,2,...,N$ event times. $\delta_i = \{0,1\}$ indicates right-censoring on terms remaining in the function at time t.

Equations (8.27), (8.28) and (8.29) permit (8.30) to be re-parameterized as

$$L = \prod_{i=1}^{N} \hat{\mu}(\tau_i, m_i(\tau_i \beta, \hat{z}_i(\tau_i)), \gamma(\tau_i, \beta), Q(\tau_i, \beta))^{\delta_i}$$

$$\times \exp\{-\int_0^{\tau_i} \hat{\mu}(u, m_i(u, \beta, \hat{z}_i(u)), \gamma(u, \beta), Q(u, \beta))du \prod_{j=1}^{k_i} (2\pi)^{-n/2} |\gamma_i(t_{j-}, \beta)|^{-\frac{1}{2}} \quad (8.31)$$

$$\exp\{-\frac{1}{2}(z_i(t_j) - m_i(t_{j-}, \beta))^* \gamma^{-1}(t_{j-}, \beta)(z_i(t_j) - m_i(t_{j-}, \beta))\},$$

where β is the vector of all unknown parameters in (8.27), (8.28), and (8.29), and are left-hand limits of $m(t,b)$ and $\gamma(t,\beta)$ when $t \uparrow t_j$. In (8.31), τ_i is known – or adjusted for censoring.

8.7. Generalizations for dependent observed and unobserved processes

The MWY model can be generalized to describe more complex processes and observational plans. Suppose an individual's hazard is a function of a composite process $Z(t) = \{X(t), Y(t)\}$, with $X(t)$ observed and $Y(t)$ unobserved. Assume both processes quadratically (but with different parameters) influence mortality, i.e.,

$$\mu(X(t),Y(t),t) = (X'(t),Y'(t)) \begin{bmatrix} Q_{11}(t) & Q_{12}(t) \\ Q_{21}(t) & Q_{22}(t) \end{bmatrix} \begin{bmatrix} X(t) \\ Y(t) \end{bmatrix} + \mu_0(t) \quad (8.32)$$

where $Q_{11}(t), Q_{22}(t)$ are positive-definite symmetric matrices and $Q_{12}^T(t) = Q_{21}(t)$.

Assume $X(t)$ and $Y(t)$ are solutions of systems of linear stochastic differential equations

$$d\begin{bmatrix} Y(t) \\ X(t) \end{bmatrix} = \left(\begin{bmatrix} a_{01}(t) \\ a_{02}(t) \end{bmatrix} + \begin{bmatrix} a_{11}(t) & a_{12}(t) \\ a_{21}(t) & a_{22}(t) \end{bmatrix} \begin{bmatrix} Y(t) \\ X(t) \end{bmatrix} \right) + \begin{bmatrix} b(t) \\ B(t) \end{bmatrix} d\begin{bmatrix} W_1(t) \\ W_2(t) \end{bmatrix} \quad (8.33)$$

where $W_1(t)$ and $W_2(t)$ are Wiener processes independent of $X(0)$, $Y(0)$, and $b(t)$, $B(t)$ are time-dependent scale matrices. $X(t)$ is observed K times. In a longitudinal study of aging, for example, values of covariates on any individual are measured a maximum of K times. Values of other influential factors, $Y(t)$, are never measured. If both processes describe the homeostatic mechanism for an individual their age trajectories may be dependent (i.e. $a_{21}(t) \ne a_{12}(t)$). The MWY model can represent this dependence by specifying the quadratic hazard function to depend on observed characteristics $X(t)$ of the homeostatic process. Let $\hat{x}(t)$ be the observation vector $X(t_1),..., X_i(t_j(t))$, where $t_j(t) = \sup\{t_m : t_m \le t\}$ with the hazard given by (8.32). Define

$$S(t,\hat{x}) = P(T > t \mid \hat{x}(t)), \quad (8.34)$$

given $\hat{x}(t)$ and let

$$\bar{\mu}(\hat{x}(t),t) = -\frac{\partial}{\partial t}\ln S(t,\hat{x}) \quad (8.35)$$

be its right-continuous hazard function between observations. The hazard from (8.27) is

$$\bar{\mu}(t,\hat{x}(t)) = m'(t)Q(t)m(t) + tr(Q(t)\gamma(t)) + \mu_0(t), \quad (8.36)$$

where

$$m(t) = \begin{bmatrix} m_1(t) \\ m_2(t) \end{bmatrix}$$

and

$$\gamma(t) = \begin{bmatrix} \gamma_{11}(t) & \gamma_{12}(t) \\ \gamma_{22(t)} & \gamma_{22}(t) \end{bmatrix},$$

which satisfy the differential equations for the means and covariances

$$\frac{dm(t)}{dt} = a_0(t) + a(t)m(t) - 2\gamma(t)Q(t)m(t), \quad (8.37)$$

and

$$\frac{d\gamma(t)}{dt} = a(t)\gamma(t) + \gamma(t)a^*(t) + b(t)b^*(t) - 2\gamma(t)Q(t)\gamma(t), \quad (8.38)$$

on intervals $t_j \le t \le t_{j+1}$, where,

$$a_0(t) = \begin{bmatrix} a_{01}(t) \\ a_{02}(t) \end{bmatrix},$$

$$a(t) = \begin{bmatrix} a_{11}(t) & a_{12}(t) \\ a_{21}(t) & a_{22}(t) \end{bmatrix},$$

$$m(t) = \begin{bmatrix} m_1(t) \\ m_2(t) \end{bmatrix},$$

$$\gamma(t) = \begin{bmatrix} \gamma_{11}(t) & \gamma_{12}(t) \\ \gamma_{21}(t) & \gamma_{22}(t) \end{bmatrix}.$$

At t_j, $j = 1,\ldots, k$, initial values are covariate means adjusted for the autoregressive functions where $\gamma_{12}(t_{j-})\gamma_{22}^{-1}(t_{j-})$ represent the auto-regression coefficients

$$m_1(t_j) = m_1(t_{j-}) + \gamma_{12}(t_{j-})\gamma_{22}^{-1}(t_{j-})(X(t_j) - m_2(t_{j-})),$$

$$m_2(t_j) = X(t_j),$$

and, where the variance is

$$\gamma_{11}(t_j) = \gamma_{11}(t_{j-}) - \gamma_{12}(t_{j-})\gamma_{22}^{-1}(t_{j-})\gamma_{21}(t_{j-}),$$

$$\gamma_{22}(t_j) = 0$$

$$\gamma_{12}(t_j) = \gamma_{21}(t_j) = 0.$$

For n individuals, the likelihood is

$$L = \prod_{i=1}^{n} \bar{\mu}(\hat{x}(T_i),\alpha,T_i)^{\delta_i} e^{-\int_0^{T_i}\bar{\mu}(\hat{x}(u),\alpha,u)du} \times \prod_{j=0}^{k_i} |\gamma_{i22}(t_{j-},\alpha)|^{-\frac{1}{2}} \quad (8.39)$$

$$\times \exp[-\frac{1}{2}[X_i(t_j) - m_{i2}(t_{j-},\alpha,\hat{x}_i(t_{j-}))] \times \gamma_{22}^{-1}(t_{j-},\alpha)[X_i(t_j) - m_{i2}(t_{j-},\alpha,\hat{x}_i(t_{j-}))]],$$

where m and γ are given by (8.37) and (8.38) and α is a vector of unknown parameters. Equations (8.37), (8.38), and (8.39) define a Kalman filter for multidimensional stochastic dynamic systems with state-dependent failure mechanisms influenced by observed and unobserved covariates. Generalizing these equations for continuously observed processes is straightforward.

8.8. Examples: longitudinal surveys and population studies

The likelihood in (8.31) cannot be optimized in the usual way since $m(t,\beta)$ and $\gamma(t,\beta)$ are not explicit functions of β. Modified procedures (based, for example, on Newton's method) are needed, e.g., an iterative maximization procedure where (8.28) and (8.29) are solved at each iteration with parameters taken equal to the current value of parameter estimates. Calculation of the information matrix is complicated because it involves partial derivatives of $m(t, \beta)$ and $\gamma(t,\beta)$ with respect to components of β. These are solutions to differential equations produced from (8.28) and (8.29) by differentiating both parts with respect to β_i with zero initial conditions for each observation interval. For each individual these equations are solved once for optimal parameter values determined by (8.31).

To illustrate the MWY approach when both covariate dynamics and times to failure T are measured, we review analyses of a.) the 34-year Framingham Heart Study follow-up and b.) the 1982, 1984, and 1989 NLTCS. In both, survival, conditional on covariates, is analyzed to ages by which most of the initial population has died. Though measured variables, $Z(t)$, are often information rich, unobserved variables may have important age-related mortality effects. The age dependence of the hazard is represented by (8.22), where time (age) effects can be factored into an exponential term (i.e., $e^{\theta t}$)

$$\mu(Z(t),t) = (\mu_0 + Z^*(t)QZ(t))e^{\theta t}. \tag{8.40}$$

where Q is a constant matrix of hazard coefficients and μ_0 is a constant.

Eqn. (8.40) is a generalization of a Gompertz hazard $\eta e^{\theta t}$, where η is a function of the process $Z(t)$. $e^{\theta t}$ represents the age-related influence of unobserved variables (i.e., those other than $Z(t)$). In this form the proportionality, or scale, factor η is a quadratic function of a multivariate process, $Z(t)$, with deterministic and random components. Since $Z(t)$ represents age-related changes in observed covariates, the value of θ in (8.40) characterizes how much information remains in the age dependence of unobserved risk-factor dynamics on survival, i.e., θ in (8.40) is larger than when θ is conditionally estimated on $Z(t)$. If all age-related covariates could be measured frequently enough and in sufficient detail, estimates of θ could approach 0.0. In practice, in longitudinal studies of the failure of complex multidimensional biological systems (e.g., humans) only a limited number of factors associated with aging are measured. Consequently, even conditional estimates of θ will tend to be significant. If θ is significant the coefficients in (8.40) are, themselves, functions of age, i.e., $Q \cdot e^{\theta t} = Q(t)$. The coefficients of the stochastic dynamic equations describing $Z(t)$ represent age-related changes in physiology prior to death. Trajectories of covariates define individual aging processes.

Alternate specifications of the effect of aging are possible. The effect of the unobserved variable on Q could be represented by a Weibull failure process (e.g. $Q(t) = Q \cdot t^m$). The selection of the exponential form in (8.40) was based on theoretical arguments that overall mortality at late ages adjusted for stochastic risk differentials can be explained by a Gompertz process (cf. e.g., Strehler, 1977; Strehler and Mildvan, 1960; Sacher and Trucco, 1962). Though others argue for a Weibull failure model (e.g., Rosenberg et al., 1973; Economous, 1982), the Gompertz has more empirical support as a model of mortality from ages 30 to 85 in humans – in its ability, for example, to describe adult mortality across human populations and subpopulations and for animal species (e.g., Finch 1990; Finch and Pike, 1996). Thus, theoretical arguments and ancillary data are both necessary in model specification for multivariate latent processes.

8.8.1. The Framingham Heart Study

In this study observations were made at fixed intervals of the same length. If intervals are short, logistic (or Cox) regression might be applied, assuming events in each interval are generated conditionally independent of events in other intervals (cf. e.g., Wu and Ware, 1979) (i.e., when covariate dynamics between measurements do not strongly effect outcomes) and one does not wish to have cause-specific hazard functions. Those procedures are not applicable if time- or age-dependent unobserved covariates influence time to failure.

In the 34-year Framingham follow-up, 10 risk factors were measured biennially (pulse pressure (in mm of Hg; the difference of systolic and diastolic BP); diastolic BP (DBP, in mm/Hg); body mass index (BMI weight in Kg divided by height in meters squared), cholesterol (mg/dl); blood glucose (mg %); hematocrit (%); vital capacity index (VCI; cl/ht in meters squared); smoking (cigarettes/day); left ventricular hypertrophy; ventricular rate) – in addition to age, sex, and date of death. To model risk-factor dynamics, a linear autoregressive process was estimated where each of 10 risk factors measured at time $t+1$ is a function of their values measured at t, a constant, and age at t. The 10 dynamic state variable equations were estimated from 16 pairs of measurements of the risk factors made over 34 years. Some risk factors (e.g., BMI) are stable (i.e., dominated by autoregression). Others (e.g., ventricular rate) were variable. Certain covariates show strong age trends (e.g., VCI declined with age) while others showed gender differences. The trajectories of yet other factors were influenced by the values of risk factors at a prior time (e.g., blood glucose at $t+1$ was positively biologically related to BMI at t, possibly related by effects on insulin production or tissue sensitivity to insulin).

Risk factors often have U- or J-shaped relations to mortality. Very low and very and high values, for example, are both positively related to mortality (cf. e.g., Witteman et al., 1994; Manton et al., 1994a). Thus, the quadratic hazard in (8.40) is used to approximate the conditional hazard function. In estimating the vector of risk factors, $Z(t)$ is augmented with a 1.0. The $k+1$ element vector $Z^+(t)$ defines a hazard matrix

$$Q^+ = \begin{bmatrix} \mu_0 & \dfrac{c}{2} \\ \dfrac{c^*}{2} & Q \end{bmatrix},$$ where μ_0 is the constant and Q is the matrix of quadratic coefficients

in (8.40). c are linear coefficients reflecting the location of the point of minimum risk in the risk-factor space at age t. Thus, Q^+ is of dimension $(k+1) \times (k+1)$, where μ_0 represents constant mortality, c is a k element vector of linear location parameters, and Q is a $k \times k$ matrix of hazard coefficients. The quadratic hazard can be expressed as

$$\mu(Z^+(t),t) = (Z^{+*}(t)Q^+ Z^+(t))e^{\theta t}. \qquad (8.40a)$$

In this case, the likelihood in (8.39) can be used. Parameters estimated include those of a linear process describing temporal and age changes in risk factors, diffusion, hazard coefficients and θ – the average age-related effect of unobserved variables on mortality. The vector and matrix coefficients $a_0(t)$, $a_1(t)$, $b(t)$ are assumed constant, i.e., a_0, a_1, b. Q^+ is assumed positive-definite and symmetric with constant entries. Estimation is discussed in Manton and Stallard (1988).

Table 8.1. Chi-squared values associated with risk factors, x_t, and with the senescence process θ for total mortality in Framingham 34 year follow-up

	Framingham; 10 risk factors			
	Males	χ^2/χ_1^2	Females	χ^2/χ_1^2
1. Full process (θ and x_t)	2,174.8	100.0%	2,047.8	100.0%
2. Effects of x_t, net of θ	1,518.8	69.8%	1,445.5	70.6%
3. Effect of θ, net of x_t	656.0 (θ=8.05%) 9.0 years	30.2%	602,3 (θ=8.12%) 8.9 years	29.4%
4. θ alone (no x_t in model)	1,350.4 (θ=9.39%) 7.7 years	62.1%	1,406.1 (θ=10.02%) 7.0 years	68.7%

The model's fit to mortality (conditional on the realized outcome of $Z(t)$), the size of θ, its standard error, and the reduction of θ due to the introduction of observed risk factors into the hazard are given in Table 8.1.

Table 8.1 presents log likelihood ratio χ^2 approximations. The null hypothesis against which χ^2 is assessed is that mortality is constant (i.e., is described by μ_0). First, we tested improvements in χ^2 when a Gompertz function is estimated, i.e., the shape parameter θ was estimated. θ improved the fit of the age trajectory of male mortality risks by 1350.4 χ^2 points with one degree of freedom (62.1% of the maximum χ^2 achievable with all information (line 4 in Table 8.1)) and is highly significant. For females the χ^2 was 1406.1 for one degree of freedom; or 68.7% of the χ^2 for the complete information model. The estimated percent increase in mortality per year of life (θ) is 9.4% for males and 10.0% for females – both θs have a high degree of precision and have highly significant effects for both genders.

If effects represented by θ can be described by $Z(t)$ then the following can be examined directly: covariate interactions over time; which covariates best predict risk; which change rapidly; how optimal covariate interventions might be designed. In a second test we estimated quadratic hazard coefficients for 10 risk factors with $\theta = 0.0$, i.e. with no age effect independent of temporal changes in $Z(t)$. The change over the null hypothesis is 1518.8 χ^2 points (69.8% of the total) for 65 degrees of freedom (i.e., the upper triangle of the 11 x 11, Q^+ matrix; there are 10 risk factors and the constant) for males; and *1445.5 χ^2 points for females for 65 degrees of freedom (70.6% of the total).* Thus, the covariates and their dynamics significantly predict survival by themselves (i.e., in a non-age-dependent fashion). In the example, a_0, a_1, and b, which describe the age dynamics of Z_t, were fixed at levels determined by maximum likelihood.

Third, we determined if θ significantly effected mortality beyond what is explained by the quadratic function of the 10 risk factors and their dynamics. We tested whether the age trajectory of the hazard is described by Q^+ – or whether hazard coefficients need to be dependent on unobserved age-related factors, i.e., $Q^+(t) = Q^+ \cdot e^{\theta t}$.

Line 3 in Table 8.1 shows that θ improved the fit over using only the 10 risk factors in the quadratic hazard by 656.0 χ^2 points with one degree of freedom – or 30.2% of the total. For females the effect of θ, net of the 10 risk factors, is 602.3 χ^2 points with one degree of freedom –29.4% of the total. Ideally (i.e., when all observed covariates are informative about aging) all age variation in mortality would be accounted for by the Z_t, so that θs net effect would be negligible. However, the χ^2 changes of 656.0 and 602.3 (one degree of freedom) suggest that effects of unobserved processes associated with age are still potent – even after conditioning on the 10 observed covariate processes. Thus, the hazard matrix is itself age dependent (i.e., $Q^+(t)$). Models not representing effects of age-related, unobserved variables produce coefficient estimates in Q^+ which can be biased in complex ways.

The 10 risk factors reduced the per annum effect, θ, of unobserved variables on mortality from 9.4% to 8.1% for males; and from 10.0 to 8.1% for females. Thus, the mortality doubling time, conditional on the dynamics of the 10 risk factors, increased from 7.7 to 8.9 years (13.5%) for males and from 7.3 to 8.9 years (18.0%) for females.

The effects of observed covariates on mortality are represented by specific coefficients in $Q^+(t)$, e.g., the diagonals of $Q^+(t)$ represent the quadratic effects of each observed variable. The product of the constant times each covariate are their linear effects. The product of risk factors with each other represents pairwise interactions. The dominant effects in the $Q^+(t)$ are the 10 quadratic terms. Some interaction terms had large effects on mortality (e.g., ventricular rate x left ventricular hypertrophy, which is theoretically meaningful in that thickened ventricular walls have effects on cardiac dynamic parameters). Some interactions were negative, suggesting that the effect of one risk factor on mortality declined as the level of a second risk factor declined (e.g., blood glucose in mg % and hematocrit, as might be found in diabetics). There were significant gender differences for some effects. For example, the quadratic effect on mortality of hematocrit was larger for males. The age increase in the effects of some risk factors was large enough that mortality selection could cause their population mean and variance (e.g., cholesterol) to stabilize, or even decline, at advanced ages (95+; Manton et al., 1994).

8.8.2. *The National Long Term Care Surveys*

The NLTCS are large longitudinal surveys that were carried out in 1982, 1984, and 1989 (overall $N = 30,308$) to assess temporal changes in chronic disability in the U.S. elderly population. Chronic disability was assessed using the same questions in all three surveys. The sample in each survey year was drawn from lists of Medicare-enrolled persons. Details of the sampling process and design are discussed in Manton et al. (1993).

The NLTCS data raise additional issues. First, the measures of disability were discrete responses to 27 questions about the ability to perform specific self-maintenance activities (e.g., eating, dressing, bathing, moving around inside). To translate 27 discrete activity measures into a smaller set of continuous dimensions of function/dysfunction a multivariate procedure designed for discrete variables was applied (Woodbury et al., 1994). This procedure was used to reduce the dimensionality of the measurements rather than, say, principle components, because it was explicitly designed to evaluate discrete measures. After the multivariate analysis, the effects of the 27 measures on mortality were represented by continuously-scaled scores on the seven disability dimensions defined in an analytic procedure to be constrained to a convex space (Manton et al., 1994a). The dynamic equations describe changes in those scores over time.

One of the seven disability scores represents persons with complete functioning. The others represent different degrees and types of disability (i.e., functional loss). If functional loss is related to the risk of death, then a nonzero score on any of the six disability dimensions indicates an increased risk of death. Thus, the scores influence a multidimensional convex hazard function which is approximated by a time-dependent quadratic hazard function, $Q^+(t)$, except that a separate constant "variable" is not introduced because of the global convexity constraints imposed on the parameter space by the multivariate analysis (Manton et al., 1994). The quadratic hazard thus has a well-defined, natural origin (i.e., point of minimum mortality) corresponding to the value of 1.0 on the first dimension.

When using parameter estimates for the two processes to calculate life-table functions or to adjust for the truncation of the variation of scores by mortality selection and by convexity constraints on the parameter space, a matrix rescaling procedure was used to preserve approximate normal variability over time (Manton et al., 1994b). This rescaling can be viewed as a dynamic, multidimensional generalization of normalizing functions applied to the error distribution for discrete dependent variables over "short" time intervals (Woodbury et al., 1996).

The first disability dimension represents the degree to which a person has moderate physical, but no cognitive, impairments. The second disability dimension represents mild cognitive, but no physical, impairment. The third disability dimension indicates loss of the physical ability to live independently (e.g., the ability to do laundry, grocery shopping, etc., without help). The fourth dimension indicates loss of the ability to maintain basic physical functions (e.g., bathing, eating, dressing without help). The fifth dimension represents the degree of physical frailty (e.g., limitations on the ability to perform basic physical movements such as using one's hands, legs). The last indicates disability so severe that institutional care is needed (Manton et al., 1994a).

Modeling the rate at which processes change is more complex in the NLTCS since survey intervals were not equal (two years elapsed from 1982 to 1984 and five from 1984 to 1989). Thus, the time dependence of disability score changes must be reparameterized to combine covariate dynamics for different length intervals. This is difficult in logistic, or Cox, regression because of the location dependence of the hazard function (Pekkanen et al., 1992). The NLTCS population is elderly (all persons are 65+)

and mortality risks, the number of dimensions, and the degree of disability increase with age. The Cox model does not have parameters describing covariate age- and time-dependent rates of change subject to random perturbation (Law et al., 1994a,b) within long (relative to the rate of occurrence of health events at late ages) and unequal intersurvey periods. Though the time/age rate of change of many traits is known from physiological (e.g., age dependence of cardiac function; Kasch et al., 1993), clinical, and epidemiological studies, the trajectory for an individual is unique because of genetic, environmental, and other influences. Longitudinal studies show that the dynamics of health variables are a mix of deterministic trends and stochastic influences (cf. e.g., Law et al., 1994a,b; Manton et al., 1994a). Thus, modeling individual covariate trajectories and their influences on survival is important in longitudinal studies when trajectories are incompletely observed.

In the stochastic process model of mortality with observed and unobserved dynamic covariates used to analyze the NLTCS data, seven scores represented an individual's impairment on six sets of activities satisfying stochastic differential equations such as (8.23). Coefficients $a_0(t)$, $a_1(t)$, $b(t)$ are constants. The conditional hazard is given by (8.32), where θ, elements of the matrix Q^+ and a_0, a_1, b are estimated using a likelihood such as (8.31).

Optimization had to be constrained. That is, to maximize (8.31) with unequal intervals ordinary nonlinear differential equations (8.29) and (8.30) are solved for each iteration. If (8.29) and (8.30) have analytic solutions, then $\bar{\mu}(t)$ is an explicit function of unknown parameters, and maximization is straightforward. In the general situation, methods such as that of Runge-Kutta are needed to solve the differential equations for m and γ between measurements. For individuals entering the study in, say, 1989, values of m_0 are set to the values of covariates for these individuals in 1989. Values of γ_0 are set to zero. For those becoming 65 between 1989 and 1994, m_0 and γ_0 are assumed equal to the mean and covariance matrix of covariate values calculated for 65 year-old individuals in 1989. This allows us to include in the likelihood information on, e.g., persons who turn 65 between 1989 and 1994 but who die before 1994.

The effect of age and the covariates on mortality are presented in Table 8.2.

The hypotheses examined for the NLTCS are logically the same as those examined for Framingham (Table 8.1). The first hypothesis compared θ against the null hypothesis of constant mortality. θ increased χ^2 by 2622.2 points with one degree of freedom for males; χ^2 increased 4966.0 points (line 1 in Table 8.2) with one degree of freedom for females. θ estimates were 8.2% for males and 9.1% for females.

With θ set to 0.0 and the disability covariates entered in a quadratic hazard, a χ^2 of 3821.5 points with 27 degrees of freedom (a Q^+ matrix with the seven scores used as

Table 8.2. 1982-1984-1989 NLTCS; seven functional scores: total mortality

	Males	χ^2/χ_1^2	Females	χ^2/χ_1^2
1. Full process (θ and $\underset{\sim}{x}_t$)	4,837.9	100.0%	7,493.8	100.0%
2. Effects of $\underset{\sim}{x}_t$, net of θ	3,821.5	79.0%	6,550.5	87.4%
3. Effect of θ, net of $\underset{\sim}{x}_t$	1,016.4 (θ=5.28%) 13.4 years	21.0%	943.3 (θ=4.75%) 14.9 years	12.6%
4. θ alone (no $\underset{\sim}{x}_t$ in model)	2,622.2 (θ=8.15%) 8.9 years	54.2%	4,966.0 (θ=9.1%) 8.0 years	59.6%

covariates) was produced for males; a χ^2 of 6550.5 points with 27 degrees of freedom for females. The first and second models are not nested but the inclusion of the disability scores produces a higher χ^2 than using only θ. When testing this hypothesis we kept the parameters a_0, a_1, and b, which describe the dynamics of Z^+ at their maximum likelihood estimates.

We examined the effect of θ, net of disability scores, by examining differences between the model with risk factors with $\theta = 0.0$ and a model with both covariates and θ. The χ^2 increment due to θ is large (1016.4 χ^2 points with one degree of freedom for males; 943.3 χ^2 points with one degree of freedom for females), though proportionately smaller than in Framingham. Declines in θ due to the introduction of the disability scores were larger: from 8.2 to 5.3% for males and 9.1 to 4.8% for females. Thus, the seven functional status dimensions in the NLTCS were more informative about age-related mortality changes than the 10 Framingham risk factors – even though the time between measurements was, on average, two and a half times longer.

In the Q^+ there were large differences in the mortality risk of the different dimensions. The nondisabled (base) dimension always had the lowest mortality. The most frail had the highest mortality. Some disabled groups were relatively young with mortality associated with acute cardiopulmonary conditions. These tended either to recover without lasting disability -- or to die rapidly. The highest mortality risk was found for a frail – but not institutionalized – group. The ratio of the size of the coefficients for this group to those for the nondisabled group was 8 to 1 for both males and females – though females had baseline mortality half that of males. Females also tolerated disability better. That is, mortality coefficients for scores representing greater disability were smaller for females than males.

8.9. General properties of the age-dependent quadratic hazard

Age and time dynamic properties of the quadratic hazard (8.31) are shown in Figure 8.1.

The hypothetical mortality for a quadratic hazard with a one-dimensional covariate process $Z(t)$ is shown for ages 50 and 95. θ is 8.1% in the top figure (from the Framingham Study) and 4.8% in the bottom figure (from the NLTCS). The hazard becomes more "sensitive" to changes in covariate values with age. The "real" age trajectory of the hazard is represented by the dashed line in Figure 8.1: When the covariate changes from the value Z_1 at age 50 to the value Z_2 at age 95, mortality changes from A to B. These changes are larger than in the quadratic hazard without dynamics. Not only are covariate increases important – but the deviation of covariate values from the optimal point with age increases risk more than for the conditional Gompertz – or a quadratic hazard with constant parameters.

The disability scores reduced age-related uncertainty more than risk factors in the Framingham Study even though NLTCS inter-survey intervals are longer. This may be because disability has temporally more proximate effects on mortality than risk factors in very elderly populations (Manton et al., 1991). Disability also predicts risk-factor changes well. For example, declines in activity predict changes in pulmonary function, blood pressure, cholesterol, and vascular tone – as well as endpoints like stroke (Colantonio et al., 1992), pneumonia, and CVD. Even so, the effects of age-related unobserved variables remain significant in the NLTCS, so that methods not adjusting for their effects will produce biased coefficient estimates for observed covariates.

8.10. Summary

Population-based data on aging and survival manifest the mutual influence of two effects. One involves the mortality selection process because "the frail die first". The other reflects the operation of a multiplicity of homeostatic mechanisms in the individuals comprising a population. Many of these mechanisms have been carefully investigated in separate biological, physiological, or epidemiological studies. How can the results of those studies be used in analyses of longitudinal population data on aging and survival? Random effect (frailty) survival models used in some demographic and biostatistical applications represent effects of differences in survival due to unobserved fixed differences between individuals. These models do not take into account the

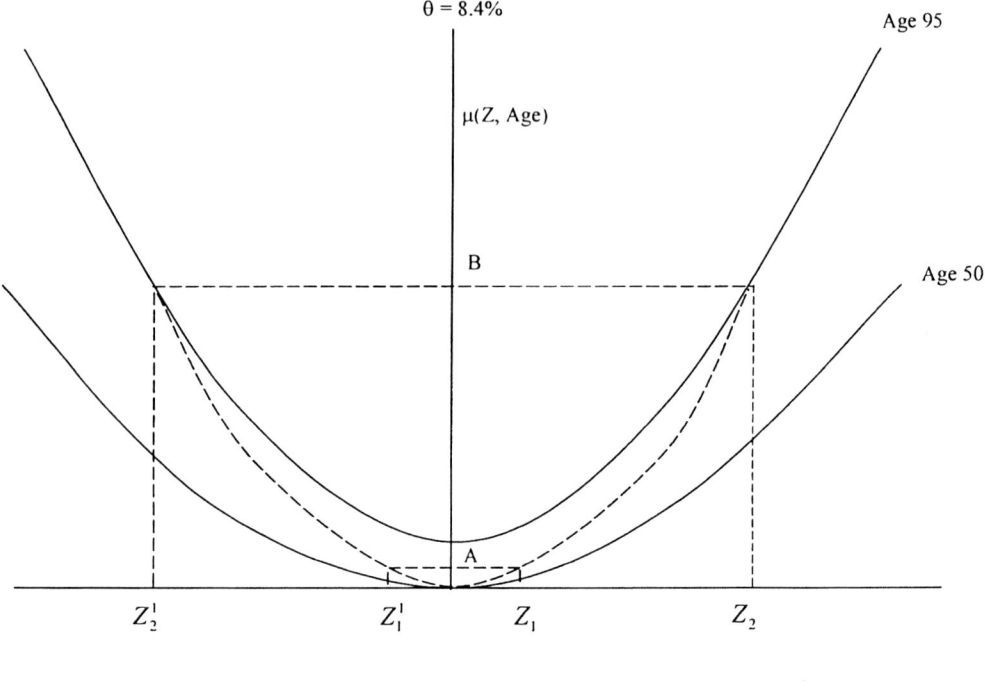

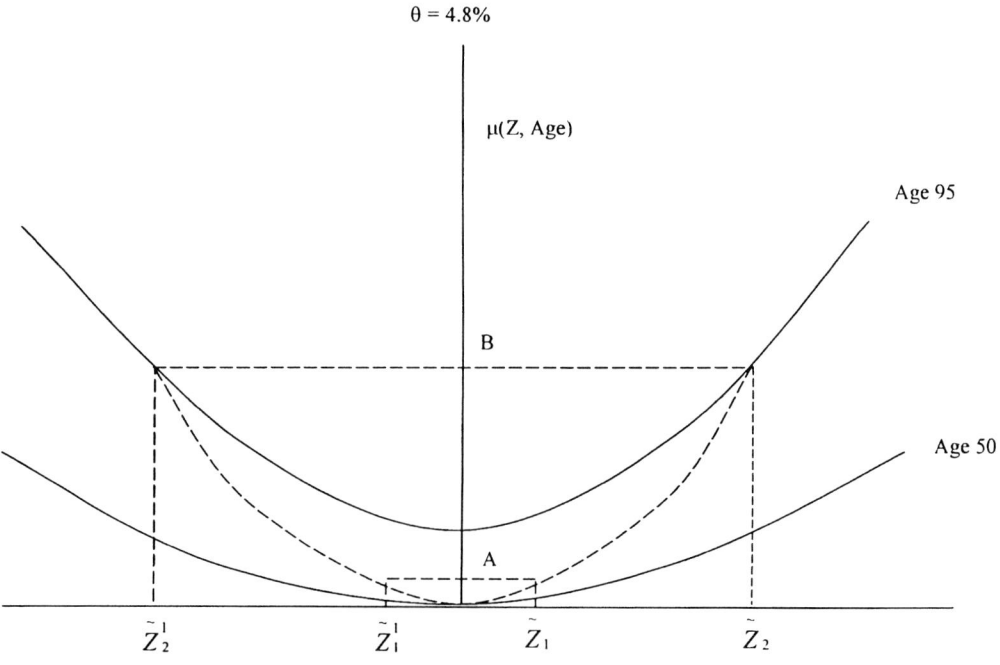

Figure 8.1. Quadratic hazard functions at ages 50 and 95 when covariate information is informative (θ= 8.1% Framingham) and highly informative (θ=4.8% NLTCS) about senescence processes θ.

dynamics of these mechanisms, i.e., they represent individual susceptibilities to disease and death as a fixed frailty distribution.

A more serious limitation is the assumption that unobserved random effects are independent of observed covariates. Since hidden factors may be genetic, and they may influence observed covariates, such assumptions may be unrealistic. Fixed-frailty models also do not represent the changing effects of homeostatic forces – or knowledge about a risk function: Many studies show that risk is often a U- (or J-) shaped function of risk factors. Hormesis effects, observed in studies of external influential factors, are consistent with such U-shaped hazard functions (Stebbing, 1987).

It appears that the quadratic-hazard, stochastic process model of aging and survival avoids many of these limitations and can be applied to the analysis of longitudinal data on aging where stochastically changing covariates may be partly observed at selected points of an individual's life. In longitudinal studies, effects of the evolution of observed and unobserved covariates over age cannot be ignored. Logistic or Cox regressions do not represent these influences. A stochastic process model based on a parametric specification of the conditional hazard and randomly changing covariates is needed. When the conditional hazard is a quadratic function of covariates, both Cameron-Martin (Myers, 1981; Yashin, 1985, 1993) and the martingale versions of MWY (Woodbury and Manton, 1977; Yashin, 1980, 1985) procedures can be used to calculate marginal survival functions.

The martingale version of MWY is preferable for several reasons. First, parameter estimates can be recursively updated when new measurements are made. Second, covariate dynamics are better represented (cf. e.g., Woodbury and Manton, 1977; Yashin, 1985; Yashin et al., 1986a,b) because all data on the evolution of the covariate in a longitudinal study is used. Third, knowledge from prior studies can be used to define the probabilistic regularities of the stochastic evolution of unobserved covariates, e.g., by specifying the conditional survival function from other longitudinal studies where hazards are estimated as functions of measured covariates. This is important because the marginal survival function is calculated by averaging the conditional one. Influential variables can satisfy stochastic differential equations representing random environmental influences, and they can describe forces preserving the equilibrium (homeostasis) of multidimensional, physiological processes. Thus, knowledge of the structure of the conditional hazard can be applied when covariates are unobserved – or incompletely observed. Thus, a.) a probabilistic description of covariate dynamics with possibly free parameters and b.) specification of the conditional survival function given the trajectories of the covariates, allow the MWY approach to be used in many types of longitudinal studies, as well as allowing comparisons of parameter estimates across study populations and for different sets of covariates.

These model properties were illustrated for two longitudinal studies with very different data structures (NLTCS and Framingham). The model performed well in each case and demonstrated the presence of information in the dynamics of both observed and unobserved covariates that standard survival analyses do not utilize. Thus, modeling and estimation strategies for failure processes with time-varying covariates may better describe the state dynamics of multivariate systems – and their failure – and can improve the understanding of complex system failure, interventions in failure processes, and forecasts of distributions of times to system failure.

IX. Population models of human aging and mortality

9.1. Life-table equations

In Chapter VIII we described a two-component model of the physiological dynamics of aging and mortality for individuals with different observed or unobserved attributes in a longitudinally followed cohort. This is a statistically efficient way of extricating unbiased estimates of parameters of physiological changes for individuals and contemporaneous mortality from longitudinal, heterogeneous cohort population data.

To use this model to describe aging changes and mortality for a national population one must specify life-table equations for all birth cohorts represented in the population. The set of transitions generated from the cohorts can be used to describe changes in survival and in the statistical moments of the conditional state-variable distribution arising from the simultaneous effects of state-variable dynamics and state-variable-dependent mortality on the population and its state-variable structure (Manton et al., 1994). These life-table equations can be applied to both bounded and unbounded state-variable processes, depending upon the assumptions made about the diffusion components of the processes.

9.2. Cohort life tables for multidimensional state processes

To combine the dynamic and mortality processes for individuals, differential equations derived from the multidimensional Fokker-Planck equation adjusted for systematic mortality loss (Woodbury and Manton, 1977) have to be formulated for temporal changes in the state-variable distribution for a heterogeneous population under selection. The process equations in prior chapters provide parameters for the system of simultaneously solved differential equations that represents the ensemble of dynamic and selective forces acting on the multidimensional state-variable distribution for the multi-cohort population.

The first life-table parameter to be calculated for cohort y is the probability of survival to age $t+1$,

$$^y\ell_{t+1} = {}^y\ell_t \, |I + V_t Q_t|^{-\frac{1}{2}} \exp\left[\frac{\mu_t(^y m_t) + \mu_t(^y m_t^*)}{2} - 2\mu\left(\frac{^y m_t + {}^y m_t^*}{2} \right) \right] \quad (9.1)$$

where $\mu_t(\cdot)$ is the cohort mortality rate from the quadratic hazard for the vector of risk factors set at their means at the prior time t ($^y m_t$), Q_t is the submatrix of the hazard function reflecting quadratic effects and second-order interactions multiplied by the exponential term reflecting unobserved factors correlated with age, and V_t is the variance-covariance matrix of the J risk factors. The vector of means is the average value of risk-factor values among the subset of persons expected to survive the age interval t to $t+1$.

In equation (9.1) cohort survival is a function of both the time-dependent hazard function (i.e., $Q_t = Q \exp^{Age_{it}}$) and its effects on the dispersion matrix (V_t) and on the means ($^y m_t$) of survivors to age t on J state variables.

The change in the means of the state variables due to systematic mortality "selection" is described for cohort y by,

$$_y m_t^* = {}^y m_t - V_t^*(q_t + Q_t \ {}^y m_t), \quad (9.2)$$

where q_t are the linear coefficients from the quadratic hazard function. The dispersion or (variance-covariance) matrix change due to mortality needed to solve (9.2) (and subsequently equation (9.1)) is described by,

$$^y V_t^* = (I + {}^y V_t Q_t)^{-1} \ {}^y V_t \ . \quad (9.3)$$

The dynamic changes in $^y m_t^*$ (i.e., changes in the means of the state variables due to the dynamics among cohort survivors from age t to $t+1$) is,

$$^y m_{t+1} = (\mu_0 + \mu_1 Age_{t+1}) + (R_1 \ {}^y m_t^*) + (R_t Age_t \ {}^y m_t^*). \quad (9.4)$$

Here u_0 is the constant in the autoregressive process, u_1 is the change in the constant due to age, R_1 is the matrix of autoregressive coefficients for the J basic state variables and are age-dependent coefficients for the J covariates. The update variance-covariance variable is adjusted for age-dependent state-variable dynamics by including the age effects in an expanded ^+R_t,

$$^y V_{t+1} = {}^+R_t \ {}^y V_t^* \ {}^+R_t^T + \Sigma_t \quad (9.5)$$

where Σ_t is the diffusion matrix (covariance matrix of residual terms from the process).

Population aging reflects the fact that a population's state-variable characteristics are a dynamic mixture of the distribution of attributes for each of an ensemble of birth cohorts whose size is changing with time. Each birth cohort has potentially different overall age trajectories and distributions on physiological parameters, which are described by equations (9.1) to (9.5).

In such a population aging and mortality model we need to examine temporal changes due to the changing mixes of cohort-specific aging processes. The effects of the mixture of age trajectories on population changes has its own implications, which are of scientific and public-policy interest. One way in which an aging population changes is due to the differential size of birth cohorts as they enter age ranges of interest, e.g., the large size of the 1946 to 1964 U.S. birth cohorts. Differences in cohort sizes differentially weight cohort differences in the population dynamics of health and mortality changes. There may be cohort differences in early health, risk-factor exposures, or gene expression generating cause of death differentials (Manton, 1996) – some of which may be manifest in the age-specific dynamics of state variables, some due to the influence of unobserved factors on mortality, and some due to cohort differences in the mortality rates for cause k where the kth component of the quadratic hazard, adjusted for age factors, is,

$$Q_{kt} = Q_k \exp^{\theta Age_t}. \tag{9.6}$$

The cause-specific crude mortality rate for cause c_k is then calculated from

$$[\mu_{kt}(m_t) + \mu_{kt}(m_t^*)]/2 + \frac{1}{2}\ell n|I + V_t Q_t|Tr[V_t Q_{kt}]/Tr[V_t/Q_t], \tag{9.7}$$

(Manton et al., 1992) with cohort life tables generated for the k causes by,

$$^y\ell_{t+1} = {^y\ell_t} \exp\left(-\sum_{k=1}^{K} \bar{\mu}_{kt}\right). \tag{9.8}$$

Clearly, by eliminating a term in the summation of K one produces a life table with a given cause elimination.

Applications of these equations to model cause elimination in the different mortality of cohorts are found in Manton and Stallard (1988) and Manton et al. (1997). Below we examine extensions of the model for cohort y to differentially weighted mixtures of Y cohort models to determine how realistic the behavior of the mixed model is for a national population.

9.3. Age trajectories in cohorts, diffusion and mortality selection

It is useful to examine the age trajectory of mortality in individual cohorts and how they vary as a function of specific parameters. This is illustrated in Table 9.1 for different assumptions made about diffusion effects on the cohort trajectory of functional status and mortality.

As diffusion is reduced (between scenarios 1 and 2 diffusion is updated less frequently), the age trajectory of mortality is changed. As mortality increases with age, it increases for some dimensions of disability faster than for others due to their greater variance (the variance is a dynamic balance of systematic mortality selection and

Table 9.1. Life tables and age trajectory of the averages of three disability intensity scores (i.e., for active persons with no disability; frail persons with high levels of disability; and socially dependent persons in institutions) for females in the U.S. NLTCS followed 1982 to 1991

Age	(1) MONTHLY			(2) ANNUAL			(3) Discrete State, Time Markov Process	
	Residual Life Expectancy	Active	Frail + Institutional	Residual Life Expectancy	Active	Frail + Institutional	Active	Frail + Institutional
65	20.8	.926	.012	20.1	.917	.018	.904	.022
75	14.1	.832	.039	13.3	.799	.054	.791	.058
85	8.65	.647	.132	7.6	.544	.172	.514	.206
95	5.42	.523	.255	4.4	.332	.379	.215	.498
105	4.0	.573	.220	3.33	.375	.336	.063	.855

Scenario (1): Process updated monthly; parameter estimates based on linearly interpolated data for all months between each pair of observations and linearly extrapolated data for all months following last observation.

Scenario (2): Process updated annually; parameter estimates based on data assumed constant for all years following a given observation, but prior to next observation.

Scenario (3): Process updated quinquennially; parameter estimates based on pairs of observed statuses in 1984 and 1989.

diffusion – or random changes in variance). The dimensions for which the variance increases most rapidly are those where functioning is most impaired – possibly because of greater damage to homeostatic mechanisms and because mortality is highest. In Table 9.1 for scenario 1 (monthly updates of state-variable variance) the frail and institutionalized proportion of the female population grows to 25.5% at age 95 and then declines to 22.0% at age 105.

When diffusion is evaluated for a specific cohort on a yearly (rather than monthly) basis there is a drop off in the proportion of frail individuals at late ages – but the proportion reaching those frail states before declining is higher (e.g., model 2; 37.9% are frail at age 95). This is because the dynamic model with only annual variance adjustments does not reflect as much short-term stochastic change in disability status as does a monthly adjustment – and consequently, the former has less effect on mortality selection. The discrete state process (scenario 3) has a very different age trajectory because no disability heterogeneity is modeled within groups (all heterogeneity is between groups) and there is no diffusion process to help re-inflate the between-group variance.

To understand the structure of these cohort dynamics we conducted a population experiment by dividing the gender-specific state dynamics into high- and low-education groups. Education is a measured covariate whose effects we can assume to be fixed at late ages. It may also represent, in part, genetic endowments, i.e., the level of education achieved could be a function of genetic traits affecting personality and general intellectual endowment, as well as socio-economic differentials in access to education. The effects of education at early ages may reflect different processes than at late ages, where education (as well as occupation) reflects, for example, physiological differentials in risk of dementia (Stern et al., 1994).

In Table 9.2, the proportion surviving in a healthy state declines more rapidly for people with high education because the force of mortality for the frail state is lower for the better educated than for the less well-educated groups, both male and female. However, there is an increase in the ratio of healthy to frail persons after age 95 (column 4) – an increase that is much larger for people with higher education, both male and female.

One of the useful features of the cohort model is that it has a built-in formal test (described in Chapter 8) of the effects of physiological senescence: $^y\theta$ represents the average effects of unobserved risk factors correlated with age on the mortality of cohort y. As the set of observed risk factors, ^yZ_t, is improved (as are estimates of Q_t), the value of $^y\theta$ declines. Though in an information-poor environment the model approximates a Gompertz, $^y\theta$ declines as information is increased until, at $^y\theta = 0$, the mortality model

Table 9.2. Male and female life tables calculated from the three NLTCS and mortality 1982 to 1991 for high and low education subgroups

Age		(1) l_x	(2) $(g_1 \times l_x)$	(3) $(g_6 \times l_x)$	(4) Ratio of $g_1 \times l_x/g_6 \times l_x$	(5) $Q_x \times 12$	(6) e_x	(7) Mild Impairment/ Unimpaired	(8) Instrumentally Impaired with/without Physical Impairment	(9) Moderate ADL & IADL Impaired	(10) Frail/Inst
65	High Education										
	Males	1.000	.950	.0052	182.63	0.025	16.26	.9691	.0155	.0051	.0103
	Females	1.000	.951	.0047	202.32	0.012	24.39	.9711	.0148	.0049	.0092
	Low Education										
	Males	1.000	.807	.0049	164.78	0.024	14.33	.8955	.0728	.0247	.0070
	Females	1.000	.815	.0052	156.81	0.024	16.82	.9059	.0620	.0234	.0087
75	High Education										
	Males	0.710	.583	.0118	49.46	0.048	10.76	.9218	.0166	.0218	.0398
	Females	0.896	.675	.0208	32.48	0.012	16.59	.8687	.0265	.0360	.0689
	Low Education										
	Males	0.619	.276	.0528	5.24	0.060	9.94	.7034	.0866	.0639	.1461
	Females	0.731	.584	.0175	33.33	0.036	11.12	.8796	.0341	.0293	.0570
85	High Education										
	Males	0.353	.233	.0157	14.83	0.108	6.48	.7759	.0509	.0392	.1341
	Females	0.679	.348	.0336	10.37	0.048	10.07	.6485	.0496	.0770	.2249
	Low Education										
	Males	0.278	.171	.0207	8.24	0.108	6.29	.7409	.0540	.0432	.1619
	Females	0.383	.231	.0210	11.02	0.096	6.50	.7001	.0545	.0615	.1838
95	High Education										
	Males	0.077	.043	.0055	7.90	0.192	4.33	.7220	.0433	.0718	.1628
	Females	0.298	.069	.0310	2.23	0.132	6.34	.3072	.0504	.0889	.5535
	Low Education										
	Males	0.057	.026	.0094	2.77	0.228	3.58	.5629	.0901	.0653	.2817
	Females	0.085	.041	.0059	6.87	0.204	3.78	.5494	.0506	.0556	.3443
105	High Education										
	Males	0.007	.004	.0001	27.97	0.288	3.03	.6629	.0189	.2702	.0481
	Females	0.063	.023	.0033	6.96	0.180	4.84	.4081	.0415	.0648	.4856
	Low Education										
	Males	0.003	.001	.0005	2.28	0.396	2.23	.5517	.1056	.0814	.2613
	Females	0.005	.002	.0003	7.48	0.360	2.53	.5460	.0402	.0593	.3545

is no longer Gompertzian but is driven solely by the empirical dynamics of the state variables – dynamics which may be the mixture of m genetically defined strata (Manton et al., 1994). Thus, the projected survival of a cohort, starting at age 30, produces a broad range of estimated ages of death reflecting the heterogeneity of the population due to $^y\theta$, to observed risk-factor differentials, and to differences in cohort state distributions and dynamics, and differences in cause-of-death structures.

This is illustrated in Figure 9.1 for projections based on the assumption that risk factors could be controlled after 20 years to reduce mortality in a series of cohorts aged 30+ in 1990, with new cohorts aging in every two years.

This simulation might reflect what a change in human longevity, as reflected by favorable changes in the distribution and dynamics of 10 risk factors, could produce in a population. In effect, the change in the dynamics and diffusion of the risk factors represents an expression of additional phenotypic variation in the state variables inducible by environmental modification of measured risk factors.

The $^y\theta$, which are estimated to be consistent with the variation represented by the J-dimensional auto-regressive processes, represent factors that may be genetically controlled. Genetic factors could also be represented by changing coefficients in the dynamic equations, i.e., the rate of change of risk factors may be genetically determined. Evolutionary effects could be represented if different models were constructed for each birth cohort y in a population. Then changes in the dynamics could reflect environmentally induced phenotypic variation, while cross-cohort differences in $^y\theta$ (or cause-specific components of $^y\theta$, estimated net of the dynamics) – if they reflect a systematic progression of traits across cohorts – might reflect changes in senescent processes. That is, $^y\theta$ might need to be indexed by birth cohort (Manton et al., 1997), and if possible, the relation of $^y\theta$ to cohort birth date should be parameterized. Another issue would be how $^y\theta$ correlates with cohort changes in fertility rates and age patterns over time (Langreth, 1998).

The results of the projections with the simulated risk-factor changes are presented in Figure 9.2.

In 2010, the median age at death is 85.1 years for females and 79.5 years for males. The two standard deviation range for the age-at-death distribution is from 46 to 97 years – i.e., 95% of the deaths in the population over age 30 occur in that range. This variation in the age at death is in part due to risk-factor variance, and in part to mortality effects associated with the Gompertz-type age parameter $^y\theta$.

By 2040, when interventions in $^y\underset{\sim it}{x}$ (i.e., shifts towards the means observed at age 30 and with reduction in risk-factor variance by improved intervention s on persons with extreme values) have had more time to become manifest, the 95% distribution of deaths

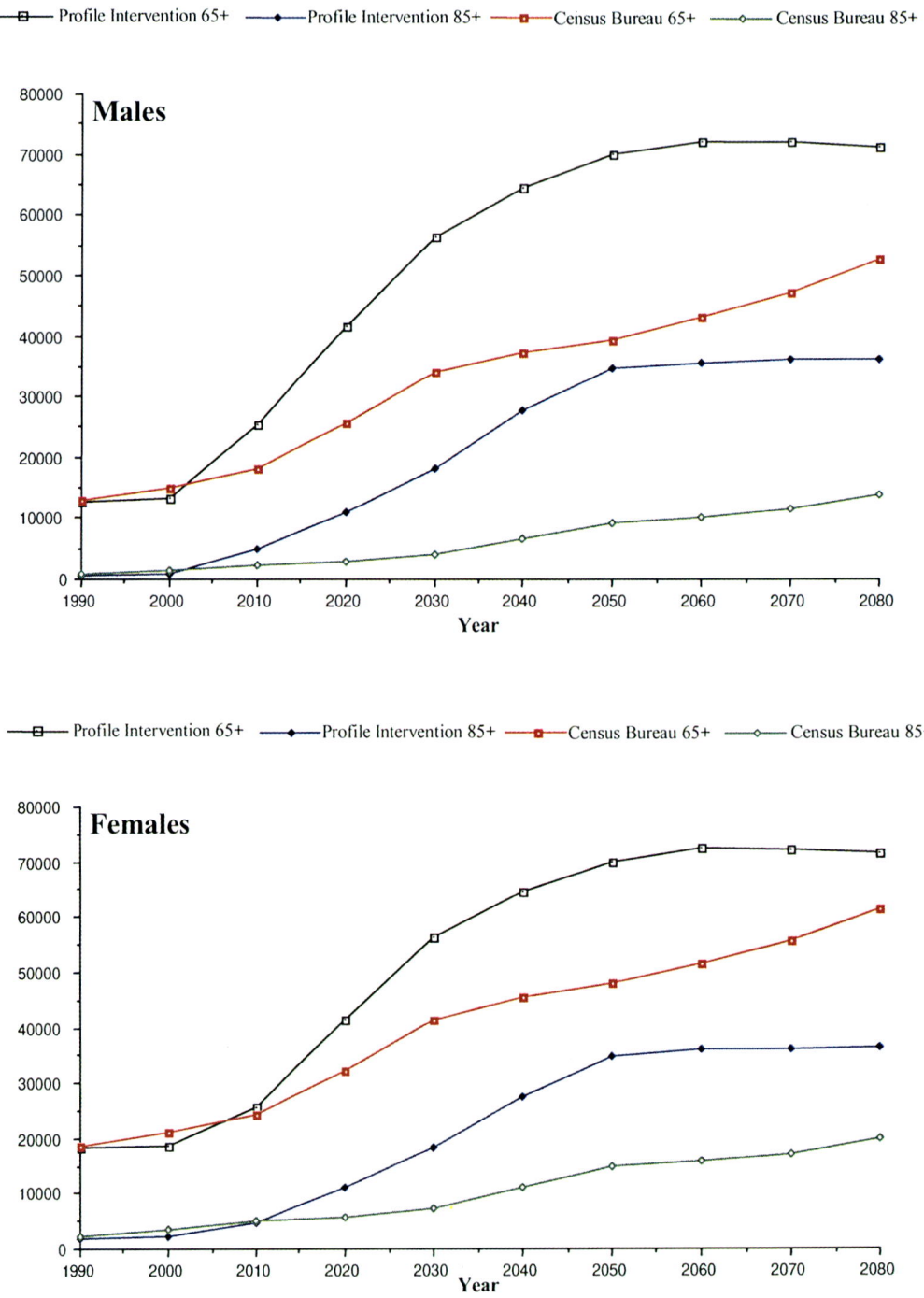

Figure 9.1. Trajectories of the population aged 65+ and 85+ for males and females, optimal intervention and highest Census Bureau series.

143

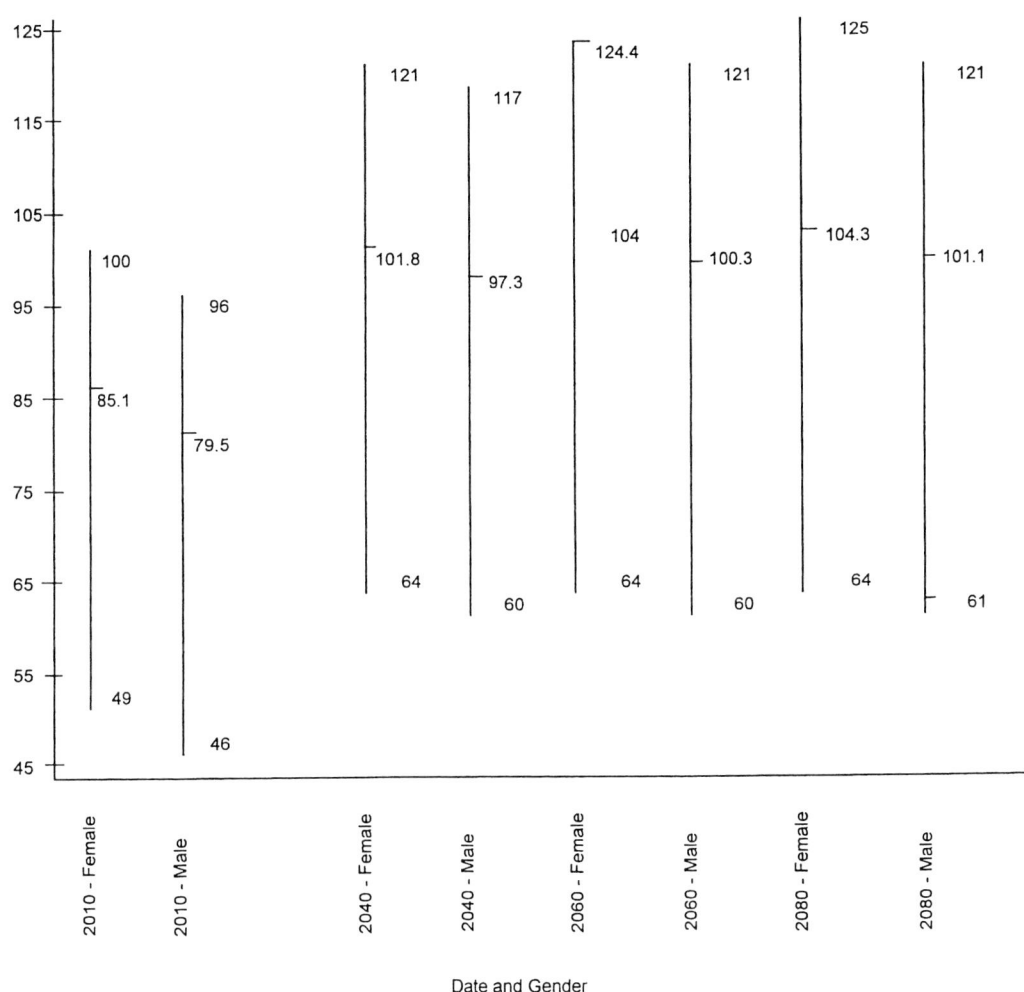

Figure 9.2. Gender specific ranges of populations in 2010, 2040, 2060, and 2080 assuming a longevity change due to risk factor interventions phased in over 20 to 40 years; median ages and 95% population bounds.

while the median age of death for death occurring above age 30 increased to 101.8 years for females and 92.3 years for males.

Further changes in the age-at-death distribution in the population aged 30 and above are expressed between 2060 and 2080. The lower 2.5% bound to the 95% age-at-death distribution is 64 for females and 60 for males. In 2060 the median age at death above age 30 has increased to 104.0 years and 100.3 years for females and males, respectively. The upper 2.5% limit to the age at death distribution has increased 3-1/2 to 4 years to 124.4 and 121 years.

Thus, between 2060 to 2080 there are modest changes in the age-at-death distribution. The range for the 95% distribution of ages at death changes relatively little. The increase in the median age of death (for all deaths above age 30) also changes little. The corresponding projections for 2080 of the age for the last 2.5% of deaths are 118 years for males and 120 years for females. This could, of course, be altered by assuming that changes in risk-factor values were programmed to occur more slowly or only to occur below, say, age 90.

Though there is a significant upward shift in the age-at-death distribution when the dynamics of the 10 variables are modified, the model preserves a high degree of variability in ages at death – the range of ages at death increases, with 2.5% of deaths occurring below age 60 to 64 and 2.5% occurring at ages 118 to 120 in 2080; 95% occur between ages 65 and 117. Thus, the model does not generate improved mortality by reducing individual differences in mortality – individual mortality differences actually increase.

One of the crucial ways in which such differences in aging and mortality affect the population is by changing the proportion that is elderly, i.e., above age 65. This has effects on entitlement programs (e.g., Social Security and Medicare in the U.S.) as well as on general social and economic factors. This is examined in Table 9.4, where we compare Census Bureau projections (Day, 1993) and projections based on a different risk-factor projection model, where risk factor means are controlled to stay at their age-30 values. Their variance in this scenario is reduced by only 50%.

Table 9.3 lists values for the Census Bureau's 1993 middle, high life expectancy and high population projections (Day, 1993). The difference in estimates is largest at ages 85+. Twenty-five percent of the Japanese population was projected (in 1982) to be age 65+ by the year 2025 – assuming life-expectancy limits several years lower (for females) than the life expectancies achieved in Japan by 1993 (Nihon University, 1982). Thus, the proportions expected to be age 65+ in the U.S. projections based on the risk-factor intervention model in Figure 9.4 are not much higher than the proportion age 65+ already projected for Japan by 2025.

Table 9.3. A comparison of projections (in millions of persons) based on control of multiple risk factors, a 2% continuing decline in mortality and two Census Bureau variants

Age	Males 1986	2010	2040	2060	2080	Females 1986	2010	2040	2060	2080	Total 1986	2010	2040	2060	2080
						Risk Factor Control[1] (20-Year Delay)									
65+	11,8	19,8	62,1	72,0	71,0	17,5	25,6	65,4	74,3	73,3	29,3	45,4	127,5	146,3	144,3
85+	0,8 (6,8)	2,3 (11,6)	25,4 (40,9)	35,3 (49,0)	36,0 (50,7)	2,1 (12,0)	4,8 (18,8)	28,5 (43,6)	37,5 (50,5)	37,9 (51,7)	2,9 (9,9)	7,1 (15,6)	53,9 (42,3)	72,8 (49,8)	73,9 (51,2)
						2% Continuing Decline in Mortality[2]									
65+			38,5					48,3					86,8		
85+			9,2 (23,9)					14,3 (29,6)					23,5 (27,1)		
						Census Bureau Highest Variant (Series 9)[3]									
65+	11,8	18,1	37,1	43,1	52,5	17,5	24,4	45,5	51,7	61,4	29,3	42,5	82,6	94,8	113,9
85+	0,8 (6,8)	2,2 (12,2)	6,6 (17,8)	10,0 (23,2)	13,9 (26,5)	2,1 (12,0)	4,9 (20,1)	11,2 (24,6)	15,7 (30,4)	20,0 (32,6)	2,9 (9,9)	7,2 (16,9)	17,9 (21,7)	25,6 (27,0)	33,9 (29,8)
						Census Bureau Low Mortality (Series 5; Middle Fertility/Immigration Assumption)[3]									
65+			N.A.					N.A.			29,3	42,3	80,1	N.A.	93
85+			N.A.					N.A.			2,9 (9,9)	7,2 (17,0)	17,7 (22,1)	N.A.	30,6 (32,9)

Source: Duke University, Center for Demographic Studies[1]; Guralnick, 1988[2]; Spencer, 1989[3].

Figure in parentheses are percentage of persons over age 65 that is age 85+.

9.4. Summary

We examined the effects of the mixing of multiple cohort dynamics and mortality structure on a national population health-state distribution, and its age-at-death distribution. The results show the dramatic effect of mixing cohorts to represent changes in aging in an aggregate national population. The magnitude of between-cohort differences in health and survival assumed in the above projections is not much greater than the cohort differences observed for male cohorts from 1825 to 1844 (Civil War veteran) and those from 1890 to 1920 (roughly WWII veteran). This suggests that unbiased estimates of individual aging dynamics must be made from longitudinal studies of individuals in defined birth cohorts. This also suggests, however, that the projection of population distributions must reflect a very complex, and changing mix of the traits of specific birth cohorts. Thus, there is a considerable difference between the problems of estimating the parameters of human aging and mortality – and of knowing what those parameters will mean for public health policy and the aggregate need for health services over time.

X. Discussion

10.1. Aging as a dynamic adaptive process

The purpose of this monograph has been to elucidate recent trends, findings and innovations in population studies of human mortality and aging. These investigations were motivated by the desire to better understand i) the regularities of survival processes among adults – especially at extremely late ages, where empirical data is currently limited (e.g., for ages 95 to 120); ii) the biological mechanisms which shape the age patterns of mortality observed in demographic and epidemiological studies; iii) the effects of an individual's health state (susceptibility to diseases and death; or physical frailty) on changes in late-age survival; iv) the use of models to predict survival outcomes which employ biological knowledge and theory and which can be combined with new data (e.g., data from longitudinal studies of aging) to improve certain parameter estimates; v) the assumptions traditionally used in demographic studies (e.g., assumptions about there being an identical chance of survival for all individuals in the population, independence of the life spans of individuals, independence of observed and omitted covariates, etc.); vi) dynamic and adaptive aspects of individual susceptibility to diseases and death in survival models.

These investigations are possible because of recent improvements in vital statistics, additional information about physiological and biological changes in individual organisms with age being collected in the longitudinal studies of aging and survival, advances in epidemiology of aging and etiology of chronic degenerative diseases, as well as the recent results of molecular epidemiological and experimental studies which help clarify the role of genes and the environment in aging processes.

In addition, we examined several approaches to studying genetic factors, as well as the dynamics of physiological and biological characteristics that may affect human morbidity and mortality at late ages. These approaches allowed us to develop mathematical models and statistical methods to evaluate the contribution of these characteristics to morbidity, disability and mortality. We showed how survival data on related individuals may be used to evaluate genetic contributions to the variability of individual susceptibility to disease and death in human populations. We also described how evolutionary forces might have produced the genetic determinants of the types of chronic diseases that dominate at ages 85+ (e.g., congestive heart failure, multiple myeloma, prostate cancer, Alzheimer's disease). After all, these, even more than the "standard" chronic diseases (e.g., diabetes mellitus; stroke), are unlikely to have been directly shaped by genotypic selection before the 20th century. A genetically related disease like amyloid restrictive cardiomyopathy (which is prevalent at ages 90 to 99) could not have been selected against in the 19th century, since relatively few members of the population made it past age 90. The spectrum of genetically related diseases observed recently among survivors to old age may depend on how improvements in the mortality rate occurred. Individual health-state dynamics may influence the genetic potential for such late age diseases. Finally, we reviewed selected aspects of aging dynamics and provided some insights on how these aspects may be related to each other.

10.2. The biology and epidemiology of human aging processes

The decline of human mortality observed in most developed countries of the world after WWII has made it mandatory to extend the age range of demographic research on aging and mortality (30-85 years) far beyond age 85 – ages for which the Gompertz-Makeham approximations of the age-dependence of the mortality rate are no longer appropriate. Special efforts are required to improve the quality of mortality data for the oldest old – and to have adequate samples to evaluate the shape of the mortality curve at very late ages (95+). In contrast to traditional demographic approaches, the use of biologically motivated statistical methods is unavoidable when studying mortality at such late ages.

The nature and regularities of the aging process continue to be the subject of intensive study in biology, epidemiology, gerontology and other research disciplines. We must admit, however, that despite numerous earlier efforts to find a biological justification for the Gompertz-Makeham mortality curve over the traditional age-interval (30 to 85 years) of adult mortality and aging and later attempts to explain changes in survival chances over the whole age interval (up to age 115 or so), large gaps between demographic and biological studies remained. Insights provided by evolutionary theories of aging might help to establish a closer connection between two approaches.

The desire to find the biological basis of the observed age-specific chances of survival over the entire human life span requires new models of mortality. Many models exploit the notion of individual susceptibility to disease and death. This notion is often described in terms of unobserved random effects, hidden frailty, liability, or omitted variables. It is also widely used in analyses of human morbidity, mortality, and aging. The introduction of this intermediate variable might improve many aspects of population studies of aging. So modified, demographic methods and ideas can contribute to the evaluation of biological regularities of aging. Likewise, biological findings about aging processes may be used for better evaluation and prediction of demographic characteristics.

The current trend in the demography of aging is to use more information from other scientific fields and to explore novel sources of longitudinal data. This, however, generates novel analytic problems for researchers. For example, data from the National Long Term Care Survey (NLTCS) or from the Duke Longitudinal Study of Aging (DLSA) involve many non-traditional (for demography) measures of individual health and changes therein with age. These may require new methods and approaches for their analysis. These new data have to be combined with the knowledge accumulated in biology, physiology, epidemiology and other disciplines about regularities of human aging, in order to make this process at least partly controllable – or to make survival predictions more accurate.

The importance of the effects of multiple genes on the aging process must also be recognized. It is often assumed that susceptibility to disease and death (frailty) has, in part, a genetic origin. To study the specific roles of genes and environment in aging some demographic procedures must be revised extensively. The assumption that individual survival outcomes are independent does not apply when analyzing biologically related individuals. Population-based studies of aging and mortality benefit greatly from analyses of data on related individuals (e.g., twins). Many methods for analyzing such studies already exist. The use of multivariate survival models which explore the concepts of correlated individual susceptibility to diseases and death (i.e. correlated frailty) allows the analyst to address genetic questions in studying longevity (Yashin et al., 1996).

Some standard biostatistical assumptions are violated when studying questions about the effects of genotype. For example, the assumption of independence between observed covariates and unobserved random effects (hidden frailty) employed in proportional hazard models is often unrealistic when genetic factors, only partly represented by frailty, influence the dynamics of covariates. These genetic factors provide motivation for further development of survival analysis in biostatistics and related disciplines.

Biological studies of aging show that characteristics of individual susceptibility to diseases and death are likely to change with age. To test hypotheses about regularities of such changes one needs a model of changing biological susceptibility (frailty, risk factors, health status). These changes may represent the age dynamics of genetic expression, changes in physiological functions with age, or the dynamics of environmental conditions and changes (in risk of exposure) with age. A review of such biological effects as hormesis suggests that the quadratic hazard model of human mortality and aging seems to be biologically appropriate for the description of dynamic changes in both observed and unobserved influential factors.

Quadratic hazard models satisfy several other important requirements. They can describe the dependence between observed and latent covariates. They may describe the correlation of outcomes across persons, which makes this model appropriate for analyzing survival data on families (i.e., pedigree data). They may describe the influence of gene-environment interactions and their correlation with the chances of survival. They allows for the analysis of demographically non-standard data sets such as the National Long Term Care Survey data (from the years 1982, 1984, 1989, and 1994) and the data on Longitudinal Studies of Aging and it permits the efficient integration of such data into more traditional demographic mortality (time to death) data by developing models of longitudinal data with informative censoring. They makes parameter estimation problems in such models computationally tractable. The results of data analyses showed the relevance of such approaches for population-based studies of aging.

10.3. The contribution of genes and the environment to the aging process

The role of genes and of the environment and the effect of gene-environment interactions in the aging process are still not well understood. In demographic and epidemiological analyses the contribution of environmental changes has been emphasized. Fogel's (1994) study of chronic diseases implies that much of the change in chronic diseases over the 75 years from 1910 to 1985 is due to early nutritional effects on maternal and fetal health and on early growth patterns reflected in changes in both stature and BMI. Thus, these changes may not reflect genetic changes in human aging.

On the other hand, a systematic evaluation of human physiology and chronic disease is required if we are to understand the rapid changes in health since 1950. These changes have led to biomedical strategies which can manipulate the human genotype as it currently exists to improve health and to increase the life span at late ages. For example, the genetic potential of the immune system is now being exploited by various immunization strategies to alter, in a fundamental way, the susceptibility of humans to a wide range of infectious disease processes. In the U.S., for instance, no endogenous case of polio has been documented since 1979 – implying that immunization has rendered the U.S. population nearly impervious to the polio virus.

We may expect that the genotype will be expressed differently in the near future. That is, as the life expectancy of the population changes, the traits of what we call "aging" are better exposed and described. For example, heart disease was once viewed as a natural concomitant of human aging. Now we know that the nature of heart disease changes in dramatic ways over age. Heart disease in early middle age may strongly implicate neuroendocrine factors and socio-psychological stress in its pathophysiology. Heart disease in late middle age may be dominated by atherosclerotic changes in cardiac and cerebrovascular circulation. Heart disease in the late 70s and 80s reflects the accumulation of small trauma and insults (e.g., chronic hypertension, mild atherosclerosis) to the myocardium, which is expressed in LVH and congestive heart failure. Recently, the role of amyloid protein in restrictive cardio-myopathies for persons aged 90+ was linked to genetic factors not usually expressed until age 80+. Chemotherapeutic regimes to treat amyloid pathologies have only been recently developed and the alert for increased clinical awareness of these very late-age pathologies is also very recent (Jacobson et al., 1997; Benson, 1997). Analogous conditions exist for the types and degrees of aggressiveness of neoplastic disorders dominant at later ages.

The changing traits associated with aging must be constantly evaluated both for changes due to the direct influence of environmental factors and for changes in the expression of human genes resulting from changes in environmental factors. The future of aging studies depends on the ability of researchers to link and systematize the results obtained in different research areas. Statistical models which allow for the combination of accumulated knowledge and theory with new data may serve as a tool for realizing this idea.

References

Aalen O: On phase-type distributions in survival analysis. *The Scandinavian Journal of Statistics* 22(4):447-464, 1995.

Abkowitz JL, Catlin SN and Guttorp P: Evidence that hematopoiesis may be a stochastic process in vivo. *Nature Medicine* 2(2):190-197, 1996.

Abrams PA and Ludvig D: Optimality Theory, Gompertz Law and the Disposable Soma Theory of Senescence. *Evolution* 49:982-985, 1995.

Adlercreutz H, Honjo J, Higashi A, Fotsis T, Hamalainen E, Hasegawa T and Okada H: Urinary excretion of lignans and isoflavonoid phytoestrogens in Japanese men and women consuming a traditional Japanese diet. *American Journal of Clinical Nutrition* 54:1093-1100, 1991.

Ainsleigh HG: Beneficial effects of sun exposure on cancer mortality. *Preventive Medicine* 22:132-140, 1993.

Andersen A, Glattre E, and Johansen BV: Incidence of cancer among lighthouse keepers exposed to asbestos in drinking water. *American Journal of Epidemiology* 138(9):682-687, 1993.

Anderson TW: *An Introduction to Multivariate Statistical Analysis.* John Wiley & Sons, New York, 1958.

Anderson TJ, Meredith IT, Yeung AC, Frei B, Selwyn AP, and Ganz P: The effect of cholesterol-lowering and antioxidant therapy on endothelium-dependent coronary vasomotion. *New England Journal of Medicine* 332(8):488-493, 1995.

Antiplatelet Trialists Collaboration: Collaborative overview of randomized trials of antiplatelet therapy– I: Prevention of death, myocardial infarction, and stroke by prolonged antiplatelet therapy in various categories of patients. *British Medical Journal* 308:81-106, 1994.

Antonovsky A: Social class and the major cardiovascular diseases. *Journal of Chronic Disease* 21: 65-106, 1968.

Arjas E: Survival models and Martingale dynamics. *Scandinavian Journal of Statistics* 16:177-225, 1989.

Armitage P and Doll R: Stochastic models for carcinogenesis. In *Proceedings of the Fourth Berkeley Symposium on Mathematical Statistics and Probability* (Neyman J, Ed.). University of California Press, pp. 19-38, 1961.

Barker DJP and Martyn CN: The maternal and fetal origins of cardiovascular disease. *Journal of Epidemiology and Community Health* 46:8-11, 1992.

Barker DJP, Meade TW, Fall CHD, Lee A, Osmond C, Phipps K, and Stirling T:

Relation of fetal and infant growth to plasma fibrinogen and factor VII concentrations in adult life. *British Medical Journal* 304:148-52, 1992.

Bayo FR and Faber JF: Mortality rates around age one hundred. *Transactions of the Society of Actuaries* 35:37-59, 1985.

Beard RE: Some experiments in the use of the incomplete gamma function for the approximate calculation of actuarial functions. Centenary assembly of the Institute of Actuaries, 1950.

Beard RE: A theory of mortality based on actuarial, biological and medical considerations. International Population Conference (1961), New York, 1963.

Benditt EP and Benditt JM: Evidence for monoclonal origin of human atherosclerotic plaques. *USA*, pp. 1753-1756, 1973.

Benson MD: Aging, amyloid, and cardiomyopathy. *New England Journal of Medicine* 336(7), 502-504, 1997.

Benzuly KH, Padgett RC, Kaul S, Piegors DJ, Armstrong ML, and Heistad DD: Functional improvement precedes structural regression of atherosclerosis. *Circulation* 89(4):1810-1818, 1994.

Berdanier CD and Hargrove JL: *Nutrition and Gene Expression*. Boca Raton: CRC Press, 1993.

Beregi E, Regius O, and Rajczy K: Comparative study of the morphological changes in lymphocytes of elderly individuals and centenarians. *Age and Ageing* 20:55-59, 1991.

Bourgeois-Pichat J: Future outlook for mortality declines in the world. *Population Bulletin of the United Nations* 11:12-41, 1978.

Boushey CJ, Beresford SAA, Omenn GS, and Motulsky AG: A quantitive assessment of plasma homocysteine as a risk factor for vascular disease. *Journal of the American Medical Association* 274(13), 1049-1057, 1995.

Bowden M, Crawford J, Cohen H, and Noyama O: A comparative study of monoclonal gammopathies and immunoglobulin levels in japanese and United States elderly. *Journal of The American Geriatrics Society* 41:11-14, 1993.

Brattstrom L, Israelsson B, Norring B, Bergquist V, Thorne J, Hultberg B , and Hamfelt A: Impaired homocysteine metabolism in early onset cerebral and peripheral occlusive arterial disease. *Athersclerosis* 81:51-60, 1990.

Brenner H: A birth cohort analysis of the smoking epidemic in West Germany. *Journal of Epidemiology and Community Health* 47:54-58, 1993.

Brody S: The kinetics of senescence. *Journal of General Physiology* 6:245-257, 1923.

Brooks A, Lithgow G, and Johnson T: Mortality rates in a genetically heterogeneous population of Caenorhabditis elegans. *Science* 263:668-671, 1994.

Browner WS, Pressman AR, Nevitt MC, Cauley JA, and Cummings SR: Association between low bone density and stroke in elderly women: The Study of osteoporotic fractures. *Stroke* 24(7):940-946, 1993.

Buja LM and Willerson JT: Role of inflammation in coronary plaque disruption. *Circulation* 89:503-505, 1994.

Bush DE and Finucane TE: Permanent cardiac pacemakers in the elderly. *Journal of the American Geriatrics Society* 42:326-334, 1994.

Calow P: Homeostasis and fitness. *American Naturalist* 120:416-419, 1982.

Cameron R and Martin W: The Wiener measure of Hilbert neighborhoods in the space of real continuous functions. *Journal of Mathematical Physics* 23:195-209, 1944.

Capron L: Chlamydia in coronary plaques -- hidden culprit or harmless hobo? *Nature Medicine* 2(8), 856-857, 1996.

Carey JR, Liedo P, Orozco D, and Vaupel JW: Slowing of mortality rates at older ages in large medfly cohorts. *Science* 258:457-460, 1992.

Carlquist JF and Anderson JL: HLA, autoimmunity, and rheumatic heart disease: Apparent or real association. *Circulation* 87(6):2060-2062, 1993.

Carson DA and Ribeiro JM: Apoptosis and disease. *The Lancet* 341:1251-1254, 1993.

Casper M, Wing S, Strogatz D, Davis CE, and Tyroler HA: Antihypertensive treatment and US trends in stroke mortality, 1962 to 1980. *American Journal of Public Health* 82(12):1600-1606, 1992.

Cerami A: Hypothesis: Glucose as a mediator of aging. *Journal of the American Geriatrics Society* 33:626-634, 1985.

Charlesworth B: Optimization Models, Quantitative genetics and Mutation. *Evolution* 44: 520-538, 1990.

Clayton DG: A model for association in bivariate life tables and its application in Epidemiological studies of familial tendency in chronic disease incidence. *Biometrika* 65(1):141-51, 1978.

Clayton DG and Cuzick J: Multivariate generalizations of the proportional hazards model (with Discussion). *J Roy Stat Soc* 148 (Series A):82-117, 1985.

Coale AJ and Rives N: A statistical reconstruction of the black poulation of the United States 1880-1970. *Population Index* 39:3-36, 1973.

Colantonio A, Kasl SV, and Ostfeld AM: Level of function predicts first stroke in the elderly. *Stroke* 23(9):1355-1357, 1992.

Cole P and Rodu B: Declining cancer mortality in the United States. *Cancer* 78(10):2045-2048, 1996.

Comfort A: *The Biology of Senescence*. Rinehart and Co., Inc., 1956.

Condran GA, Himes CL, and Preston SH: Old-age mortality patterns in low-mortality countries: An evaluation of population and death data at advanced ages, 1950 to the present. *Population Bulletin of the United Nations* 30:23-60, 1991.

Corder EH, Guess HA, Hulka BS, Friedman GD, Sadler M, Vollmer RT, Lobaugh B, Drezner MK, Vogelman JH, and Orentreich N: Vitamin D and prostate cancer: a prediagnostic study with stored sera. *Cancer Epidemiology and Biomarkers Prevention* 2(5):467-472, 1993.

Cortopassi G and Liu Y: Genotypic selection of mitochondrial and oncogenic mutations in human tissue suggests mechanisms of age-related pathophysiology. *Mutat Res* 338:151-159, 1995.

Curtsinger JW, Fukui HH, Townsend DR, and Vaupel JW: Demography of genotypes: Failure of the limited-lifespan paradigm in Drosophila Melanogaster. *Science* 258:461-463, 1992.

Cutler RG and Semsei I: Development, cancer and aging: Possible common mechanisms of action and regulation. *Journal of Gerontology: Biological Sciences* 44(6):25-34, 1989.

Davis DL, Dinse GE, and Hoel DG: Decreasing cardiovascular disease and increasing cancer among whites in the United States from 1973 through 1987: Good news and bad news. *Journal of the American Medical Association* 271(6):431-437, 1994.

Dawkins R: *The Selfish Genes*. Oxford University Press: Oxford, 1990.

Day JC: Population projections of the United States, by Age, Sex, Race, and Hispanic origin: 1993 to 2050. Series P25-1104. U.S. Government Printing Office: 1993.

DeFries JC and Fulker DW: Multiple regression analysis of twin data: Etiology of deviant scores versus individual differences. *Acta Geneticae Medicae et Gemellologiae* 37:205-16, 1988.

Diggle P and Kenward MG: Informative drop-out in longitudinal data analysis. *Applied Statistics* 43(1):49-93, 1994.

Dubey SD: Some percentile estimators of weibull parameters. *Technometrics* 9:119-129, 1967.

Dubos R: *Man Adapting*. Yale University Press: New Haven and London, 1965.

Dudman NPB, Wang WJ, Lynch JF, and Lundberg P: Disordered methionine homocysteine metabolism in premature vascular disease: Its occurence, cofactor therapy, and ezymology. *Arteriosclerosis and Thrombosis* 13(9):1253-1260, 1993.

Dzau VJ, Gibbons GH, Cooke JP, and Omoigui N: Vascular biology and medicine in the 1990s: Scope, concepts, potentials, and perspectives. *Circulation* 87(3):705-719, 1993.

Eastell R, Yergery A, Vieira N, Cedel S, Kumar R, and Riggs B: Interrelationship among vitamin D metabolism, true calcium absorption, parathyroid function, and age in women: evidence of an age-related intestinal resistance to 1, 25 dihydroxyvitamin A action. *Journal of Bone Mineral Research* 6:125, 1991.

Economos AC: Systems analysis of mechanisms relating to life-span determination. Technical Report for NASA. Technology Incorporated, Houston, 1977.

Economos AC: A non-Gompertzian paradigm for mortality kinetics of metazoan animals and failure kinetics of manufactured products. *Age* 2:74-76, 1979a.

Economos AC: Systems analysis of physiological adaptation to weightlessness and dependence of adaptation capacity on biological age. Technical Report for NASA. Technology Incorporated, Houston, 1979b.

Economos AC: Rate of aging, rate of dying, and the mechanisms of mortality. *Archives of Gerontological Geriatrics* 1:3-27, 1982.

Economos AC and Miquel J: Analysis of population mortality kinetics with application to the longevity follow-up of the Navy's '1000 Aviators'. *Aviat. Space Environ. Med.* 50:697-701, 1979.

Eisman JA, Martin TJ, MacIntyre I, and Mosely JM: 1.25 Dihydroxy vitamin D receptor in breast cancer cells. *The Lancet* 2:1335 1336, 1979.

Elayda MAA, Hall RJ, Reul RM, Alonzo DM, Gillette N, Reul GJ, and Cooley DA: Aortic valve replacement in patients 80 years and older: Operative risks and long-term results. *Circulation* 88 (Part 2):11-16, 1993.

Elbers C and Ridder G: True and spurious duration dependence: The identifiability of the proportional hazards model. *Rev Econ Stud* 49:403-409, 1982.

Fagan SC, Morganstern LB, Petitta A, Ward RE, Tilley BC, Marler JR, Levine SR, Broderick JP, Kwiatkowski TG, Frankel M, Brott TG, and Walker MD: Cost-effectiveness of tissue plasminogen activator for acute ischemic stroke. *Neurology* 50:883-890, 1998.

Failla G: The aging process and cancerogenesis. *Annals of the New York Academy of Science* 71:1124-1140, 1958.

Falconer J, Hollenbeck CB, Jeppesen J, Chen IY-D, and Reaven GM: Insulin resistance and cigarette smoking. *The Lancet* 339:1128-1130, 1992.

Fiatarone MA, O'Neill EF, Doyle N, Clements KM, Roberts SB, Kehayias JJ, Lipsitz LA, and Evans WJ: The Boston FICSIT study: The effects of resistance training and nutritional supplementation on physical frailty in the oldest old. *Journal of the American Geriatrics Society* 41(3):333-337, 1993.

Fiatarone MA, O'Neill EF, Ryan ND, Clements KM, Solares GR, Nelson ME, Roberts SB, Kehayias JJ, Lipsitz LA, and Evans WJ: Exercise training and nutritional supplementation for physical frailty in very elderly people. *New England Journal of Medicine* 330(25):1769-1775, 1994.

Finch CE: *Longevity, Senescence, and the Genome.* University of Chicago Press: Chicago, 1990.

Finch CE and Pike MC: Maximum life span predictions from the Gompertz mortality model. *Journal of Gerontology: Biological Sciences* 51A(3):B183-194, 1996.

Flatz G: Genetics of lactose digestion in humans. *Advances in Human Genetics* 16:1-77, 1987.

Fleming JF, Walton JK, Dubitsky R, and Bensch KG: Aging results in an unusual expression of Drosophila heat shock proteins. *Proceedings National Academy of Science, USA* 85:4099-4103, 1988.

Fogel RW: Economic growth, population theory, and physiology: The bearing of long-term processes on the making of economic policy. *American Economic Review* 84(3):369-395, 1994.

Folkman J: Angiogenesis in cancer, vascular, rheumatoid and other disease. *Nature Medicine* 1(1), 27-31, 1995.

Forman D: Helicobacter pylori infection: A novel risk factor in the etiology of gastric cancer. *Journal of the National Cancer Institute* 83(23):1702-1703, 1991.

Frankel S, Elwood P, Sweetnam P, Yarnell J, and Smith GD: Birthweight, body-mass index in middle age, and incident coronary heart disease. *The Lancet* 348, 1478-1480, 1996.

Franken DG, Vreugdenhil A, Boers GHJ, Verrips A, Blom HJ, and Novakova IRO: Familial cerebrovascular accidents due to concomitant hyperhomocysteinemia and protein C deficiency type 1. *Stroke* 24(10):1599-1600, 1993.

Freedman AR, Zhu H, Levine JD, Kalams S, and Scadden DT: Generation of human T lymphocytes from bone marrow CD34+ cells in vitro. *Nature Medicine* 2(1), 46-51, 1996.

Friedman DM, Lazarus HM, and Fierman AH: Acute myocardial infarction in pediatric systemic lupus erythematosus. *Journal of Pediatrics* 117(2), 263-266, 1990.

Fries JF: The compression of morbidity: Near or far? *Milbank Quarterly* 67(2), 208-232, 1989.

Gavrilov LA and Gavrilov NS. *The Biology of Life Span: A Quantitative Approach.* New York: Harwood Academic Publishers, 1991.

Ghali JK, Cooper R, and Ford E: Trends in hospitalization rates for heart failure in the United States, 1973-1986. *Archives of Internal Medicine* 150:769-776, 1990.

Gilbert EM, Sandoval A, Larrabee P, Renlund DG, O'Connell JB, and Bristow MR: Lisinopril lowers cardiac adrenergic drive and increases b-receptor density in the failing heart. *Circulation* 88(2):472-480, 1993.

Gill RD: Discussion of the paper by D. Clayton and J. Cuzick. *J Roy Statist Soc Ser A* 148:108-9, 1985.

Gonzalez F and Nebert D: Evolution of the P450 gene superfamily: animal-plant 'welfare' molecular drive, and human genetic differences in drug oxidation. *Trends in Genetics* 6:182-186, 1990.

Gottesman MM: Report of a meeting: Molecular basis of cancer therapy. *J Natl Cancer Inst* 86:1277-1285, 1994.

Gottlieb S, Goldbourt U, Boyko V, Barbash G, Mandelzweig L, Reicher-Reiss H, Stern S, and Behar S: Improved outcome of elderly patients with acute myocardial infarction from 1981-1983 to 1992-1994 in Israel. *Circulation* 95, 342-350, 1997.

Gralnick HR: von Willebrand factor, integrins, and platelets: Their role in cancer. *Journal of Laboratory and Clinical Medicine* 119:444-447, 1992.

Grayston JT: Chlamydia in atherosclerosis. *Circulation* 87(4):1408-1409, 1993.

Greenspan EM: The cure of breast cancer by combination chemotherapy. *Cancer Investigation* 14(Supp. 1), 70-73, 1996.

Hales CN, Bartker DJP, Clark PMS, Cox LJ, Fall C, Osmond C, and Winter PD: Fetal and infant growth impaired glucose tolerances at age 64. *British Medical Journal* 303:1019-1022, 1991.

Hambright Z: Comparison of information on death certificates and matching 1960 census records: Age, marital status, race, nativity and country of origin. *Demography* 6(4):413-423, 1969.

Hamilton WD: The moulding of senescence by natural selection. *Journal of Theoretical Biology* 12:12-45, 1966.

Henney AM, Wakeley PR, Davies MJ, Foster K, Hembry T, Murphy G, and Humphries S: Localization of stromelysin gene expression in atherosclerotic plaques by in situ hybridization. *Proceedings National Academy of Science USA* 88:8154-8158, 1991.

Hilme E, Hansson L, Sandberg L, Söderström T, and Herlitz H: Abnormal immune function in malignant hypertension. *Journal of Hypertension* 11:989-994, 1993.

Hoffmeister H, Mensink, GBM, and Stolzenberg H: National trends in risk factors for cardiovascular disease in Germany. *Preventive Medicine* 23:197-205, 1994.

Holcombe C, Omotara BA, Eldridge J, and Jones DM: Helicobacter pylori, the most common bacterial infection in Africa: A random serological study. *American Journal of Gastroenterology* 87:28-30, 1992.

Holman RL, McGill HC, Strong JP, and Geer JC: The natural history of atherosclerosis: The early aortic lesions as seen in New Orleans in the middle of the 20th century. *American Journal of Pathology* 34:209-235, 1958.

Hosking MP, Warner MA, Lodbell CM, Offord KP, and Melton LJ: Outcomes of surgery in patients 90 years of age and older. *Journal of the American Medical Association* 261:1909-1915, 1989.

Hosking SW, Ling TKW, Yung MY, Cheng A, Chung SCS, Leung JWC, et al.: Randomized controlled trial of short term treatment of eradicate Helicobacter pylori in patients with duodenal ulcer. *British Medical Journal* 305:502-504, 1992.

Hosking SW, Ling TKW, Chung SCS, Yung MY, Cheng AFB, Sung JJY, and Li AKC: Duodenal ulcer healing by eradication of helicobacter pylori without anti-acid treatment: Randomized controlled trial. *The Lancet* 343: 508-510, 1994.

Hougaard P: A class of multivariate failure time distributions. *Biometrika* 73(3):671-78, 1986.

Hougaard P: Modelling multivariate survival. *Scand J Statist* 14:291-304, 1987.

Hughes GRV: The antiphospholipid syndrome: Ten years on. *The Lancet* 342:341-344, 1993.

Iachine IA: Parameter estimation in the bivariate correlated frailty model with observed covariates via EM-algorithm. Population Studies of Aging No. 16 (research report). Denmark: Odense University, pp. 1-21, July 1995a.

Ichihara A, Suzuki H, and Saruta T: Effects of magnesium on the renin-angiotensin-aldosterone system in human subjects. *Journal of Laboratory and Clinical Medicine* 122(4):432-440, 1993.

Ikegami N and Campbell JC: Medical care in Japan. *New England Journal of Medicine* 333(19):1295-1299, 1995.

Jacobson DR, Pastore RD, Yaghoubian R, Kane I, Gallo G, Buck FS, and Buxbaum JN: Variant-sequence transthyretin (isoleucine 122) in late-onset cardiac amyloidosis in black Americans. *New England Journal of Medicine* 336(7):466-473, 1997.

Jeune, B: Centenarians - tail or tale? (in Danish) *Gerontologi og Samfund* 10(1):4-6, 1994.

Joffe BI, Panz VR, Wing JR, Raal FJ, and Seftel HC: Pathogenesis of non-insulin-dependent diabetes mellitus in the black population of southern Africa. *The Lancet* 340:460-462, 1992.

Johnson CL, Rifkind BM, Sempos CT, Carroll MD, Bachorik PS, Briefel RR, Gordon DJ, Burt VL, Brown CD, Lippel K, and Cleeman JI: Declining serum total cholesterol levels among US adults: The National health and nutrition examination surveys. *Journal of the American Medical Association* 269(23):3002-3008, 1993.

Jones HB: A special consideration of the aging process, disease and life expectancy. *Advanced Biological Medical Physics* 4:281-337, 1956.

Joossens J, Hill M, Elliott P, Stamler R, Stamler J, Lesaffre E, et al.: Dietary salt, nitrate, and stomach cancer mortality in 24 countries. *International Journal of Epidemiology* 25(3):494-504, 1996.

Kannisto V: Development of Oldest-Old Mortality, 1950-1990: Evidence from 28 Developed Countries. Odense Monograph on Population Aging, 1. Odense University Press, Odense, Denmark, 1994.

Kannisto V: The Advancing Frontier of Survival: Life Tables for Old Age. Odense Monograph on Population Aging, 3. Odense University Press, Odense, Denmark, 1996.

Kaplan EL: Global assessment of rheumatic fever and rheumatic heart disease at the close of the century. Influences and dynamics of populations and pathogens: A failure to realize prevention? *Circulation* 88(4):1964-1972, 1993.

Kaplan GA and Keil JE: Socioeconomic factors and cardiovascular disease: A review of the literature. *Circulation* 88(4):1973-1998, 1993.

Kasch FW, Boyer JL, Van Camp SP, Verity LS, and Wallace JP: Effect of exercise on cardiovascular ageing. *Age and Ageing* 22:5-10, 1993.

Kautsky JE: Woman of History. NC Catholic, March 12, p. 13, 1995.

Keene GS: Mortality and morbidity after hip fractures. *British Medical Journal* 307:1248-1250, 1993.

Kendall MG and Stuart A: *The Advanced Theory of Statistics, Vol .1, Distribution Theory*. New York: Hafner, 1969.

Kerr JF, Wyllie AH, and Currie AR: Apoptosis: A basic biological phenomenon with wide-ranging implications in tissue kinetics. *British Journal of Cancer* 26:239-257, 1972.

Kestenbaum Bert: A Description of the extreme aged population based on improved Medicare enrollment data. *Demography* 29(4):565-581, 1992.

Kim J, Steck P, et al.: Suppression by retinoic acid of epidermal growth factor receptor autophosphorylation and glycosylation in cultured human head and neck squamous carcinoma cells. *Journal of the National Cancer Institute Monographs* 13:101-110, 1992.

Kirkwood TBL: The disposable soma theory of aging. In *Genetic Effects of Aging II*. Telford Press: Caldwell, 9-19, 1990.

Kitagawa E and Hauser P: Differential Mortality in the United States: A Study in Socio-Economic Epidemiology. In APHA Monograph Series; Harvard University Press: Boston, 1973.

Klag MJ, Whelton PK, and Seidler AJ: Decline in US stroke mortality: Demographic trends and anti-hypertensive treatment. *Stroke* 20(1):14-21, 1989.

Klein JP: Semiparametric estimation of random effects using the Cox model based on the EM-algorithm. *Biometrics* 48:795-806, 1992.

Knudson AJ: Mutation and cancer: Statistical study of retinoblastoma. *Proceedings of the National Academy of Sciences, USA* 68:820-823, 1971.

Knudson AG: Hereditary cancer: Two hits revisited. *Journal of Cancer Research and Clinical Oncology* 122(3), 135-140, 1996.

Ko W, Gold JP, Lazzaro R, Zelano JA, Lang S, Isom OW, and Kreiger KH: Survival analysis of octogenarian patients with coronary artery disease managed by elective coronary artery bypass surgery versus conventional medical treatment. *Circulation* 86(Suppl. II):II-191-II-197, 1992.

Kokoglu E, Karaarslan I, Karaarslan HM, and Baloglu H: Elevated serum Lp(a) levels in the early and advanced stages of breast cancer. *Cancer, Biochemistry and Biophysics* 14:133-136, 1996.

Kramer J, Fulop T, Rajczy K, Tuan NA, and Fust G: A marked drop in the incidence of the null allele of the B gene of the fourth component of complement (C4B*Q0) in elderly subjects: C4B*Q0 as a probable negative selection factor for survival. *Human Genetics* 86(6):595-598, 1991.

Kramer J, Rajczy K, Hegyi L, Fulop T, Mohacsi A, Mezei Z, Keltai M, Blasko G, Ferenczy E, Anh-Tuan N, and Fust G: C4B*Q0 allotype as risk factor for myocardial infarction. *British Medical Journal* 309:313-314, 1994.

Kusaka Y, Kondou H, and Morimoto K: Healthy lifestyles are associated with higher natural killer cell activity. *Preventive Medicine* 21:602-615, 1992.

LaBuda MC, DeFries JC, and Fulker DW. Multiple regression analysis of twin data obtained from selected samples. *Genetic Epidemiology* 425-33, 1986.

Lakatta EG: Health, Disease, and Cardiovascular aging. In: *America's Aging: Health in An Older Society*. Washington, DC: National Academy Press pp. 73-104, 1985.

Lander ES and Schork NJ: Genetic dissection of complex traits. *Science* 265:2037-48, 1994.

Lang CA, Naryshkin S, Schneider DL, Mills BJ, and Lindeman RD: Low blood glutathione levels in healthy aging adults. *Journal of Laboratory and Clinical Medicine* 120(5):720-725, 1992.

Langreth R: Women having fewer children may live longer. *The Wall Street Journal*. Section B, December 24, 1998.

Lanska DJ and Mi X: Decline in US stroke mortality in the era before antihypertensive therapy. *Stroke* 24(9):1382-1388, 1993.

Law MR, Wald NJ, Wu T, Hackshaw A, and Bailey A: Systematic under-estimation of association between serum cholesterol concentration and ischaemic heart disease in observational studies: Data from the BUPA study. *British Medical Journal* 308:363-366, 1994a.

Law MR, Wald NJ, and Thompson SG: By how much and how quickly does reduction in serum cholesterol concentration lower risk of ischaemic heart disease? *British Medical Journal* 308:367-373, 1994b.

Le Bras H: Lois de Mortalité et Age Limité. *Population* 31:655-692, 1976.

Lew EA and Garfinkel L: Mortality at ages 75 and older in the cancer prevention study. (CPSI). *Cancer Journal for Clinicians* 40(4):210-224, 1990.

Lian JB and Stein GS: Vitamin D regulation of osteoblast growth and differentiation. Chapter 8 in *Nutrition and Gene Expression* (Berdanier CD, Hargrove JL, Eds.). CRC Press: Boca Raton, pp. 391-430, 1993.

Linnanmäki E, Leinonen M, Mattila K, Nieminen MS, Valtonen V, and Saikku P: Chlamydia Pneumoniae– specific circulating immune complexes in patients with chronic coronary heart disease. *Circulation* 87(4):1130-1134, 1993.

Lipster R and Shiryayev A: *Statistics of Random Processes*. Springer-Verlag: New York, 1977.

Louhija J, Miettinen HE, Kontula K, Tikkanen MJ, Miettinen TA, and Tilvis RS: Aging and genetic variation of plasma apolipoproteins: Relative loss of the apolipoprotein E4 phenotype in centenarians. *Arteriosclerosis and Thrombosis* 14:1084-1089, 1994.

MacGregor GA and Cappuccio FP: The kidney and essential hypertension: A link to osteoporosis? *Journal of Hypertension* 11(8):781-785, 1993.

Makeham W: On the law of mortality and construction of annuity tables. *Journal of the Institute of Actuaries* 8:301, 1867.

Manton KG: The demography of aging. Chapter 8 in *Principles and Practice of Geriatric Medicine Third Edition* (Pathy, MSJ, Ed.), John Wiley & Sons, Ltd: England, 1996.

Manton KG: The future of old age. Chapter 3 in *Textbook of Geriatric Medicine and Gerontology*, 5E (Brockhurst JC, Tallis RC, Fillit HM, Eds.). Churchill Livingstone: London, 1998.

Manton KG: Longevity and Long-Lived Populations. In *Encyclopedia of Gerontology* (Birren JE, Ed.). Academic Press: San Diego, 1996.

Manton KG: National Long Term Care Survey (New). In *Encyclopedia of Aging* (Maddox GL, Ed.). Springer: New York, 1996.

Manton KG, Corder L, and Stallard E: Chronic disability trends in the U.S. elderly populations 1982 to 1995. *Proceedings of the National Academy of Sciences* 94:2593-2598, 1997.

Manton KG, Corder L, and Stallard E: Monitoring changes in the health of the U.S. elderly population: Correlates with biomedical research and clinical innovations. *FASEB Journal* 11(12):923-930,1997.

Manton KG and Stallard E: *Chronic Disease Modeling: Measurement and Evaluation of the Risks of Chronic Disease Processes*. Charles Griffin Ltd., London, 1988.

Manton KG and Stallard E: Demographics (1950-1987) of breast cancer in birth cohorts of older women. *Journal of Gerontology* 47 (Special Issue):32-42, 1992.

Manton KG and Stallard E: A two-disease model of female breast cancer: Mortality in 1969 among white females in the United States. *J Nat Cancer Inst* 64(1):9-16, 1980.

Manton KG and Stallard E: Heterogeneity and its effects on mortality measurement. Chapter 12 in *Methodologies for the Collection and Analysis of Mortality Data* (Vallin J, Pollard JH, Heligman L, Eds.). International Union for the Scientific Study of Population, Ordina Editions, pp. 265- 299, 1984.

Manton KG and Stallard E: Nonwhite and white age trajectories of mortality: Evidence from extinct cohort analysis, 1950 to 1992. Chapter 2 in *Minorities, Aging, and Health* (Markides K, Miranda M, Eds.). Sage Publications, 1996b.

Manton KG and Stallard E: Assessment of the quality of age reporting on U.S. death certificates for cohorts born 1860-1864 to 1890-1894 followed 1962-1990. Working manuscript, Center for Demographic Studies, Duke University, Durham, N.C., 1996.

Manton KG and Stallard E: Longevity in the U.S.: Age and sex specific evidence on life span limits from mortality patterns: 1962-1990. *Journal of Gerontology: Biological Sciences* 51A:B362-B375, 1996a.

Manton KG and Stallard E: The effects of health changes on the projections of future health costs. Submitted to *Journal of the American Medical Association*, 1997.

Manton KG, Stallard E, and Corder L: Changes in the age dependence of mortality and disability; cohort and other determinants. *Demography* 34(1):135-157, 1997.

Manton KG, Stallard E, and Liu K: Forecasts of active life expectancy: Policy and fiscal implications. *Journals of Gerontology* 48 (Special Issue):11-26, 1993.

Manton KG, Stallard E, and Singer BH: Methods for projecting the future size and health status of the U.S. elderly population. Chapter 2 in *Studies of the Economics of Aging* (Wise D, Ed.). National Bureau of Economic Research, University of Chicago Press: pp. 41-77, 1994a.

Manton KG, Stallard E, and Singer BH: Projecting the future size and health status of the U.S. elderly population. *International Journal of Forecasting* 8:433-458, 1992.

Manton KG, Stallard E, and Tolley HD: Limits to human life expectancy: Evidence, prospects, and implications. *Population and Development Review* 17(4):603-638, 1991.

Manton KG, Stallard E, and Vaupel JW: Alternative models for the heterogeneity of mortality risks among the aged. *Journal of the American Statistical Association* 81:635-644, 1986.

Manton KG, Stallard E, and Vaupel JW: Methods for comparing the mortality experience of heterogeneous populations. *Demography* 18:389-410, 1981.

Manton KG, Stallard E, Woodbury MA, and Dowd JE: Time-varying covariates in models of human mortality and aging: Multidimensional generalization of the Gompertz. *Journal of Gerontology: Biological Sciences* 49:B169-B190, 1994b.

Manton KG and Vaupel JW: Survival after the age of 80 in the United States, Sweden, France, England, and Japan. *New England Journal of Medicine* 333:1232-1235, 1995.

Manton KG, Corder LS, and Stallard E: The limits of longevity and their implications for health and mortality in developed countries. Presented at the Symposium on Health and Mortality, Brussels, Belgium, November 19-22, 1997.

Manton KG and Yashin AI: Inequalities of Life. Center for Demographic Studies, Working Paper M614, Duke University, Durham, N.C., 1998.

Marcovina SM, Albers JJ, Jacobs DR, Perkins LL, Lewis CE, Howard BV, and Savage P: Lipoprotein[a] concentrations and apolipoprotein[a] phenotypes in Caucasians and African Americans: The CARDIA study. *Arteriosclerosis and Thrombosis* 13:1037-1045, 1993.

Marenberg ME, Risch,N, Berkman LF, Floderus B, and de Faire U: Genetic susceptibility to death from coronary heart disease in a study of twins. *New England Journal of Medicine* 330(15):1041-1046, 1994.

Marriotti S, Sansoni P, Barbesino G, Caturegli P, Monti D, Cossarizza A, Giacomelli T, Passeri G, Fagiolo U, Pinchera A, and Franceschi C: Thyroid and other organ-specific autoantibodies in healthy centenarians. *The Lancet* 339:1506-1508, 1992.

Martin NG, Eaves LJ, and Heath AC. Prospects for detecting genotype X environment interactions in twins with breast cancer. *Acta Genet. Med. Gemellol* 1987; 36:5-20.

Martyn CN, Barker DJP, and Osmond C: Mothers' pelvic size, fetal growth, and death from stroke and coronary heart disease in men in the UK. *The Lancet* 348, 1264-1268, 1996.

Materson BJ and Preston RA: Angiotensin-Converting enzyme inhibitors in hypertension: A dozen years of experience. *Archives of Internal Medicine* 154:513-523, 1994.

McCord, JM: Is iron sufficiency a risk factor in ischemic heart disease? *Circulation* 83(3):1112-1113, 1991.

McCully KS: Homocysteine theory of arteriosclerosis: Development and current status. *Atherosclerosis Review* 2:157-246, 1983.

McCully KS: Homocysteine and vascular disease. *Nature Medicine* 2(4), 386-389, 1996.

McGeer PL, Schulzer M, and McGeer EG: Arthritis and anti-inflammatory agents as possible protective factors for Alzheimer's disease: A review of 17 epidemiologic studies. *Neurology* 47, 425-432, 1996.

McGue M: When assessing twin concordance rate, use the probandwise not the pairwise rate. *Schizo Bull* 1992; 18(2):1982.

McKeigue PM, Shah B, and Marmot MG: Relation of central obesity and insulin resistance with high diabetes prevalence and cardiovascular risk in South Asians. *The Lancet* 337:382-386, 1991.

McKeigue PM, Laws A, Chen YD, Marmot MG, and Reaven GM: Relation of plasma triglyceride and ApoB levels to insulin-mediated suppression of nonesterified fatty acids: Possible explanation for sex differences in lipoprotein pattern. *Arteriosclerosis and Thrombosis* 13(8):1187-1192, 1993.

Medawar PB: *An Unsolved Problem in Biology*. London: H.K. Lewis, 1952.

Medvedev ZA: An attempt at a rational classification of theories of aging. *Biological Review* 65:375-398, 1990.

Melnick JL and Schattner A: Viruses and atherosclerosis*. *Israel Journal of Medical Science* 28:463-465, 1992.

Melnick JL, Adam E, and DeBakey ME: Possible role of cytomegalovirus in atherogenesis. *Journal of the American Medical Association* 263(16), 2204-2207, 1990.

Mercer MJ and Van Nieker CH: Clinical characteristics of childhood asthma. *South African Medical Journal* 79:77-79, 1991.

Moon J, Bandy B, and Davison AJ: Hypothesis: Etiology of atherosclerosis and osteoporosis: Are imbalances in the calciferol endocrine system implicated. *Journal of the American College of Nutrition* 11(5):567-583, 1992.

Mooradian AD and Wong NC: Molecular biology of aging part I: An introduction to laboratory techniques of molecular biology. *Journal of the American Geriatrics Society* 39:717-723, 1991a.

Mooradian AD and Wong NC: Molecular biology of aging Part II: A synopsis of current research. *Journal of the American Geriatrics Society* 39:717-723, 1991b.

Moser M: An overview of the meta-analyses of the hypertension treatment trials. Commentary. *Archives of Internal Medicine* 151:1277-1279, 1991.

Mozar HN, Bal DG, and Farag SA: The natural history of atherosclerosis: An ecologic perspective. *Atherosclerosis* 82:157-164, 1990.

Mueler LD and Rose MR: Evolutionary Theory Predicts Late-Life Mortality Plateus. *Proc.Nat. Acad. Sci. USA* 93:15249-15253, 1996.

Myers LE: Survival functions induced by stochastic covariate processes. *Journal of Applied Probability* 18:523-529, 1981.

Myers GC and Manton KG: Compression of morbidity: Myth or reality? *Gerontologist* 24:346-53, 1984a.

Myers GC and Manton KG: Recent changes in the U. S. age at death distribution: Further observations. *Gerontologist* 24:572-75, 1984b.

Nab H, Hop W, Crommelin M, Kluck H, Van der Heijden L, and Coebergh J: Changes in long term prognosis for breast cancer in Dutch Cancer Registry. *British Medical Journal* 309:83-86, 1994.

National Center for Health Statistics: Health United States 1994. Public Health Service: Washington, D.C., 1995.

National Center for Health Statistics: The change in mortality trends in the United States. Public Health Service (Series 3 No. 1): Washington, D.C., 1964.

Neuts MF: Probability distribution of phase-type. In: Liber Amicorum Prof. Emeritus H. Florin, 173-206. Dept. Mathematics, Univ. Louvain, Belgium, 1975.

Niedobitek G and Young L: Epstein-Barr virus persistence and virus-associated tumors. *The Lancet* 343:333-335, 1994.

Nightingale TE, Gruber J: Helicobacter and human cancer. *Journal of the National Cancer Institute* 86(20):1505-1509, 1994.

Nihon University: Population aging in Japan: Problems and policy issues in the 21st century. In: Kuroda T, Ed. *International conference on an aging society: Strategies for the 21st century Japan*. Nihon University, Japan: Nihon University Population Research Institute, 1982.

Oakes D: Bivariate survival models induced by frailties. *J Am Stat Soc* 84:487-503, 1989.

Oakes D: Semiparametric inference in a model for association in bivariate survival data. *Biometrika* 72(2):353-61, 1986.

Okamoto Y: Health care for the elderly in Japan: Medicine and welfare in an aging society facing a crisis in long term care. *British Medical Journal* 305:403-405, 1992.

Olivotto IA, Bajdik CD, Plenderleith IH, Coppin CM, Gelmon KA, Jackson SM, Ragaz J, Wilson KS, and Worth A: Adjuvant systemic therapy and survival after breast cancer. *New England Journal of Medicine* 330(12):805-810, 1994.

Olshansky SJ, Carnes BA, and Cassal C. In search of Methuselah: Estimating the upper limits to human longevity. *Science* 250(4981):634-40, 1990.

Olshansky SJ, Rudberg MA, Carnes BA, Cassel CK, and Brody JA: Trading off longer life for worsening health: Expansion of morbidity hypotheses. *Journal of Aging and Health* 3:194-216, 1991.

Omran AR: The Epidemiologic Transition: A theory of the epidemiology of population change. *Milbank Quarterly* 49(4):509-538, 1971.

Pancharuniti N, Lewis CA, Sauberlich HE, Perkins LL, Go RCP, Alvarez JO, Macaluso M, Action RT, Copeland RB, Cousins AL, Gore TB, Cornwell PE, and Roseman JM: Plasma homocyst(e)ine, Folate, and Vitamin B_{12} concentrations and risk for early-onset coronary artery disease. *American Journal of Clinical Nutrition* 59:940-948, 1994.

Paolisso G, D'Amore A, Giugliano D, Ceriello A, and Varricchio M: Pharmacologic doses of Vitamin E improve insulin action in healthy subjects and non-insulin-dependent diabetic patients. *American Journal of Clinical Nutrition* 57:650-656, 1993.

Parsonnet J: Helicobacter pylori in the stomach– A paradox unmasked. *New England Journal of Medicine* 335(4):278-280, 1996.

Pathobiological Determinants of Atherosclerosis in Youth (PDAY) Research Group: Relationship of atherosclerosis in young men to serum lipoprotein cholesterol concentrations and smoking. *Journal of the American Medical Association* 264:1018-1024, 1990.

Paul SD, Kuntz KM, Eagle KA, and Weinstein MC: Costs and effectiveness of angiotensin converting enzyme inhibition in patients with congestive heart failure. *Archives of Internal Medicine* 154:1143-1149, 1994.

Pearl R, and Peard RD: *The Ancestry of the Long-Lived.* The Johns Hopkins Press: Baltimore, 1934.

Pekkanen J, Manton KG, Stallard E, Nissinen A, and Karvonen M: Risk factor dynamics, mortality and life expectancy differences between eastern and western Finland: the Finnish cohorts of the Seven Countries Study. *International Journal of Epidemiology* 21(2): 406-419, 1992.

Peller S: Carcinogenesis as a means of reducing cancer mortality. *The Lancet* 2:552-556, 1936.

Peller S and Stephenson CS: Skin irritation and cancer in the United States navy. *American Journal of Medical Science* 194:326-333, 1937.

Perera F: Molecular epidemiology: Insights into cancer susceptibility, risk assessment, and prevention. *Journal of the National Cancer Institute* 88(8):496-509, 1996.

Perks W: On some experiments in the graduation of mortality statistics. *Journal of the Institute of Actuaries* 63:12, 1932.

Pletcher SD and Curtsinger JW: Mortality Plateaus and the Evolution of Senescence: Why Are Old-Age Mortality Rates So Low? *Evolution* 52(2):454-464, 1998.

Prasad KN and Edwards-Prasad J: Vitamin E and cancer prevention: Recent advances and future potentials. *Journal of the American College of Nutrition* 11(5):487-500, 1992.

Preston S: Cohort succession and the future of the Oldest Old. In *The Oldest Old* (Suzman R, Willis D, and Manton K, Eds.). Oxford University Press: New York, pp. 50-57, 1992.

Psaty BM, Savage PJ, Tell GS, Polak JF, Hirsch CH, Gardin JM, and McDonald RH: Temporal patterns of antihypertensive medication use among elderly patients: The cardiovascular health study. *Journal of the American Medical Association* 270(15):1837-1841, 1993.

Radl J, Sepers J, Skvaril F, Morell A, and Hijmans W: Immunoglobulin patterns in humans over 95 years of age. *Clinical Experimental Immunology* 22:84-90, 1975.

Ramsey MJ, Moore DH, Briner JF, Lee DA, Olsen LA, Senft JR, and Tucker JD: The effects of age and lifestyle factors on the accumulation of cytogenetic damage as measured by chromosome painting. *Mutat Res* 338:95-106, 1995.

Rath M and Pauling L: Hypothesis: Lipoprotein(a) is a surrogate for ascorbate. *Proceedings of the National Academy of Science* 87:6204-6207, 1990.

Rosenberg B, Kemeny G, Smith LG, Skurnick ID, and Bandurski MJ: The kinetics and thermodynamics of death in multicellular organisms. *Mechanisms of Ageing and Development* 2:275-293, 1973.

Rosenwaike L and Logue B: Accuracy of death certificate ages for the extreme aged. *Demography* 20:569-585, 1983.

Ross R: The pathogenesis of atherosclerosis — An update. *New England Journal of Medicine* 314:488-500, 1986.

Ross R, Bernstein L, Lobo R, Shumizu H, Stanczyk F, Pike M, and Henderson B: 5-alpha reductase activity and risk of prostate cancer among Japanese and US white and black males. *The Lancet* 339:887-889, 1992.

Ross RK and Henderson BE: Do diet and androgens alter prostate cancer risk via a common etiologic pathway? *Journal of the National Cancer Institute* 86(4):252-254, 1994.

Rubenstein LZ and Josephson KE: Hospital based geriatric assessment in the United States: The Sepulveda VA Geriatric Evaluation Unit. *Gerontology: Special Supplement* 7:74-79, 1989.

Sacher GA: Life table modification and life prolongation. In *Handbook of the Biology of Aging* (Birren, J and Finch, C, Eds.). Van Nostrand Reinhold: New York, pp. 582-638, 1977.

Sacher GA and Trucco E: The stochastic theory of mortality. *Annals of the New York Academy of Sciences* 96:985, 1962.

Safe AF, Warren B, Corfield A, McNulty CA, Watson B, Mountford RA, and Read A: Helicobacter pylori infection in elderly people: Correlation between histology and serology. *Age and Ageing* 22:215-220, 1993.

Sahi T, Launiala K: More evidence for the recessive inheritance of selective adult type lactose malabsorption. *Gastroenterology* 73:231-232, 1977.

Schachter F, Cohen D and Kirkwood T: Prospects for the genetics of human longevity. *Human Genetics* 91:519-526, 1993.

Self SG and Prentice RL: Incorporating random effects into multivariate relative risks regression models. In Moolgvkar SH, and Prentice RL, Eds., *Modern Statistical Methods in Chronic Disease Epidemiology*. Wiley: New York, 167-177, 1986.

Selhub J, Jacques PF, Wilson PWF, Rush D, and Rosenberg IH: Vitamin status and intake as primary determinants of homocysteinemia in an elderly population. *Journal of the American Medical Association* 270(22):2693-2698, 1993.

Sellers TA, Bailey-Wilson JE, Elston RC, Wilson AF, Elston GZ, Ooi WL, and Rothschild H: Evidence for mendelian inheritance in the pathogenesis of lung cancer. *Journal of the National Cancer Institute* 82:1272-1279, 1990.

SHEP Cooperative Research Group: Prevention of stroke by antihypertensive drug treatment in older persons with isolated systolic hypertension. *Journal of the American Medical Association* 265:3255-3264, 1991.

Shock NW, Greulich RC, and Andres R: Normal Human Aging: The Baltimore Longitudinal Study on Aging. NIH, Washington DC (Pub No. 84-2480), 1984.

Siegel JS: Recent and prospective demographic trends for the elderly population and some implications for health care. In Haynes SG and Feinleib M, Eds., *Epidemiology of Aging*. National Institute on Health Publication No. 80-969, U.S. Government Printing Office: Washington, D.C., pp. 17-82, 1980.

Simms H: The use of measurable causes of death (hemorrhage) for the evaluation of aging. *Journal of General Physiology* 26:169-178, 1942.

Singpurwalla ND: Survival in dynamic environments. *Statistical Science* 10(1):86, 1995.

Social Security Administration: Life Tables for the United States Social Security area 1900-2080 (Actuarial study 107). Social Security Administration (SSA Pub No. 11-11536) August, 1992.

Society of Actuaries: *1994 Group Annuity Mortality Table and 1994 Group Annuity Reserving Table*. Society of Actuaries, Schaumburg, IL (Exposure Draft, 1994).

Sonnenberg A: Temporal trends and geographical variations of peptic ulcer disease. *Ailment Pharmacol Ther* 9(2):3-12, 1995.

Sonneborn TM: The origin, evolution, nature, and causes of aging. In *The Biology of Aging*. Academic Press: New York, 361-374, 1978.

Sorlie P, Rogot E, Anderson R, Johnson NJ, and Backlund E: Black-White mortality differences by family income. *The Lancet* 340:346-350, 1992.

Spiegelman M: *Introduction to Demography*. Harvard University Press: Cambridge, Mass., 1968.

Stebbing ARD: Growth hormesis: A by-product of control. *Health Physics* 52(5):543-547, 1987.

Stern MP: The recent decline in ischemic heart disease mortality. *Annals of Internal Medicine* 91:630-640, 1979.

Stern Y, Gurland B, Tatemichi TK, Tang MX, Wilder D, and Mayeux R: Influence of education and occupation on the incidence of Alzheimer's disease. *Journal of the American Medical Association* 271(13), 1004-1010, 1994.

Stevenson R, Ranjadayalan K, Wilkinson P, Roberts R, and Timmis AD: Short and long prognosis of acute myocardial infarction since introduction of thrombolysis. *British Medical Journal* 307:349-353, 1993.

Stewart S: The biodistribution of stealth liposomes in patients with solid tumors and the implications for targeted chemotherapy. *Cancer Insvestigation* 15:58-59, 1997.

Strehler BL: *Time, Cells and Aging*. Academic Press: New York, 1977.

Strehler BL: Deletional mutations are the basic cause of aging: Historical perspectives. *Mutat Res* 338:3-17, 1995.

Strehler BL and Mildvan AS: General theory of mortality and aging. *Science* 132:14-21, 1960.

Sullivan J: Antioxidant and coronary heart disease. *The Lancet* 337: 432-433, 1991.

Sverre JM: Secular trends in coronary heart disease mortality in Norway, 1966-86. *American Journal of Epidemiology* 137(3):301-310, 1993.

Takata H, Suzuki M, Ishii T, Sekiguchi S, and Iri H: Influence of major histocompatability complex region genes on human longevity among Okinawan-Japanese centenarians and nonagenarians. *The Lancet* 2(8563):824-826, 1987.

Tango T, Kurashina S: Age, period and cohort analysis of trends in mortality from major diseases in Japan, 1955 to 1979: Peculiarity of the cohort born in the early show a era. *Statistics in Medicine* 6:709-726, 1987.

Thieszen SL, Hixson JE, Nagengast DJ, Wilson JE, and McManus BM: Lipid phenotypes, apolipoprotein genotypes and cardiovascular risk in nonagenarians. *Atherosclerosis* 83:137-146, 1990.

Thoms WS: *Human Longevity, Its Facts and Its Fictions*. John Murray: London, 1873.

Tolley HD and Manton KG: Intervention effects among a collection of risks. *Transactions of the Society of Actuaries* 43:443-468, 1991.

Treasure CB, Klein JL, Weintraub WS, Talley JD, Stillbower ME, Kosinski AS, et al.: Beneficial effects of cholesterol-lowering therapy on the coronary endothelium in patients with coronary artery disease. *New England Journal of Medicine* 332(8):481-487, 1995.

Tulley et al.: The steroid hormone receptors and their mechanism of action. *Nutrition and Gene Expression*. CRC Press: Boca Rotan, pp. 549-567, 1993.

Vagero D, Ringback G, and Kiveranta H: Melanoma and other tumors of the skin among office, other indoor and outdoor workers in Sweden 1961-1979. *British Journal of Cancer* 53:507-512, 1986.

Vallin J: Enquête IPSEN 1990-1992. Presented at the Research Workshop on Oldest-Old Mortality. Duke University, March 4-6, 1993.

Van der Wal AC, Becker AE, Van der Loos CM, Das PK: Site of intimal rupture or erosion of thrombosed coronary atherosclerotic plaques is characterized by an inflammatory process irrespective of the dominant plaque morphology. *Circulation* 89:36-44, 1994.

Vaupel JW and Jeune B: The emergence and proliferation of centenarians. In *Exceptional Longevity* (Jeune B and Vaupel JW, Eds.). Odense Monograph on Population Aging, 2. Odense University Press, Odense, Denmark, 1995.

Vaupel JW, Manton KG, and Stallard E: The impact of heterogeneity in individual frailty on the dynamics of mortality. *Demography* 16:439-454, 1979.

Vaupel JW and Lundström H: Longer life expectancy? Mortality reductions at older ages in Sweden. In *The Economics of Aging* (Wise D, Ed.), pp. 79-104. University of Chicago Press: Chicago, 1994.

Vaupel JW and Yashin AI: Heterogeneity ruses: Some surprising effects of selection on population dynamics. *American Statistician* 39:176-185, 1985.

Vaupel JW, Yashin AI, Lundström H, Lee PJ: Mortality at older ages in Sweden. Paper presented at Population Association of America meeting in Denver, Colorado, U.S.A., April 29-May 2, 1992.

Vile RG: p53: A gene for all tumors? *British Medical Journal* 307:1226-1227, 1993.

Von Eckardstein A, Malinow R, Upson B, Heinrich J, Schulte H, Schonfeld R, Kohler E, and Assmann G: Effects of age, lipoproteins, and hemostatic parameters on the role of homocyst(e)inemia as a cardiovascular risk factor in men. *Arteriosclerosis and Thrombosis* 14(3):460-464, 1994.

Wallace DC: Mitochondrial genetics: A paradigm for aging and degenerative disease? *Science* 256:628-632, 1992.

Warner HR, Fernandes G, and Wang E: A unifying hypothesis to explain the retardation of aging and tumorigenesis by caloric restriction. *Journal of Gerontology: Biological Science* 50A:B107-B109, 1995.

Webb AR and Holick MF: The role of sunlight in cutaneous production of vitamin D3. *Annual Review of Nutrition* 8:375-399, 1988.

Weber K and Brilla C: Pathological hypertrophy and cardiac intersittium. *Circulation* 83(6):1849-1865, 1991.

Wetterstrand W: Parametric models for life insurance mortality data: Gompertz's law over time. *Transactions of the Society of Actuaries* 33:159-175, 1981.

Weismann A: *Essays on Heredity*. Clarendon Press: Oxford, 1891.

Williams GC: Pleiotrophy, natural selection, and the evolution of senescence. *Evolution* 11:398-411, 1957.

Witteman JC, Grobbee DE, Valkenburg HA, van Hemert AM, Stijnen T, Burger H, and Hofman A: J-shaped relation between change in diastolic blood pressure and progression of aortic atherosclerosis. *The Lancet* 343:504-507, 1994.

Woodbury MA and Manton KG: A random walk model of human mortality and aging. *Theoretical Population Biology* 11:37-48, 1977.

Woodbury MA and Manton KG: A theoretical model of the physiological dynamics of circulatory disease in human populations. *Human Biology* 55:417-441, 1983.

Woodbury MA, Manton KG, and Tolley HD: A general model for statistical analysis using fuzzy sets: Sufficient conditions for identifiability and statistical properties. *Information Sciences* 1:149-180, 1994.

Woodbury MA and Manton KG: Modeling complex biological systems using fuzzy set principles: Methods and models. Comments on *Theoretical Biology* 4(1):1-29, 1996.

Woodhouse PR, Khaw KT, Plummer M, Foley A, and Meade TW: Seasonal variations of plasma fibrinogen and factor VII activity in the elderly: Winter infections and death from cardiovascular disease. *The Lancet* 343:435-439, 1994.

World Health Organization: *World Health Statistics Annual*. Geneva, Switzerland, 1994.

Wu MC and Carroll RJ: Estimation and comparison of changes in the presence of informative right censoring by modeling the censoring process. Department of Statistics: Chapel Hill, 1987.

Wu M and Ware J: On the use of repeated measurements of regression analysis with dichotomous responses. *Biometrics* 35:513-521, 1979.

Yashin AI: Conditional Gaussian estimation of dynamic systems under jumping observations. *Automat. and Rem. Control (translated from Russian),* 5. 1980.

Yashin AI: *Dynamics in Survival Analysis: Conditional Gaussian Property Versus Cameron-Martin Formula. Statistic and Control of Stochastic Processes.* Springer-Verlag: New York, 1985.

Yashin AI: Extension of the Cameron-Martin result. *Journal of Applied Probability* 30:247-251, 1993.

Yashin AI and Arjas E: A note on random intensities and conditional survival functions. *Journal of Applied Probability* 25:630-635, 1988.

Yashin AI and Iachine IA: How long can human live? Lower bound for biological limit of human longevity calculated from Danish twin data using correlated frailty model. *Mechanisms of Ageing and Development* 80:147-169, 1995a.

Yashin AI and Iachine IA: Genetic analysis of durations: Correlated frailty model applied to survival of Danish twins. *Genetic Epidemiology* 12:529-538, 1995b.

Yashin AI and Iachine IA: Mortality models with application to twin survival data. In: Halin J, Karplus W, and Rimane R, Eds., *CISS-Proceedings of First Joint Conference of International Simulation Societies* ETM. Zurich, Switzerland, 22-25 August 1994.

Yashin AI, Manton KG, and Lowrimore G. Evaluating partially observed survival histories: Retrospective evaluation and projections of covariate trajectories. *Applied Stochastic Models and Data Analysis* 13(1):1-13, 1997.

Yashin AI, Manton KG, and Iachine IA: Genetic and environmental factors in the etiology of chronic diseases: Multivariate frailty models and estimation strategies. *Journal of Epidemiology and Biostatistics* 1(2):115-120, 1996. Presented at WHO Mathematical Modeling Group Consultation and European Institute of Oncology meeting 27-29 November in Milan.

Yashin AI, Manton KG, and Stallard E: Dependent competing risks: A stochastic process model. *Journal of Mathematical Biology* 24:119-140, 1986.

Yashin AI, Vaupel JW, and Iachine IA: Correlated individual frailty: An advantageous approach to survival analysis of bivariate data. *Mathemat Pop Stud* 5(2):1-15, 1995.

Yashin AI, Vaupel JW, and Iachine IA: A duality of aging: The equivalence of mortality models based on radically different concepts. *Mechanisms of Ageing and Development* 74:1-14, 1994.

Yki-Järvinen H: Pathogenesis of non-insulin-dependent diabetes mellitus. *The Lancet* 91-5:91-94, 1994.